RADIO

VARI

SC

Published Weekly at 154 West 46th St., New York, N.
Entered as second-class matter December 22, 1905 at
COPYRIGHT, 1935, BY VARI

Vol. 119   No. 5

NEW YORK, WED

STICKS NI

Cry for 'Author' of Five Plays
On B'way Will Get No Response

NOT IN
IN FA

EEN   STAGE

IETY

PRICE
15¢

Variety, Inc., Annual subscription, $6. Single copies, 15 cents
Office at New York, N. Y., under the act of March 3, 1879.
1935. ALL RIGHTS RESERVED

SDAY, JULY 17, 1935   72 PAGES

K HICK PIX

RESTED

M DRAMA

Stars Favor Own Picture Firm
For Tax Conservation Purposes

World's Worst   Trend for self-production by the

THE *VARIETY*
HISTORY
OF SHOW
BUSINESS

BY THE EDITORS OF VARIETY
INTRODUCTION BY PETER BART
DESIGNED BY J.-C. SUARÈS
EDITED BY J. SPENCER BECK

A *VARIETY* BOOK

HARRY N. ABRAMS, INC., PUBLISHERS

Photo Editor: SUSAN EVANS

Design Coordinator: GATES SISTERS STUDIO

Production Editor: ANDERSON TEPPER

Special thanks to: THOMAS PHILLIPS, PAUL YOUNG,
MAX ALEXANDER

Library of Congress Cataloging-in-Publication Data

The Variety History of Show Business / by the editors
    of Variety; introduction by Peter Bart; edited by
    J. Spencer Beck
        p.   cm.
    "A Variety book."
    Includes index.
    ISBN 0-8109-3926-6
    1. Performing arts—United States—History—
20th century. 2. Performing arts—History—20th
century. I. Beck, J. Spencer. II. Variety
(New York, N.Y.)
PN2266.V35 1993
791'.0973'0904—dc20   93-9401
                                          CIP

Published in 1993 by Harry N. Abrams, Incorporated,
New York
A Times Mirror Company

Printed and bound in the United States of America

FACING PAGE

Mary Pickford, circa 1917.

PAGE 1

Charlie Chaplin, Mary Pickford, Douglas Fairbanks, and D.W. Griffith sign the papers creating United Artists, 1919.

PAGE 4

Greta Garbo and John Barrymore on the set of *Grand Hotel*, 1932.

PAGE 10

Marlon Brando, circa 1951.

PAGE 224

Joan Crawford and Wallace Beery on the set of *Grand Hotel*, 1932.

CONTENTS

INTRODUCTION

Those of us at *Variety* who cover the entertainment business day-by-day are all too aware of one over-riding reality: namely, that show biz is on the threshold of immense and startling change. Any month now the floodgates will open and the typical household will be able to access hundreds of TV channels. The consumer will be literally awash in entertainment via phone lines, personal computers, satellites, whatever. The deluge will be so great that we will likely have to depend on electronic memories to sift through our options and present us with a menu of past preferences to guide us.

As we all start thumbing our way down the much-heralded "electronic superhighway" of the future, the onrush of new experience may all but obliterate the past. Channel surfing through a myriad of choices, we will surely forget the calmer, more intimate encounters that marked the show biz of times past: the serenity of a one-on-one encounter with one's radio set, for example. Or the mindless joys of vaudeville.

To the fretful viewer, struggling to cope with the multimedia demands of interactive TV, threading his way through a maze of electronic mixed messages, the simple joys of the past might seem almost medieval. "History is just one great dustheap," one seer instructed us, but before the show-biz dustheap disappears from our collective memory, we at *Variety* decided to try to recapture some fleeting memories and random moments—turning points in the history of entertainment. There is no grand design at work here; our history is scattershot, but then so is show business. We asked our writers to search out the momentous events, the lightning bolts, the grand moments before they are buried in time.

Perhaps the act of revisiting this glorious dustpile one last time will give us some solace in our struggle to derive some entertainment from future technologies. Perhaps, channel surfing through the night, we will recall a brief interlude when show biz was simpler, communication more direct, and when wit, rather than electronics, drove our emotions.

PETER BART

Fade Out New York, Cut to California

In 1913, silent-film studios were hardly new to southern California. Sometimes independent companies, sometimes the offspring of Eastern studios, they had been vigorously flourishing for ten years. Moviemaking, rudimentary but ambitious, was already big business. On wooden stages before primitive cameras, pantomiming performers emoted outdoors against upright flats under sunlight-diffusing muslin, with props painted directly on the canvas-covered backdrops. When a piece of dialogue was to be spliced into the picture, the director sang out, "Speak your title!" and the actor would say the words aloud to the deaf camera.

Retired merchant Jacob Stern's home lay in the heart of sleepy Hollywood among the lemon groves and graceful pepper trees. Just to the south, at Vine Street and Selma Avenue, he had an L-shaped barn and yard. This was where Cecil B. De Mille, creative maestro of the motion picture world, would supervise the first smasharoo feature-length western to be made in Hollywood, the Jesse L. Lasky Feature Play Company's *The Squaw Man.*

The ninety-minute film took initiative and courage, and its preeminence is based not on its being the area's first feature, which it was not, but on its enormous commercial impact. Its influence would launch a mighty film studio in an idyllic, puritanical country town where residents chinned about farming and land values. No one could foresee that the lazy Los Angeles suburb would someday be the company town for the American entertainment industry. *The Squaw Man* put Hollywood on the map.

Prior to the second decade of this century, New York, New Jersey, and Chicago were the true centers of filmmaking. But harsh winters, sparse sunlight, and costly labor halted outdoor filming. Plus, the Motion Picture Patents Company—or the "Trust," as it was known—controlled licenses on all patents for cameras and projectors and had a stranglehold on raw film stock. Formed in 1908, the Trust had been using rash methods, from threats to hooliganism, to interfere with the "indies," as unlicensed independent filmmakers were then known.

Hollywood, with its unpaved roads, had yet really to compete even with its

FACING PAGE

The Pioneers: Cecil B. De Mille, *right,* and co-director Oscar Apfel pose for a twenty-fifth anniversary reunion in 1938 of the original cast and crew of *The Squaw Man,* Hollywood's first feature-length film. When "director-general" De Mille insisted the picture be shot in the real West—not New Jersey— modern Hollywood was born.

southern California neighbors in the film business. Nestor, the first studio of record in somnolent Hollywood itself, was set up in 1911 at a failed tavern on Sunset Boulevard. It put up an open-air stage on a vacant lot behind the structure, the derivation of filmdom's term "back lot."

Annexed by Los Angeles in 1910, Hollywood was peopled with pious, retired midwesterners. Real estate was up, but labor costs were much lower than in the East, and Indian, Mexican, and Asian populations enriched the countryside. Nearby ocean beaches and rolling surf, Catalina and Death Valley, snow-laden mountains, blue lakes and meandering streams, and mile after square mile of uncluttered land were part of the package, and the world looked fresh. In summer, hills turned ochre from the blazing heat, and torrential rains flooded the land in January, but for the most part, California was golden.

The word, given a mighty assist by the L.A. Chamber of Commerce, was out that California offered opportunity. The Bank of Italy, forerunner of the Bank of America, was interested in underwriting adventuresome filmmakers, the natives were friendly, and the Trust was a continent away.

Vaudeville producer Jesse L. Lasky, onetime reporter, promoter, and once even part of "a blackface cornet act with his sister," as *Variety*'s Abel Green described him, would be one of the creative geniuses behind Paramount Pictures in years to come. He and his close friend playwright-actor De Mille, with whom he had produced several plays, were having lunch in 1913, 3,000 miles from sunny California at New York's Claridge Grill. With the theater in the doldrums, De Mille was thinking of chucking the whole thing. Lasky, concerned about De Mille's depression, suggested that Lasky's eager brother-in-law, glove salesman Sam Goldfish, might be right: it might be a smart move to get into the picture business.

Using the Claridge menu, the two men jotted down a blueprint for the Jesse L. Lasky Feature Play Company. Lasky would head the operation, Goldfish would be the salesman, De Mille, whose experience was strictly theater, would be director general. One provision: They would be making, instead of the customary two- and three-reel films, feature-length narrative moving pictures.

Goldfish arranged for De Mille to spend an afternoon at the Edison Studio in the Bronx observing the shooting of a movie; that was the extent of the director general's film schooling. Lasky and De Mille, deciding it would be wise to film a well-known stage play, fixed on Edwin Milton Royle's hit *The Squaw Man*, a western set in Wyoming with outdoor settings requiring minimum expense. Lasky and Goldfish put up $7,500 apiece, but De Mille, with a wife, daughter, and no income, was broke; he could offer only his vitality, imagination, and, to use his own words, "youthful confidence." That was enough.

Royle agreed to their terms, and matinee idol Dustin Farnum signed on as leading man. Oscar C. Apfel, a young but experienced director, and cameraman Alfred Gandolfi, a graduate of Italian and Pathé films, joined the company, as did Fred

Kley, Farnum's dresser. The destination of the five-man company was Flagstaff, Arizona, a substitute for Wyoming.

De Mille, who had left his family in New York after hocking the family silver to cover expenses, and Apfel worked on the scenario on the train ride west. For years, legend has had it that Flagstaff was in the middle of a rainstorm when they arrived, but that is not true. The weather was beautiful, but in no way did Arizona resemble what they had in mind for the movie. Wrote De Mille in a *Life* magazine article, "We saw instantly that for our purposes Arizona—beautiful, healthful, sunny Arizona—was all wrong." He saw high mountains, but he wanted plains with mountains in the distance. Farnum suggested going on to Los Angeles, where there were all sorts of scenery. The company, hopping back on the same train, headed for L.A., where they arrived on December 20, 1913.

Two "enterprising gentlemen" told De Mille that they had leased a laboratory in Hollywood at Vine and Selma and that they would develop their film. Adjacent to the lab was a large, yellow barn and an open-air stage. Jacob Stern had leased the property to the two men. Wiring Lasky and Goldfish for the okay, De Mille sublet it from them for $250 a month. Stern insisted on continued use of the barn for his horses and carriage; otherwise, the Jesse L. Lasky Feature Play Company had itself an office and dressing rooms—except for those times when Stern's carriage was being washed.

New York actress Winifred Kingston travelled West to play the lead opposite Farnum. De Mille hired the rest of the company locally, casting Sioux Indian Princess Redwing and, among bit players, Art Acord, who would become an early western star, and H. E. Roach, later better known as Hal, a comedy king whose pictures would showcase Will Rogers, Laurel and Hardy, and the Our Gang kids. *The Squaw Man* used San Pedro Harbor, San Fernando Valley's open spaces, and a mansion on West Adams in L.A. for locations; dramatic action took place on the outdoor stage outside Stern's barn.

De Mille ordered an extra negative shot on every scene after seeing a strip of film stock flare up when a cigarette touched it. (Intensely involved in all phases of the production, he even bought an inexpensive, secondhand British machine for punching sprocket holes in the film.) Sharing a cottage with a cast member, a protective prairie wolf, De Mille took the second negative home at night. (When Mrs. De Mille and their daughter moved west, they all moved to a house in the Cahuenga Pass, and the wolf went to the zoo.) The wolf was not an affectation. Since the Lasky Company was not a member of the Trust, it was in jeopardy: one morning De Mille stepped into the darkened lab and discovered scraps of torn film on the floor.

Obviously, a saboteur had slipped into the lab, and it did not take much imagination to figure out who had sent him. A bed was set up in the small lab, and De Mille and other members of the troupe took turns as guards. De Mille soon began receiving anonymous threatening letters warning him to get out of the movie business or lose his life. The director general, sporting jodhpurs and boots and riding horseback to work over the rough road through Cahuenga Pass, carried his lunch in

Jesse L. Lasky, *right*, whose Jesse L. Lasky Feature Play Company produced *The Squaw Man,* poses at the 1947 Academy Awards with Adolph Zukor, *center*, and Jack Warner. Lasky and Zukor formed Paramount Pictures in 1917.

Variety called *The Squaw Man,* which starred veteran stage actor Dustin Farnum, *left,* a "genuine masterpiece." It was remade in 1918, making De Mille the first director to make a remake of his own original.

a satchel; he used the same satchel to bring home the extra negatives. He also began packing a revolver in case the Trust's goons were tracking him. Twice he was shot at from thickets lining the canyon; he fired back, but nothing came of it.

The production ended after eighteen anxiety-ridden days. Lasky arrived in L.A. to see the opus, while an enthusiastic Goldfish continued his successful selling of the film from New York. The first showing was in the barn, with the executives, cast, and crew in attendance. The room was darkened, and "The Squaw Man" appeared—briefly—before it scrambled up the makeshift screen. The opening action followed suit, climbing up out of sight. The screening was stopped; the Trust had apparently managed to ruin the negative. Lasky and De Mille had to face the bitter fact that their picture was lost.

Goldfish wired De Mille to hand-carry the negative to Philadelphia to get the opinion of optics expert Sigmund ("Pop") Lubin, head of the Lubin Manufacturing Company but also a member of the dreaded Trust. De Mille and Lasky headed east. Lubin reported in fifteen minutes what was wrong with the film: nothing. That secondhand hole puncher De Mille had bought to save money had punched holes for another type of projector. A technician, covering the film's edge with a strip of celluloid, cut the properly spaced holes; *The Squaw Man* was back on track. De Mille and Lasky never did learn why Lubin, a member of the Trust, had been so helpful. They decided it was his good nature.

Finally, the film was ready for its New York trade screening for those regional buyers who had not already succumbed to Goldfish's masterful salesmanship. France and Great Britain were already demanding the picture, and the *Variety* review set the tone:

> One of the best of all the reproductions in pictures of successful dramas is the Jesse L. Lasky Feature Play Co.'s filming of Edwin Milton Royle's *The Squaw Man* in six reels—264 scenes. It was shown for the private invitation performance at the Longacre Tuesday morning before an audience that looked like a "first night" of some legitimate show.…A makeshift machine, with sprocket holes constantly obtruding themselves, reinforced by a cracked condenser, did not contribute to the otherwise good effect. Nor did the sheet, a piece of muslin, help things along.…
>
> In spite of these handicaps, the feature film may be set down as a genuine "masterpiece" in moving picture production.…The idea of introducing the characters is new and many of the lighting effects are a radical departure from the beaten path. *The Squaw Man* as a feature film will most certainly do.

Based on the rave review and on what they had seen, exhibitors bought, and the film was released in February 1914. It was on its way to becoming a legend.

The Lasky Feature Play Company thrived for two years, delivering a film a month (five written by De Mille, who eventually recovered the family silver), before merging with New York-based Adolph Zukor's Famous Players in 1916 to create Famous Players-Lasky with Zukor as president and Lasky as vice president in charge of production. In 1912, Zukor had imported Sarah Bernhardt's four-reel *Queen Elizabeth* from France for U.S. distribution. It had been a sensation. Films suddenly had stature, and "cultured people" would attend the movies.

Thanks to Zukor's Famous Players, to theatrical producer Jesse L. Lasky, and to down-on-his-luck actor-playwright Cecil B. De Mille, Players-Lasky was already a thriving business when it was renamed in 1917. That year, Paramount Pictures was born. Zukor would be president of Hollywood's first big studio until 1936, when he became chairman of the board. At his death at 103 in 1976, he was chairman of the board emeritus.

Samuel Goldfish, who had his disagreements with Zukor, stayed only briefly with the new company. He and producer-director Edgar Selwyn formed Goldwyn Productions in 1917, taking the name from Goldfish's first syllable and Selwyn's second. (Goldfish so liked the new moniker that he legally changed his own name in 1918 to Goldwyn.) In 1922, that company merged with Metro Pictures and Louis B. Mayer Productions to form MGM—without Goldwyn himself, who went on to form a company of his own.

Jesse L. Lasky stayed with the studio until 1932, when he turned independent producer. He ultimately returned to Paramount before dying in 1958.

De Mille stayed until 1925, then returned in 1932 for the rest of his career. He was the major creative force at Paramount, where his entertaining pictures depicted sinners redeemed by morality or, later, offered eye-filling religious spectacles. His two versions of *The Ten Commandments,* one silent, the other sound (his final film in 1956), put him in the curious position of being the only man in history to part the Red Sea twice. After seventy pictures, he still wore jodhpurs and boots, reminders of the days when he rode horseback through rugged Cahuenga Pass.

Stern's barn, which could easily have been ploughed under, remained on the same spot while the Lasky Feature Play Company expanded over two blocks. Ten years after the merger with Zukor's Famous Players, the company shifted to Melrose and Van Ness, and Lasky and De Mille saw to it that the barn moved with it. Eventually, the De Mille barn, as it became known, was moved to its present site across from the Hollywood Bowl. A museum today, it spotlights movie artifacts from the silent era.

As for the barn's original site at Vine and Selma, a handsome plaque once marked the place—well, almost the place. The plaque was tacked onto a bank building on the northeast corner of Selma and Vine—not on the southeast corner where the barn actually stood—because there was no place in a parking lot to hang it. It read: "'The Squaw Man' Was Filmed on This Site."

The bank is now a state office, the parking lot is still there, but the plaque—and the bucolic charm of old Hollywood—are long gone.

TONY SCOTT

The Brotherhood: In their heyday, Lee Shubert, *above,* and his two brothers, Sam and Jacob, *were* the American theater. Their failed ban of *New York Times* critic Alexander Woollcott paved the way for the *Times*'s eventual domination of New York's cultural life.

1 9 1 5

The Shuberts vs. The *New York Times*

Alexander Woollcott had been the *New York Times* drama critic for only a year when, in March 1915, he reviewed a German farce called *Taking Chances* at a theater owned by the surpassingly powerful Shubert brothers. Woollcott dismissed the play as "vulgar" and "quite tedious." That was as nasty as he got in the review, but the Shuberts were spoiling for a fight. After a series of preliminary thrusts and parries between the newspaper and the landlord-managers, Woollcott was refused admittance to a Shubert theater by Jacob ("Jake") Shubert himself, who was clearly eighty-sixing the *Times* man from his extensive domain.

The banishment of critics was common at the time. Theater reviews were perceived as decorations on the arm of advertising, and many critics actually doubled as sellers of advertising space. Ten years before Woollcott, James R. Metcalfe and *Life* magazine took on a consortium of New York producers who had banded together to keep Metcalfe out of their theaters. This was a very rare occurrence—a publication standing by its man—but the producers finally prevailed. A New York court succumbed to the notion that a drama critic had no more right, unbidden, to enter the theater of a man than a man had a right, unbidden, to enter the boudoir of a lady. Never mind that ladies do not advertise their boudoirs in newspapers and on billboards nor, as a general rule, sell tickets of admission, nor detail firemen at public expense to be present during performances: that was the ruling. The Shuberts, when they reigned in Chicago, had regularly punished critics for perceived apostasy. The brilliant Percy Hammond was banished for three years after he advised the brothers, then specializing in fleshy musicals, that "the human knee is a joint and not an entertainment." They barred Heywood Broun of the *World* and Gilbert Gabriel of the *Sun* in New York. According to Shubert biographer Jerry Stag, "Freedom of the press to Lee and Jacob J. was the right of the Shuberts to read favorable notices."

This time the Shuberts' target was not really the lowly, sixty-bucks-a-week Woollcott, but the ascendant *New York Times,* whose power and prestige were increasing steadily under the righteous publisher Adolph Ochs, who had been at the helm for twenty years, and his veteran managing editor, Carr Van Anda, whom one writer called "the shaping hand of the *Times'* journalistic destiny." Van Anda decided to fight the Shuberts and went to confer with Ochs about strategy. According to Woollcott biographer Samuel Adams, this Citizen Kane-ish dialogue ensued.

"Do you think Mr. Woollcott's criticism of the play was justified?" was Ochs's first question.

"That isn't the point, is it?"

"No, of course not," said Ochs after reflection. "What do you think we should do?"

"Get an injunction against the Shuberts."

"I'll call up the lawyers. Anything else?"

"Throw out the Shubert advertising."

"Do so."

The first of Ochs's directives involved engaging the Shuberts in a legal embroilment that would trundle from lower court to high. It began with Woollcott's securing an injunction, claiming that his civil rights were being violated. He showed up one blizzardy night at a Shubert production of *Trilby,* "the first instance anywhere in the world," he would claim in a *Vanity Fair* piece, "of a play being reviewed under an injunction." It was the first instance, too, of a signed review appearing in the *Times.* This was Van Anda's way of rubbing the Shuberts' noses in his temporary victory. (Woollcott liked the play.)

The Shuberts fought to have the injunction vacated, claiming that the young Woollcott had set out maliciously to injure their business, that his review of *Taking Chances* was merely one example of his biased opprobrium. They produced clips from the newspaper that they contended reflected his prejudice. In fact, they made a very poor show of it. Five of the sixteen unsigned reviews put into evidence had been written by someone other than Woollcott, two of them published even before he joined the drama staff. (His early criticisms, by the way, were balanced, painstakingly gallant, and usually reflective of a wide critical consensus. Woollcott was not then the caution he would become.)

The case was widely covered throughout the country, even by the lofty *Harvard Law Review.* Sympathy was overwhelmingly for the *Times* and for the freedom to criticize vigorously for the sake of the press and on behalf of quality theater. The *Times* itself gave the trial's highlights front-page coverage, alongside such coeval events as the sinking of the *Lusitania.* A great backlash smote the Shuberts, while the *Times* enjoyed wide popular support. ("When many papers are known to be under the thumb of the producers," went a typical editorial, "the courage and independence of the *New York Times* are inspiring.")

Most important, the *Times* continued its aggressive ban of all things Shubertian. No play managed by them or player appearing on one of their stages was mentioned in the paper. No advertising was accepted, even though that meant a loss of approximately $35,000 for the year. Withal, the *Times* continued to flourish, showing steady

LEGIT

MANAGERS MAY BAR CRITICS DECISION IN WOOLLCOTT CASE

State Court of Appeals Decides That Shuberts Have Legal Right to Refuse Admittance to Their Theatres to Time's Reviewer. Ruling of Lower Courts Affirmed.

The unalterable right to bar or remove from their theatres for any reason, excepting creed, race or color, was given theatrical managers in New York state this week when the Court of Appeals affirmed the opinion of a lower court deciding the Shuberts had the legal right to refuse admittance into any of their houses to Alexander Woollcott, dramatic editor of the New York Times.

The Times commenced an action to mandamus the Shuberts to permit its critic entrance, upon the Shuberts some months ago turning Mr. Woollcott aside when he attempted to enter the Shubert theatre on 44th street, to witness the premiere of a production in that house. The Woollcott case was repeatedly decided in favor of the Shuberts as it traveled upward toward the highest tribunal in the state. The Times rested on the Civil Rights bill enacted in New York, and which the paper believed superseded the common law on individual privilege. Through its affirmation without an opinion, the Court of Appeals virtually said the Civil Rights act only applied to race, creed and color discrimination by theatre man-

Variety, February 23, 1916.

increases in circulation and advertising lineage. Meyer Berger (*The Story of the New York Times*) reported that throughout this period the paper showed circulation gains greater than those of all other New York morning dailies combined, "and the Shuberts sensibly figured that the Ochs ban on their advertising was affecting the box office."

Despite the Shuberts' eventual failure to prove bias, however, the New York State Court of Appeals on February 22, 1916, less than a year after the meeting in Ochs's office, ruled for the landlords and their Divine Right to exclude from their premises anyone they pleased, so long as that exclusion was not based on race, creed, or color.

In the spring of 1916, Ochs and one of the Shuberts rode together by happenstance on a Philadelphia-bound train out of New York. By the time they reached the City of Brotherly Love, they had made a détente. In mid-May, the *Times* ran a little story reporting, "Lee Shubert formally notified the *New York Times* yesterday that the firm of theatrical managers of which he is a member would welcome the critic or representative of the *Times* to its theaters." Shubert sent Woollcott, who had become a celebrity on account of the attendant publicity, a box of cigars and invited him back to the Five-and-Dime. ("Yes," Woollcott told a friend, "they threw me out and now I'm basking in the fierce white light that beats upon the thrown.")

The Shuberts continued their fierce confrontations with the rest of the press, though, ousting perceived and frequently very powerful adversaries until the law that permitted such banishment was changed in 1941. But they never messed in the same way with the estimable *Times,* which emerged from World War I with redoubled cachet on account of the accuracy and excellence of its spare-no-expense coverage. A less punctilious publisher might have used revenue loss and court costs to justify capitulation to the Shuberts, but not Ochs, for whom righteousness always seemed to work ("My father guided the *Times* to success by adhering steadfastly to lofty principles," said his daughter, Iphegene). Ochs instead chose to fight on two fronts and to expel the money men from his temple. His heralded independence became a formidable attraction: the best and the brightest were drawn to his Mandarin theater pages.

After a career of more than twenty-five years, Woollcott's eventual successor, Brooks Atkinson, would remember only one time when an embarrassed Adolph Ochs asked him to delete a single too-harsh word on behalf of a friend. The Shuberts' failed ban of Woollcott prefigured the *Times*'s eventual rise to dominance in covering the cultural life of New York and the rest of the country, as well as the paper's ambivalent regard for its own considerable weight. Indeed, Atkinson was reported to have claimed, "I've got power I don't want."

LEE ISRAEL

Star Power

You hear the words "United Artists" still, and somehow they spark those synapses in the brain that connect union and fraternity, maybe even égalité and revolution, all arrayed in the solidarity of artists—those pure spirits of humankind—against the misery of bosses, who dine on the hocks of the little people. Yet, it is useful to remember that the formation of United Artists was also about money. The impulse behind it has rippled out for decades since 1919, perhaps even through the formation of the baseball players' union in the 1970s and the recognition that talent ought to be paid what the market will bear, not what the plantation owners will suffer.

The decade that ended in 1919 with the creation of United Artists was the pivotal one in the nascent film industry's history. The immigrant entrepreneurs looking for a way up had only just sidestepped Edison's Motion Picture Patents Company and General Film. In fact, the industry had barely ratcheted up to feature films from the menu of shorts insisted upon by the Neanderthal business mentality that eventually buried Patents and its subsidiary.

There was no hunkering down on the horizon, the way the Patents Company or General Film wanted to do, vainly forbidding this new gold rush. Too many people smelled fortune and sensed that the power to harness talent, rather than to control patents, was the gateway to the future. For instance, William Selig had signed up writers Rex Beach and Zane Grey, then produced Beach's Alaskan adventure, *The Spoilers,* in eight reels as the first super-picture, and finally booked it into the spanking new Strand on Broadway. Forty thousand people showed up that first week in April 1914. Exhibitors sensed that the new religion had arrived and set about building temples. No shorts need apply. Patents were for medicine, thanks.

It was the spectacle of director D. W. Griffith's *Birth of a Nation,* undertaken in 1914 by Epoch Films Corporation at a cost that would have paid for ten ordinary features, that legitimized the industry to something other than what respectable folks regarded as a garbage way to spend money and time. Epoch itself had split from a patents supplier, Mutual Films, and its founders (Harry Aitken, Griffith, and the Rev. Thomas Dixon, a pro-cracker Southerner who had written the *The Clansman* to praise the gray Caesars, not bury them) embodied the idea that a risk taken on inspiration could be earned back in multiples. The Griffith "photoplay" opened to

Charlie Chaplin was the highest paid man in the world, commanding a salary of $670,000, when he teamed up with Mary Pickford, Douglas Fairbanks, and D.W. Griffith to form United Artists in 1919.

black riots in Boston, yet whites tore through the turnstiles, paying not ten or fifteen cents but two dollars—the cost of a stage play.

All over the country, the industry was in ferment, its executives hyperactive. William Fox banked on Theda Bara for *A Fool There Was* (1915), and "vamp" entered the lexicon of sex and danger, as Bara posed bare-legged before a supine skeleton in publicity stills. Louis B. Mayer was in motion out of Haverhill, Massachusetts, on his way to meeting Marcus Loew and Sam Goldfish (aka Samuel Goldwyn). Vitagraph stumbled over Norma Talmadge and made her a star in *The Battle Cry of Peace* (1915), before she met and married producer Joseph Schenck, who turned her into a superstar. Adolph Zukor was churning out a picture a week at Paramount, Jesse Lasky one every two weeks. The Warner brothers were only a short time away from producing up a storm.

Russian immigrant and jeweler Lewis J. Selznick barged into Carl Laemmle's Universal Pictures with a case of jewels, found the company split into two warring factions, and so appointed himself an executive. When he was thrown out, he formed the World Film Corporation with Arthur Spiegel of the catalog company in Chicago, then left World with its star actress, Clara Kimball Young, and set up a company in her name. He even franchised the rights to distribute her pictures.

Essanay boasted stars G. M. ("Broncho Billy") Anderson (one of the company's founders), Francis X. Bushman, and (for one year) Charlie Chaplin. Then there was this sweet young thing Mary Pickford in the likes of *Cinderella* in 1915 for Famous Players and *The Poor Little Rich Girl* in 1917 for Artcraft.

All of it was based on talent, whether it was the ability to see in the mind's eye what could be inside the frame, or to inhabit the fantasy world that someone else imagined. The formation of United Artists only partially occurred out of the desire to control one's own work. Part of the inspiration was to refuse to let work control one's time, and part of it was, let us gently say, to share in the profits.

What might have been the first incarnation of United Artists, Triangle Pictures, a union of director giants Griffith, Thomas Ince, and Mack Sennett, coalesced to produce features that would raid the stage for stars. Triangle went to Wall Street for the immense capital it would take to drag the inflated egos of Broadway off the boards. Though it would control for a time Douglas Fairbanks, Gloria Swanson, and "Fatty" Arbuckle, Triangle failed, in part because it set off the first really big runaway inflation of talent compensation: Sir Herbert Beerbohm Tree, fresh from Broadway, made $100,000 for six months, thank you. Then it was discovered that taken from the stage and placed in front of a camera, Sir Tree was up one.

So it was not wasted on Charlotte Pickford, mother of Mary, when she happened to hear a group of Zukor's Paramount salesmen shooting the breeze, saying, "As long as we got Mary we can wrap everything around her neck." Meaning, they could condition the sale of Pickford's pictures on the sale of the rest of the lineup. Charlotte understood immediately: More money, please, Adolph.

P·368·

To meet her demands for two thousand dollars per week plus half the profits for ten pictures per annum, Paramount merely changed the entire way business was done, selling Pickford pictures as a series to exhibitors at raised prices. After word of Triangle spread all over town, Mary's price rose to one thousand dollars per day—seven thousand dollars per week. Didn't people go to movies even more on Saturday and Sundays, after all?

This made sense to Charlie Chaplin, who went to New York to reconnoiter after his contract at Essanay was up. Producer Ira Lowry trapped Chaplin in his tub at the Astor Hotel. Name your price, Lowry urged. Ten grand a week, Chaplin chirped. Okay, Lowry gulped. Out of the tub came Chaplin to sign the memo of understanding—in a year when a buck bought a steak.

But it wasn't over. Mutual's John Freuler upped Lowry's offer by $150,000, for a total of $670,000 for one year. That had a predictable result. Pickford's manager demanded Paramount meet her new price. Over at Mutual, Freuler said he would. Famous Players insisted their contract with her was still in force. Zukor also listened to her in a way that Freuler did not—by hearing the one thing that coursed beneath Pickford's desire to be paid her worth. She wanted to stop making little girl pictures. She wanted her salary of one thousand dollars per calendar day, half the profits, and to make six or eight pictures a year, not ten, so she could make better ones. Though Paramount completely reconstituted itself, and Pickford formed Artcraft to sell each of her films and pay her one million dollars a year in salary and profit participation, here at last was articulation of the artistic impulse that would eventually give rise to United Artists a few short years later in 1919.

There were permutations to come, however. Pickford moved to the first exhibitor-run production consortium, First National, for a year; Cecil B. De Mille opted to use only repertory actors; independent producers kept looking for daylight; and Griffith faltered and then outright failed with *Intolerance* (1916), an expensive attempt to recapture the spectacle and profits of *The Birth of a Nation*. When the Great War ended, filmmaking was poised to enter another era. After Armistice Day, escape was the ticket. Hollywood became a magnet for everyone who decided an abrupt change in fortunes was needed.

Enter Benjamin Percival Schulberg, who left New York in 1909 at age sixteen to take a job on the *Evening Mail*. Schulberg had thought maybe he would become a writer, but when the opportunity presented itself, he wormed his way into Zukor's studio in the story department, rising to company manager when Zukor consolidated control of Paramount and Artcraft into Famous Players-Lasky in late 1918. Schulberg, then in his mid twenties, looked at Pickford, who was now down to making three or four pictures a year, and took stock of the rest of the retinue. Fairbanks was hot, Chaplin untouchable, and Griffith was, well, Griffith, the most famous director in the world. And it hit him: United Artists, a new company of stars.

All Schulberg needed was a front man, whom he found in William Gibbs

McAdoo, former Secretary of the Treasury and son-in-law of Woodrow Wilson. Schulberg sold his concept to the four stars as a great venture in which each would produce his own pictures, retaining all rights and controls, and UA would simply take each little piggy to market. Shares would be divided among the four principals and McAdoo. In a stroke, stars became owners, no longer employees. How United Artists went bad is another story. How it was picked from the ashes by Arthur Krim and Robert Benjamin is yet another story.

Over the long course of the industry's history, subsequent generations of filmmakers imagined what Pickford, Chaplin, Fairbanks, and Griffith saw when they heard Schulberg woo them with something more seductive than the whisper of the palm trees or the little whoosh of the closing of outstretched palms around a fat check. They heard those words "United Artists." Spalding Gray even now makes jokes about it: "You can get me to do anything when you call me an artist—jump out of a helicopter, sure, no prob."

In our own time, the dream has lived on and crashed into the various mountains that bring everyone to reality, sooner or later. Who had more crazy heart than Francis Ford Coppola when he dreamed up—or, should we say, hallucinated—Zoetrope? What was First Artists, with Paul Newman, Sidney Poitier, and Barbra Streisand, if not UA Redux?

One can argue, I suppose, that stars have, by dint of their enormous wills and backed by their gazillion-dollar paychecks, regained a measure of control over their work in a kind of herky-jerk fashion. Keep plugging and you are Clint Eastwood on the way to immortality, unbound and unforgiven. Stay in front of the mirror too long, and you're Eddie Murphy, well paid, or an Axel Rose by any other name until no one can remember it anyway. Welcome to L.A.

I will never forget the morning after the shootout between United Artists and TransAmerica, the conglomerate where a decade earlier Arthur Krim had mortgaged his soul to the devil in order to delve into the hardball of Lyndon Johnson's presidency. I was a young reporter for *Variety,* covering UA. Krim and company had the night before decamped to form Orion. There sitting in the president's chair was a wee little executive whose feet noticeably didn't touch the ground. By a lot. The company never recovered, since the soul that took flight in 1919, and found a home in 1951, had split and left no instruction book behind. Because you can't teach magic, and movies and dreams are all about magical thinking.

Among my trophies from my days at *Variety* is a present the publisher once gave me: a beautiful red enamel belt buckle. Inlaid in gold are the words "United Artists." When I wear it, I actually believe I can write anything.

HARLAN JACOBSON

TREMENDOUS MONEY INTERESTS REPORTED BACKING BIG FIVE

J. P. Morgan, Henry Ford and du Ponts All Mentioned as Furnishing Capital. Ford Denies. Fairbanks With First National. Returning Magnates Review Situation.

Los Angeles, Jan. 29.

So far as can be learned here the star unit or "big five" proposition is going through, with several big money interests mentioned as backers of the scheme. Among those whose names are freely mentioned as financially interested in it are Henry Ford, who is here (but he denies the report). The names of DuPont and Morgan are also mentioned.

Any immediate working out of such plan is impossible for the reason that all the five "headliners" are more or less tied up for a lengthy period. Even Fairbanks, whose contract is supposed to have expired, is understood to have to make one more picture for Artcraft. Hart is under contract for four more and Griffith for a like number, while Pickford and Chaplin must make at least three more for First National.

When the big five finally decide to distribute their pictures through other channels, if such a thing comes to pass, both Famous and First National would withhold the pictures they had on hand of these stars and release them in competition with the later output.

Griffith is the spokesman for the stars and stated today he would have an important statement to make tomorrow.

Griffith is doing his own exhibiting here, having leased the Kinema for the showing of his "Babylon" and "The Mother and the Law," and will follow these with others. He is understood to have been dissatisfied with the distribution of his "Hearts of the World." He wanted some of the First National franchise holders to get certain terri-

Variety, January 29, 1919.

Acting Up: Actors' Equity and the Theatre Guild

By August of 1919, the union representing legitimate theater actors, the Actors' Equity Association, was nearly seven years old, but as far as producers were concerned, it might as well have been nonexistent. The concerns of actors were never regarded seriously: They were not paid during rehearsals, nor were they paid for extra performances; actors in touring productions were completely at the mercy of managers and often found themselves far from home without train fare back when a show closed. The fledgling union had not been successful in rectifying any of those conditions.

That all changed on Wednesday, August 6, 1919, when a hundred members of Equity went on strike five minutes before curtain time, astounding the Broadway theater establishment organized as the Producing Managers' Association. The issue had boiled down to one: the actors' rather polite request that matters on which they disagreed with the managers be subject to arbitration. At first the managers agreed, but then they balked and the actors walked, immediately closing down twelve shows.

Not surprisingly, given the nature of the industry involved, the actors' strike had its dramatic episodes. The managers instantly filed a half-million-dollar damages suit against the union and, in an advertisement in *Variety,* warned that "all members of the Actors' Equity Association are personally liable for all damages and losses to the Managers caused by the strike." That one never made it to the courts.

The actors were not short of dissenters, though, the most famous of whom proved to be George M. Cohan, one of the most popular entertainers in the history of American show business. He was also one of the most powerful, being a manager and producer as well. He angrily denounced Equity and pledged $100,000 of his own money to found a rival, the Actors' Fidelity League, resigning from the Producing Managers' Association in a speech that had his colleagues near tears. (The

FACING PAGE

Variety, August 11, 1919.

NEW YORK, MONDAY, AUGUST 11, 1919

11 BROADWAY HOUSES REMAIN DARK ON SUNDAY NIGHT

New Actors' Organization For Legits Reported to Be Announced Tuesday. Will Contain Resigned Members of A. E. A. Actors' Equity Loses and Gains Important Members. Managers Do Little More Than Announce, But State They Will Fight to a Finish.

Saturday night 10 Broadway theatres remained dark, owing to the strike ordered by the Actor's Equity Association. The Producing Managers' Association's members held a meeting Saturday as they had done daily during the week, but beyond announcing they were preparing to open some of the theatres during this week, with new or partially new casts, the managers appear to have done nothing of importance to stop, settle or break the strike.

That the A. E. A. had kept so many theatres dark for three days seemed to infuse much confidence into the actors and the A. E. A. Saturday was reported securing additions to its membership in large numbers.

While the managers sent out the names of several important players who had resigned from the A. E. A., the association gained several equally

ings. There is no one head directing the managers' side. The A. E. A. has systematized its operations and, from observations has fairly well regulated itself in the matter of committees, squads and so forth.

The managers hold together solidly and it is the expressed intention of them all to make the fight to a finish.

One manager stated Saturday he

without arbitration. But the managers association insists it will not deal with a body actuated by professional agitators. The A. E. A. is equally insistant that Mountford and Fitzpatrick, the men objected to by the managers, have had nothing whatsoever to do with this A. E. A. fight.

The A. E. A. stated it is not out for a closed shop and does not expect such a condition would ever attain. An Equity head said Saturday that when the final message was sent to the managers Thursday afternoon through E. H. Sothern, there was added to the message that a closed shop was not sought.

The suddenness of the walk-out, which succeeded in crippling 12 theatres on Thursday night, without the customary theatrical two weeks' notice, was the feature which crystalized the managers to fight the strike to a finish. Equity officials admitted that this move might place the holders of contracts who walked out liable to damage actions and that the officials of the A. E. A. might be liable to conspiracy actions. But they stated that

THE STRIKE SITUATION

SHOWS OPEN

*"The Royal Vagabond"—Cohan & Harris.
"A Lonely Romeo"—Casino.
"The Better 'Ole"—Booth.
"Chu Chin Chow"—Century.
"Follies"—New Amsterdam.
"John Ferguson"—Fulton.
"La La Lucille"—Henry Miller.
"Greenwich Village Follies"—Bayes.
"Scandals of 1919"—Liberty.
"39 East"—Maxine Elliott.
*"The Challenge"—Selwyn.
†"Monte Cristo, Jr."—Winter Garden.
"Midnight Whirl"—Century Roof.

SHOWS CLOSED

"East Is West"—Astor.
"Oh, What a Girl"—Shubert.
"Listen, Lester"—Knickerbocker.
"The Five Million"—Lyric.
"The Crimson Alibi"—Broadhurst.
"At 9:45"—Playhouse.
"A Voice in the Dark"—Republic.
"Nightie Night"—Princess.
"Lightnin'"—Gayety.
†"She's a Good Fellow"—Globe.
"Gaieties of 1919"—44th Street.

$100,000 never went to the league, which refused it; Cohan donated the money to the Actors' Fund instead.)

But the striking actors had an obvious advantage over the producers: they were performers. They took to the streets outside the theaters they were striking, offering for free what customers usually paid to see. They staged benefits at the Lexington Theatre, which drew packed houses to raise money, with lineups that included "the greatest opening act ever given," *Variety* reported: Marie Dressler and "Our Chorus Girls." Other performers at the benefits included Ed Wynn, W. C. Fields, Ethel and Lionel Barrymore, and Eddie Foy. Chorus girls headed to Wall Street to demonstrate. In the most boisterous event of the strike, the actors and their sympathizers marched en masse down Broadway. This is how New York Times drama critic Brooks Atkinson described the scene in his history of Broadway:

> On a rainy day in the middle of August, two thousand actors, stagehands and musicians paraded from Columbus Circle down Broadway, led by Francis Wilson, Frank Gillmore, John Cope and Grant Stewart, the prime movers of Equity. Actors who had served overseas wore their uniforms and carried American flags. Despite the rain, there were big crowds on the sidewalks. Actors and actresses enthusiastically beamed at them and they cheered in return. "No More Pay. Just Fair Play," one of the signs read.

The number of theaters affected varied from day to day during the strike, as the managers coerced chorus members not represented by Equity into performing and in some cases took to the stage themselves. However, by the end of the strike exactly thirty days after it began, thirty-seven shows in eight cities had been closed; sixteen others had canceled their openings. The losses were estimated at $3 million. And Equity, under the leadership of executive secretary Gillmore, was finally recognized as the actors' representative in contract negotiations, and its members would finally earn extra pay for extra performances, among other benefits. Broadway quickly recovered from the losses, and there would be no like confrontation for forty-one years.

One theater that was not affected by the strike was the Garrick on West 35th Street, just east of Broadway. Earlier in the year the theater's lessor, the financier Otto Kahn, had agreed to turn the six hundred-seat house over to an adventurous new group that called itself the Theatre Guild. The Guild would have many other homes during the ensuing decades, but few arrangements would match Kahn's: if a Guild show earned enough money to cover the rent, the rent would be due; if not, no rent would be paid.

The Theatre Guild was really the second incarnation of the Washington Square Players, an amateur ensemble based in Greenwich Village that prided itself on presenting more challenging fare than was being produced uptown. Writers embraced by the Players included Eugene O'Neill, Oscar Wilde, Arthur Schnitzler, and the

Variety, August 10, 1919.

European playwrights who were dragging the theater into the twentieth century: Ibsen, Chekhov, and Shaw. The Players disbanded in 1918, but three key members, Lawrence Langner, Philip Moeller, and Helen Westley, regrouped a year later. Their plan was to create a democratically run organization of actors, writers, and other talent to produce new works for a subscription audience. Guild members would share the profits of Guild productions (hence the dispensation from Equity).

The first production, Jaconto Benavente's *Bonds of Interest,* opened on April 14, 1919, and ran just thirty-two performances, losing five hundred dollars per week (most of which had been donated by members). But the second show, John Ervine's *John Ferguson,* was a hit; the melodrama ("meller," in *Variety* parlance) starred Augustin Duncan (brother of Isadora) and ran 177 performances. In fact, it wasn't very good. The actors' strike undoubtedly helped sustain its run, because so many houses were dark.

From such meager beginnings emerged the most distinguished producing organization in the history of the American theater. Many of the early plays were of European origin, but slowly the Guild came into its own not only as Shaw's American champion, but as the signatory producer of native work. The watershed was Elmer Rice's bleakly futuristic *Adding Machine,* which Langner directed in 1923. The Guild sponsored subscription series around the country and dabbled in movies as well. Its fortunes were a constant roller coaster, though, as Langner and company flirted with financial disaster, which was staved off by the occasional hit. The Guild produced both Molnár's *Liliom* and the Rodgers and Hammerstein musical based on it, *Carousel.* It produced both Lynn Riggs's *Green Grow the Lilacs* and the Rodgers and Hammerstein musical based on it, *Oklahoma!* The premiere of *Porgy and Bess* in 1935 was a Guild production.

During the 1930s the Guild, by then more or less part of the establishment, also served as the incubator for another revolutionary troupe, the Group Theatre, whose members included such writers as Clifford Odets and Paul Green, and which spawned such legendary talents as directors Harold Clurman, Lee Strasberg, and Elia Kazan. But the Guild itself was never a snobbish organization. It welcomed musical comedy authors Betty Comden, Adolph Green, and Jule Styne (*Bells Are Ringing*) along with Eugene O'Neill.

And although the Guild today exists in little more than spirit, it was for much of this century the conscience of Broadway.

JEREMY GERARD

Beyond the Horizon— Broadway Gets Serious

When Eugene O'Neill's *Beyond the Horizon* opened on Broadway at the unorthodox hour of 2:15 P.M. on February 3, 1920, the New York critics were tired, having reviewed roughly one hundred productions since the season's start in late June. The season began earlier in those days, and the hardworking critics had already recorded their opinions of thirty musicals and revues, sixty comedies and melodramas, six farces, a couple of adaptations of European classics, and a limited run of Shakespearian repertory. Moreover, they were scheduled that evening to cover the opening of an adaptation of a Georges Feydeau farce called *Breakfast in Bed*.

Nothing like "an American tragedy"—which was how *Beyond the Horizon* was billed—had ever before challenged the critics' languid spirits. Certainly they were unprepared to witness what would turn out to be a theatrical milestone.

Some of these critics had gone downtown to Greenwich Village to see the Provincetown Players' productions of the young O'Neill's one-act plays, notably *Bound East for Cardiff* (1916), *The Long Voyage Home* (1917), and *The Moon of the Caribbees* (1919) and had recognized a talented newcomer. But this was O'Neill's first full-length play to be produced: a study of two brothers—one a doomed idealist, the other a disillusioned pragmatist—tragically in love with the same woman.

The critics were impressed, if not altogether dazzled. The influential Heywood Broun, for example, wrote in the *Tribune* that *Beyond the Horizon* was "a significant and interesting play by a young author who does not yet know all the tricks." The anonymous critic for the *Herald*, while praising the play for being "profoundly human and moving in most of its scenes," found it "unnecessarily long"—a criticism O'Neill was destined to hear more than once during his lifetime.

Alexander Woollcott, on the other hand, was astute enough to praise the play warmly for many of the right reasons, writing in the *New York Times* (in both his

FACING PAGE

Dramatis Persona: Sinclair Lewis credited playwright Eugene O'Neill, *opposite,* with having transformed the American drama "utterly in ten or twelve years from a false world of neat and competent trickery to a world of splendor, fear, and greatness."

daily and Sunday pieces) that the theatrical season was "immeasurably richer and more substantial" because of *Beyond the Horizon,* which he described as "an absorbing, significant and memorable tragedy, so full of meat that it makes most of the remaining fare seem like the merest meringue." He went on to praise O'Neill—then thirty-one—as "one of our foremost playwrights" as well as "one of the most spacious men to be both gifted and tempted to write for the theater in America...In its strength, its fidelity, its color, its irony, and its pitilessness, [*Beyond the Horizon*] recalls nothing quite so much as...the tales of Thomas Hardy." Yet not even the sagacious Woollcott recognized that an event of far-reaching significance had occurred on Broadway—nor could he predict the impact of the play on Broadway's future.

Eugene O'Neill, himself, with the born ego that drives artistic genius, had never doubted that it was in his power to revolutionize the American theater, and *Beyond the Horizon* was his embryonic battle cry. Capable of working with iron-willed concentration for as much as seven hours a day, he completed the play in Provincetown, Massachusetts, in April of 1918. Ruthless in his editing, he often destroyed entire scripts he deemed unworthy; by the time he completed *Beyond the Horizon*—less than five years after he began it—he had disowned or actually torn up eight of his twenty one-act plays and five long ones.

Beyond the Horizon was the first long play he did not destroy. He sent it off to his friend and mentor, editor and drama critic George Jean Nathan, who read it and immediately took it to John D. Williams, a producer known for his efforts to counter the tingle-and-tinsel tradition of such Broadway showmen as David Belasco and Charles Frohman. Although *Beyond the Horizon* was a departure far beyond anything Williams had yet dared, Nathan thought he would have the courage and imagination to take it on.

An oddity among Broadway producers of his day, Williams was a soundly educated Harvard man and (in common with O'Neill) had attended Professor George Pierce Baker's playwriting classes. He produced plays he liked (along with those he knew would be commercial) even though he often lost money on them. "Intelligence and good taste," he acknowledged, were "fatal to successful play producing anywhere in America, because, handicapped by either of these, you are apt to produce the kind of play you think other college graduates will go to see." He went on to list more than half a dozen plays "of substance, some taste, real acting and containing some interesting angles on life" that he had produced, asking plaintively, "And what happened?"

"Every college graduate ran as fast as he could past the theaters containing these handstitched college graduate plays, put on by a college graduate," he said. "And they didn't stop running until they landed in the front row of the 'Follies'; failing that, they ran over to see 'Girls, Girls, and Nothing but Girls,' 'Oh, You Girls,' or 'The Skidding of Tottie Coughdrop.'"

Nonetheless, Williams decided once again to put his faith in substance and taste and, in what was surely one of the speediest transactions in the annals of show business, immediately sent O'Neill a check for five hundred dollars as an option for six months. And then, not uncharacteristically for the theater, nothing happened.

Though frustrated by the seemingly endless delay, O'Neill continued to work steadily on two new plays, one of them ultimately to evolve as *Anna Christie*. And he complained to friends like Professor Baker (in May 1919) that, while Williams intended to produce *Beyond* with John and Lionel Barrymore as the two brothers, their current starring vehicle, *Redemption,* was a hit that showed no sign of closing. Williams had, however, renewed his option, O'Neill said, and promised a production before December.

In December, fuming over the continued delay, O'Neill wrote to the critic Barrett Clark, "I'm still at the nerve-racking job of waiting for a production." Broadway, it appeared, was suffering from an acute theater shortage. John Williams, evidently unable to find one for *Beyond the Horizon,* had nonetheless managed to book the Morosco for a new play called *For the Defense*. In Provincetown O'Neill angrily read about this latest betrayal, never dreaming that this overwrought courtroom drama, by a young playwright named Elmer Rice, would serve as the indirect means of finally getting his play into production.

In the cast of *For the Defense* was the handsome and popular leading man Richard Bennett (two of whose daughters, Joan and Constance, became movie stars). Bennett, then forty-seven, was beginning to be dissatisfied with matinee-idol roles. Not long after the opening of the Rice play, he visited Williams's office, pulled the dusty manuscript of *Beyond the Horizon* out of a cubbyhole, and found himself greatly moved by it. He urged Williams to let him star in the play as the twenty-three-year-old Robert Mayo. He also offered a solution both for the theater shortage and for the financial risk of presenting a contemporary American tragedy. He suggested that the play be staged at the Morosco, where *For the Defense* appeared to be settled in for a long run; that as much of the cast as possible be recruited from that play; and that the new production be presented in a series of special matinees. Williams, genuinely eager to give *Beyond* a hearing, quickly calculated that he would not have to risk more than an investment in some sketchy scenery. He agreed to Bennett's plan.

Bennett persuaded three cast members of *For the Defense* to accept roles in the O'Neill play and rounded up Edward Arnold and Helen MacKellar from another successful melodrama then on Broadway to play the older brother, Andrew, and the young woman, Ruth, with whom both brothers are smitten. To these actors, appearing in *Beyond the Horizon* was an act of faith and love; it meant rehearsing a second role in addition to performing daily in their established vehicles, and then giving twelve performances a week, instead of eight. But Bennett's enthusiasm was contagious, and soon they had a creditable production.

O'Neill, having waited so long, was caught off guard by the suddenness of the venture and had little chance to object to the makeshift arrangements. Having set his heart on the still youthful John Barrymore, he was not readily reconciled to the middle-aged Bennett in the role of young Robert Mayo; nor did he think the rest of the cast ideal. He was outraged by the hastily improvised stock interior and picture-postcard exterior that Williams provided for scenery, but it was to be the impromptu matinee production or none at all. He settled sulkily for the matinee, a series of four performances a week which would, Williams promised, be installed regularly in another theater when one became available.

Hiding behind a pillar at the back of the theater to avoid recognition, O'Neill watched the audience, including his parents, Ella and James, file into the Morosco Theatre on West Forty-fifth Street on opening day. The curtain rose on a badly painted, awkwardly lighted set that was supposed to represent O'Neill's poetically conceived section of country highway, "the horizon hills...rimmed by a faint line of flame, and the sky above them [aglow] with the crimson flush of the sunset." But the shabby sets were forgotten and the audience sat in tense, respectful silence, as the grim and chaotic tale of the two brothers unfolded with uncompromising realism.

James O'Neill, himself a celebrated matinee idol in his day, sat with his wife in a box, rigidly erect with his disciplined actor's carriage, but tears streamed down his cheeks. He had often despaired of the future for the moody, willful and seemingly self-destructive Eugene. When the final curtain fell he walked, damp-eyed and beaming, to the back of the theater and patted his son. "Are you trying to send the audience home to commit suicide?" he asked huskily.

"I felt sure," Eugene O'Neill said later, "when I saw the woebegone faces on the audience on opening day that it was a rank failure. No one was more surprised than I when I saw the morning papers and came to the conclusion that the sad expressions on the playgoers' faces were caused by their feeling the tragedy I had written."

Yet few of the critics—although aware that a noteworthy event had taken place—evaluated the play accurately. They had difficulty finding a niche into which they could place it and its author. It was not that they had never seen contemporary tragedy well performed on Broadway: a number of European plays had been skillfully adapted for the commercial stage, and they had been impressed by the occasional imaginative works of such Americans as Percy MacKaye and William Vaughan Moody. But *Beyond the Horizon* was unclassifiable because it combined naturalism and tragedy with native character and contemporary expression. It employed no melodramatic tricks and did not rely on coincidence; it was built upon the development of character alone, eschewing plot for plot's sake. It was, in short, something never before attempted by an American for the Broadway theater: dramatic literature. It was written, rather than contrived, and it introduced the possibility—long since realized in Europe—that the commercial theater could express

dramatic literature, rather than serve merely as an amusement arena. O'Neill, though dismayed by the failure of most of the critics to comprehend his achievement fully, was elated with the realization that he had finally done what he had set out to do: force Broadway to accept him on his own terms. (In 1930 Sinclair Lewis, in his Nobel Prize acceptance speech, would credit O'Neill with having transformed the American drama "utterly in ten or twelve years from a false world of neat and competent trickery to a world of splendor, fear and greatness.")

Beyond the Horizon turned out to be a hit, and Williams moved it to the Criterion on February 23 for regular evening performances. It ran for 111 (a respectable run in those days) and grossed $117,071, of which O'Neill's share was only $6,264 (he had accepted a low royalty rate in his eagerness to sign a contract, but it was more money than he had ever earned before). That June the play was awarded the Pulitzer Prize (the first of O'Neill's four). Established only three years before, it had been withheld twice and given only once in the category of drama (to *Why Marry?* by Jesse Lynch Williams in 1918). To O'Neill the prize meant chiefly a windfall. Later, O'Neill (who had a lifelong affection for contemporary slang and an addiction to the exclamation mark) said:

> In 1920 I had honestly never heard of the Pulitzer Prize, or if I had, hadn't listened. So when a wire reached me…saying I had won it, my reaction was a disdainful raspberry—"Oh, a damned medal! And one of those presentation ceremonies! I won't accept it!" (I have never been fond of medals or ceremonies.) Then a wire from my agent arrived which spoke of a thousand dollars and no medal and no ceremony. Well, I practically went delirious! I was broke or nearly. A thousand dollars was sure a thousand dollars! It was the most astoundingly pleasant surprise I've ever had in my life.

In a more serious vein, O'Neill vowed to George Jean Nathan in the summer of 1920 that, despite the success and acclaim for *Beyond the Horizon,* he would not rest on his laurels. He had paved the way for his own further development (let alone the development of future American dramatists of serious intent, such as Arthur Miller and Tennessee Williams), and he would continue to grow and to oblige Broadway to grow with him. He grandly declared:

> I will not "stay put'" in any comfortable niche and play the leave-well-enough-alone game….I am young yet and I mean to grow! And in this faith I live: That if I have the "guts" to ignore the megaphone men and what goes with them, to follow the dream and to live for that alone, then my real significant bit of truth, and the ability to express it, will be conquered in time—not tomorrow nor the next day nor any near, easily attained period, but after the struggle has been long enough and hard enough to merit victory.

Barbara Gelb

Barrymore Takes Broadway!

An understated notice appeared on the entertainment page of the *New York Times* for November 16, 1922. It read: "Arthur Hopkins announces the opening performance of John Barrymore in 'Hamlet' at the Sam H. Harris Theatre. Tonight at 8 o'clock sharp. First Matinee Saturday at 2:15. Seats now on sale. Prices after opening, $3.30 to $1.10."

That Barrymore ever attempted *Hamlet* at all can be traced to the moment his sister, Ethel, only three years older but always a protective and somewhat motherly figure in his life and career, had given him a small, red Temple Edition of the play at a health spa in French Lick, Indiana. She had taken him there in the hope of lifting the gloom she knew had settled over him when his second wife, Blanche Oelrichs (who wrote poetry under the pseudonym Michael Strange), on June 28 of that year, sailed for Europe on the *Mauretania* in the company of Doris Rankin, the wife of their older brother, Lionel, both marriages being in considerable trouble. Ethel suggested to her little brother that he "learn one of the soliloquies," which he promptly did. When he performed it for her a few days later, neither of them seemed satisfied, although Ethel later claimed she "knew the spark was there."

Upon their return to New York, John journeyed on to the Greenwich, Connecticut, estate of retired concert singer Margaret Carrington, who had coached him when he played Richard III at the Plymouth Theatre early in 1920. Barrymore had gone to Carrington in the first place because his uncle, John Drew, had loathed what he called the actor's "furry" voice and felt the diva's system of vocal exercises might give him an entirely revamped instrument. "Jack [John] speaks like a ruffian from Avenue A," Drew complained. "It's a disgrace to a family. How he came by these shoddy accents, I cannot know."

Carrington, the sister of actor Walter Huston, approached each Shakespearean text as though it had never been played before, a tack that appealed to the adventurous Barrymore. She imposed her own conditions: no opening night could be selected until she had worked with him for a solid month, and, even after that, the play could not be produced until she felt sure that the actor was professionally as well as psychologically ready.

Barrymore stayed at the estate for two and a half months. "We studied the play

as we would a modern script that had never been performed," Carrington wrote. "I think this accounted for his spontaneous reading and acting throughout the various scenes and helped to banish any natural fear he might have had appearing for the first time in a part that has been the high spot in every actor's experience."

The other "team" members, designer Robert Edmond Jones (whom Carrington would marry in 1930) and Barrymore's long-standing producer, the chubby, elfin Arthur Hopkins, finally got the nod from Carrington, and the opening date of November 16 was settled upon. Hopkins hired Rosalinde Fuller, a twenty-one-year-old British ballad singer and onetime show girl, as Ophelia, at $175 a week. Blanche Yurka, blond and Czechoslovakian-born, would be the production's Gertrude, at $300. Tyrone Power Sr., the hard-drinking father of the future film star, received $675 as Claudius. Barrymore's salary was $1,000. The well-established classical troupe headed by Julia Marlowe and E. H. Sothern had recently folded, and as a result Hopkins found many of the smaller players for his *Hamlet* among the actors suddenly cast adrift by that misfortune.

Jones had played an increasingly major role in Hopkins's recent productions, and for *Hamlet* he may have overextended himself. A vast flight of stairs rose from the stage to a huge upstage arch through which the "sky" could be seen, the precise blue varying to accommodate the mood of the scene at hand. Three platforms extended left or right at various levels of the staircase, while another reached out over the orchestra pit. There were to be no footlights, with all illumination provided by overhead lamps and side spots.

The actors were required to do a good deal of staircase negotiation, and their eventual view of Jones's set depended, understandably, on their individual adroitness at climbing and scampering. The Ghost of Hamlet's Father was represented by a shimmering light and disembodied voice, a device that never satisfied Barrymore and that, in fact, he eliminated, restoring the part to a corporeal actor when he re-created the production at London's Haymarket Theatre for a successful run starting on February 19, 1925. Veteran actor Whitford Kane, who joined the company in the third week of rehearsals to play one of the grave diggers, lamented to the elegant Barrymore that Hamlet appeared to have been sired by a light bulb. Many observers felt that the set competed with Barrymore for attention; indeed, it was nicknamed "Penn Station" by the star, who had to cope each night and matinee with its peculiarities.

Extensive cutting is almost always a given with *Hamlet*. Even so, the version cobbled together by Hopkins, Carrington, and Barrymore was noteworthy in that more than 1,250 lines had been eliminated. In addition, by avoiding the cuts traditionally made, the trio had virtually reinvented certain characters, especially Laertes, Polonius, and Horatio.

Hopkins's admiration for Barrymore was boundless. "Of all the actors I have ever known," he said, he was the most conscientious and untiring in preparation. Nothing was too much trouble. He would go to the costumer, the boot maker, the wig maker, the armor maker, twenty times each, forty if necessary, to get everything right. He was the first to know his part. He would rehearse each time as though it were a performance. He was never late, never made excuses. He would rehearse scenes with other actors as long as they wanted. He never grew tired. To him perfection was the aim, and its attainment could not be too much trouble.

(One Barrymore family story puts the producer's claim that his star never tired in question. Critics praised Barrymore for delivering the initial soliloquy introspectively, from a seated position in an almost self-effacing manner. The version related to the actor's grandson John Blyth Barrymore as he grew up maintained, false or true, that Barrymore had had a courage-bolstering drink in the wings and, growing dizzy as he entered, had little alternative but to sit down for the scene.)

A Tennessee-born actor, John Lark Taylor, kept a log of the entire run of *Hamlet*, starting with an entry for the first day's rehearsal, in which he owned up to a certain trepidation about working with the star. "I rather dreaded rehearsing with Barrymore," he admitted,

> for I'd heard, from all sources, that he was a "Perfect Fiend," absolutely impossible at rehearsals and to act with. I must say he proved quite the reverse....A kinder, more considerate person at rehearsals I've never been associated with. He seemed to go out of his way sometimes to be kind and courteous. He rarely directed anyone; occasionally he would make a suggestion, and always a good one...he seemed to want each individual actor in the cast to get the most he could out of his part.

Much as Barrymore liked to refer to himself as "only an instrument in an orchestra," his Gertrude, played by Blanche Yurka, quickly came to the conclusion that every move the actor made was planned and calculated, albeit with great intelligence, and woe betied the actor or actress who failed to hit a mark or was even slightly late or early delivering a cue. Barrymore was, Yurka soon enough learned, the star, and the only competition he could tolerate came from Jones' daunting scenery. Yurka was, as it happened, some seven years younger than Barrymore, which lent a certain Freudian thrust to the scenes they played together, rendering them as love scenes in a way and to a degree Broadway audiences had never seen

> John Barrymore is said to have taken exception to the critical comment on "Hamlet" in one of the New York afternoon dailies to the effect that "Other players in the cast will agree their performance cannot be mentioned in the same breath with Mr. Barrymore's." The star is reported having posted a notice at the Sam H. Harris stating the opinion was preposterous. Also he took occasion to thank the players for their fine support. For some reason the Barrymore note was removed shortly after being posted.
>
> Fortune Gallo's San Carlo Grand Opera Company is piling up a business

Variety, December 1, 1922.

Barrymore ended his New York run of *Hamlet* on February 8, 1923. On the night of the last performance, the box office turned away over a thousand people.

before. (Sir Laurence Olivier saw Barrymore's *Hamlet* in London when he was just seventeen, and found the actor "burningly real." When he made his film version of the play in 1948, possibly remembering the heat generated by Barrymore and Yurka, Olivier selected as his Gertrude the Scottish actress Eileen Herlie, who was fully thirteen years his junior.)

While *Hamlet* was in rehearsal, Ethel Barrymore was performing just six blocks north, at the Longacre Theatre, in Gerhart Hauptmann's *Rose Bernd,* also produced by Hopkins. On *Hamlet*'s opening night, she had her cast play the Hauptmann text at breakneck speed, so that she could see at least the final scenes of her baby brother's greatest stage triumph. The response of the New York press was universally positive.

In the *New York Times,* Alexander Woollcott called it "a 'Hamlet' reborn and one that, for all its skill and graphic artfulness, is so utterly free from all that is of the state stagey. Issuing from [Barrymore's] lips, the soliloquies seemed to have been spoken for the first time." Stark Young, in the *New Republic,* wrote that Barrymore "seemed to gather in himself all the Hamlets of his generation, to simplify and direct everyone's theory of the part. His Hamlet was the most satisfying I have ever seen." Percy Hammond wrote in the *Tribune* that "Mr. Barrymore's Hamlet was so beautiful a picture, so clear in analysis, so untheatrical in impersonation, and so musical a rendering of Shakespeare's song."

Barrymore disliked the idea of wearing tights, which he called "skin-fitting jollities," and which made him feel as though he had "put on the intimate wear of Peg Woffington." He borrowed a pair of underdrawers from his brother, Lionel, to wear beneath, and they seemed to him to be a sort of good luck charm—in addition to which they were seamless and did not bunch up on his thighs. With the fiftieth *Hamlet* performance at hand, the actor's valet gently suggested a change of underwear. The star rebelled. "Damn it, no! I opened in these drawers," he roared, "and, by God, I'll close in them!"

According to Barrymore's first biographer, his friend and journalist Gene Fowler, the actor was visited in his dressing room at one point by a collection of elderly men who asked him to end the run with the ninety-ninth performance. When he asked why, he was informed that Edwin Booth had played the role on Broadway a hundred times, and they were interested in seeing to it that Booth's record remain unbroken. "Gentlemen," Barrymore replied, "I think it about time that you stop living in the past. That's what's wrong with the world. It is run by a lot of persons who keep bitching up the present by applying only the rules of a dead past. I am compelled to inform you that I shall play Hamlet for exactly 101 times. And when you see the master, give him my regards. I knew him when I was a little boy, and he'll laugh like the devil when you tell him that you saw me."

It appears that Booth's run was not the record Barrymore had to beat. A now-forgotten actor, John E. Kellerd, racked up 102 performances during the 1912-1913 season, according to a later Barrymore biographer, John Kobler, "beginning at the Garden Theater and finishing, oddly enough, at the theater where John was to appear ten years later, the Harris."

Barrymore's *Hamlet* ended its New York run on February 8, 1923, as the actor wished, since he had no formal contract with Hopkins. On the night of the last performance, the Sam H. Harris box office turned away over a thousand people. Barrymore, contrite that he had put some sixty colleagues out of work, vowed to take up the role again in the fall for a brief tour—which, true to his word, he did.

In 1925, Barrymore took his *Hamlet* to London. Hopkins, for all his professed faith in the actor, had declined to produce the show across the Atlantic; an English acquaintance had told him, "If Barrymore has the audacity to come to London in *Hamlet,* they'll assassinate him." Conquering his own doubts, Barrymore raised the money himself for a limited run of six weeks—extended to nine—and the actor not only got his $25,000 investment back, but made $10,000 more. The sole blight on the London run was that Barrymore's wife, Blanche, by now fairly well estranged from him, brought George Bernard Shaw to the opening night. Shaw became upset, not by Barrymore's performance, but by the extensive cuts, which he felt did lethal damage to Shakespeare's text. The playwright never published a review, but he wrote the actor a lengthy letter, accusing him of literary violence. "You saved, say, an hour and a half on Shakespeare by cutting," Shaw raged, "and filled it up with an interpolated drama of your own in dumb show."

Still, John Barrymore, a member of America's theater royalty, had introduced Shakespeare to many of his own countrymen for the first time, changing Broadway forever. The actor played his last *Hamlet* ever on Saturday evening, April 18, 1925, and sailed for New York the following Thursday.

JOSEPH HURLEY

Apparently the only person who didn't like Barrymore's *Hamlet,* George Bernard Shaw accused the actor of butchering the Bard's text and filling it up with an "interpolated drama of your own in dumb show."

The Jazz Singer raked in $3.5 million, saving the Warners from bankruptcy and winning a special Oscar at the first Academy Awards.

FACING PAGE

"You Ain't Heard Nothing Yet!":
When Al Jolson, playing a cantor's son, sings "Blue Skies" to his mother in this scene from *The Jazz Singer,* America's first pop star ushers in the sound era with a bang. Incredibly, only 354 words are spoken in the film, almost all of them ad-libbed by Jolson.

Hollywood Talks!

In a particularly memorable scene from Warner Bros.' revolutionary 1927 film *The Jazz Singer,* Al Jolson, playing Jackie Robin, a cantor's son with a passion for the music of the streets, finishes singing "Dirty Hands, Dirty Face," turns to a friend in the audience, and hollers over the applause: "Wait a minute. Wait a minute. You ain't heard nothin' yet!" Jolson then breaks into a rousing jazz number that brings the house down.

Later, when Jolson returns home and sings "Blue Skies" to his mother, he pauses between verses to tell her that he loves her and wants to take her to Coney Island, to move her to the Bronx, to buy her a new pink dress if and when he makes it big in show business. "Shut your eyes, Mama," he enthuses. "Shut 'em for little Jackie. Ha! I'm going to steal something." He laughs, then leans over and kisses her. "I'll give it back to you someday too—you see if I don't." In these brief, off-the-cuff bits of repartee, captured on Vitaphone's rudimentary sound-on-disc recording system by Warner Bros., Al Jolson almost single-handedly ushered in the new age in motion pictures that would change Hollywood forever.

Contrary to popular belief, *The Jazz Singer* was not the first film to introduce sound to pictures. Technically speaking, it is actually a silent picture interspersed with musical numbers and brief dialogue. Nor was it the first time movie audiences had ever heard voices that talked from the screen. There had been plenty of novelty films offering that, including a Fox-Movietone newsreel featuring an interview with the playwright George Bernard Shaw. What was so remarkable about the premiere of this sentimental movie is that it was the first time anyone had ever heard words spoken in a dramatic film. Thanks to Jolson's penchant for ad-libbing, the spontaneous conversations sounded so intimate, so unpredictable and so lifelike that audiences went crazy, lapping up every syllable, as if he were standing right in front of them delivering the lines. During the scene with Jolson and his mother, audiences in theaters across the country literally stood up and cheered. No one had ever seen—or heard—anything quite like it before.

The journey from silence to sound in films was a long one, with many detours. The story actually begins with Thomas Edison's invention of the phonograph in 1877. Edison, who pioneered the Kinetoscope, also invented the Tinfoil Phonograph, the first recording device that actually worked. As early as 1896, he was talking about uniting the two devices to make photographic representations of

operas or plays. Elsewhere around the globe, similar efforts were being made. At the 1900 Paris Exposition, attendees were able to watch crude talkies, using synchronized sound, based on the works of Edmond Rostand. Throughout the early days of movies, the news was filled with bold innovators who were constantly trying to bring sound into the cinema halls. A film of King George V's coronation in England, for instance, was shown with synchronized sound effects at the Herald Square Theatre in New York. At movie houses narrators were often hired to read the titles, and phonographs were used to play background sounds. Troupes of actors made careers out of traveling with silent movies and reading the dialogue from behind the screen. But in time, audiences found such gimmicks to be distractions, rather than enhancements. The narrators were eventually replaced with captions, and recorded sound effects were replaced with live orchestras.

Like Thomas Edison, however, hundreds of enterprising inventors explored the feasibility of liberating movies from their silence. Patents were given for devices with unusual names like Synchroscope, Projectophone, Telegraphone, Photographophone, Pallophotophone, Chronophone, Kinetophone, Titanifone, Madalatone, and the preposterous-sounding Phonocinematophone. In 1921 D. W. Griffith experimented with sound by employing sound effects in *Dream Street* at Town Hall in New York. The film used a synchronized sound system called Photokinema. Although praised for his efforts, the idea languished. It seemed the public's appetite for sound in pictures was not yet whetted. Lee De Forest was a maverick who started the Phonofilm Company in 1923 using an optical recording device that provided silent films with synchronized sound. For the most part, however, his presentations were poorly realized dramatically, and the studios initially rejected his idea. Behind their resistance to this new form of entertainment was a reluctance to mess with a sure thing. The popularity of silent pictures was unprecedented in the history of show business, and it had taken several years to achieve a level of sophistication that won the approval of critics as well as fans. The money these studios were making defied comprehension. To jeopardize a tried-and-true system seemed ludicrous.

But the Warner brothers—Sam, Harry, Albert, and Jack—thought otherwise. They were impressed by a device developed at Bell Laboratories called Vitaphone, which promised to make synchronized musical accompaniment easier and better sounding. In April 1926 Warner Bros. contracted to use the Vitaphone system to record a synchronized score for a lavish silent film they were producing—*Don Juan*—starring John Barrymore. The Warners saw in the project the genesis of a profitable subindustry. If they could conceivably "can" the music to be presented alongside their silent pictures, they could guarantee a universal level of quality at all screenings across the country, and they could own the rights to the original scores as well. They could also reap substantial profits by selling the Vitaphone equipment to the theaters. Ironically, the Warners did not yet foresee that the invention would

The first purpose-built sound stage in the world was Stage Three at Warner Bros. Studios on Sunset Boulevard in Hollywood, where shooting on *The Jazz Singer* began in 1926.

usher in a new age of talking pictures.

On August 6, 1926, Vitaphone premiered at a gala spectacle at the Warner Theatre in New York. Before the actual presentation of *Don Juan,* with an original score by William Axt, the audience was greeted by a filmed announcement by Will Hays, president of the Motion Picture Producers and Directors of America, who promised "a new era in music and motion pictures." Then Warners unveiled several Vitaphone shorts which they had laboriously produced at the Flatbush Studios and at the Manhattan Opera—including arias sung by Giovanni Martinelli (who sang "Vesti la Giubba" from *Pagliacci*), Anna Case, and the Metropolitan Opera Chorus. The great Efrem Zimbalist played the violin, while a popular dancing duo, the Cansinos (Rita Hayworth's parents), performed. The event was a sensation, and the show ran for over a year, grossing more than $800,000. But even though Vitaphone was suddenly proclaimed as "the eighth wonder of the world," it was still considered just a novelty item by the critics.

Despite their disappointment—and near bankruptcy after pouring their life savings into the venture—the Warners immediately set out to create another film to exploit the Vitaphone phenomenon. *The Better 'Ole,* a comedy, was released later that year along with a Vitaphone short of Al Jolson singing. The film got good notices, but the response to the famed vaudevillian's few minutes on screen was incredible. Mordaunt Hall, the *New York Times* film critic, predicted, "This Vitaphone [short] assuredly destroys the old silent tradition of the screen." *Variety* took a more pessimistic view, but one that proved equally prophetic: "What would happen to the class theatres with expensive orchestras and stage shows," the

Hollywood paper asked, "if any jerk water movie joint was to be able to give its patrons gorgeous feasts of music via the screen?"

This time, the Warners decided to go with a modern story that had a vaudeville hook. In 1926, Sam Warner had bought the film rights to Sam Raphaelson's hit play *The Jazz Singer,* based on his popular short story "A Day of Atonement," which had appeared in *Everybody*'s magazine. George Jessel had been the Broadway star of the immensely popular show and a shoo-in for the movie role, but negotiations over his salary broke down when he learned the film was to be a Vitaphone feature, rather than a silent. He felt he deserved more money if people were going to hear him sing. The Warners dropped him and landed Al Jolson as a replacement—a natural choice since *The Jazz Singer* was based on his life.

Raphaelson had written the play after seeing Jolson perform in *Robinson Crusoe, Jr.* in Chicago. The son of a cantor, Jolson (né Asa Yoelson) had starred in nine Broadway hits between 1911 and 1925. He was one of the first real music superstars—"the Mick Jagger of his time," as one critic put it. During the making of the picture, in between takes, Jolson kept ad-libbing lines and, delighted by the impromptu dialogue, the director, Alan Crosland, decided to keep them in. The totally unexpected result was the mania that surrounded the release of *The Jazz Singer.* Audiences were thrilled by Jolson's explosive, contagious stage presence. While the public stood up to cheer, critics lined up to offer their stamp of approval. Robert Sherwood, the movie critic for *Life* magazine wrote: "When Al Jolson starts to sing…well, bring on your super-spectacles, your million-dollar thrills, your long shots of Calvary against a setting sun, your closeups of a glycerine tear on Norma Talmadge's cheek. I'll trade them all for one instant of any ham song that Al cares to put over—and the hammier it is the better I'll like it."

"Jolson fever" swept the nation. Everyone wanted to see the eye-popping, melody-drawling minstrel sing, dance, and act (or at least try to) in his first major motion picture. Not everyone was thrilled, however. Aldous Huxley, future author of *Brave New World,* criticized the maudlin sentimentality of the film in a now-famous article entitled "Silence Is Golden," and made disparaging remarks about "the dark…Hebrews" populating the movie. But *The Jazz Singer* paid no heed, raking in a fortune for the once nearly-broke Warners and winning a special Oscar at the Academy Awards for being "the outstanding pioneer talking picture, which has revolutionized the industry."

Soon, theaters around the country were scurrying to install Vitaphone equipment. (The system was soon replaced by Fox-Movietone's more practical sound-on-film system, which stemmed from De Forest's Phonofilm.) In 1928, 157 out of 20,000 theaters were wired for sound. A year later, that number surged to 1,046. By 1931, 83 percent of all movie theaters were equipped, yet other technical hurdles had to be overcome. Camera movement was severely restricted because of the need to record the actors with stationary microphones. Fluidity of composition was cur-

VARIETY

Jessel and Jolson

Owing to the several inquiries by lay readers of Variety as to whom was whom in the play and picture versions of "The Jazz Singer," these are the facts:

George Jessel stars in the play.

Al Jolson stars in the picture.

Variety, January 4, 1928.

PIC

ACTUAL 'TALKING PICTURES' LO(
AS SCREEN POSSIBILITY SI

Paramount is preparing a sound and talking device for its pictures. Warner Brothers is reported dialoging a highly dramatic courtroom trial in a coming release and Gen-

Brewster Lonesome

Los Angeles, Nov. 22.
Eugene V. Brewster who

F. N. HOL
FOR LA

Variety, November 23, 1927.

tailed due to editing limitations. Films could be made only indoors, and the cameras had to be enclosed in soundproof cages so that their motor would not interfere with the recording. These boxes were so hot that cameramen could run them only a few minutes at a time. Then there was the problem of what to say and how to say it. Many actors and actresses had to take elocution lessons; authors were hired from Broadway and literary circles to salvage tedious scripts. But in just a few short years, numerous improvements were made. Spontaneity was restored. Composers such as Irving Berlin, George Gershwin, and Jerome Kern were persuaded to lend their talents to composing for Tinseltown, and a golden age of movie musicals and spoken dramas was on the horizon.

The first all-talking feature film was *Lights of New York,* a 1928 melodrama directed by Bryan Foy and starring Helene Costello. Poorly directed and difficult to hear, the film nevertheless became one of the biggest hits of the year. Warner Bros. quickly signed Jolson to another picture and that same year released *The Singing Fool,* another ode to sentiment in which his character sang "Sonny Boy" to his recently deceased son. A huge smash, grossing $4 million, it held the box-office record until *Gone with the Wind* surpassed it in 1939.

By 1929, all the major studios had hopped on the bandwagon. Fox announced that all of its pictures from that year on would be sound. The silent era was drawing to a close. Garbo made the leap to sound in *Anna Christie,* which boasted the legendary ad line "Garbo Talks!" Gary Cooper spoke his first screen lines in *The Shopworn Angel.* Nancy Carroll at Paramount became known as "the first star of the Talkies." Other new stars like Clark Gable, Bette Davis, Jean Harlow, John Wayne, Marlene Dietrich, and Bing Crosby appeared. Joan Crawford saw her career explode after making her first talkie, *Untamed,* in 1929. Meanwhile, old stalwarts like John Gilbert, Clara Bow, and Vilma Banky watched their careers grind to a halt as the need for eloquent voices put greater demands on actors. Charlie Chaplin held out, making *City Lights* and *Modern Times* (with a few special sound effects) as silents, but he finally saw the way the wind was blowing and released *The Great Dictator* in 1940 as a full sound feature.

MGM's first stab at a talking picture, *The Broadway Melody,* was a technical and dramatic triumph which snared the Oscar for best picture of 1929. That cinched it. The word was out. "Talkies" were here to stay. □

Despite *Show Boat*'s success, librettist Oscar Hammerstein was considered washed up by the '30s. He recouped in 1943 when he teamed with Richard Rodgers to compose the Broadway smash *Oklahoma!*

FACING PAGE

Riverboat Gamble: Producer Florenz Ziegfeld was convinced *Show Boat* would flop without the usual chorus girls and snappy dance numbers to show them off. Instead, the revolutionary "musical with a message" outshone the 270 other plays in Broadway's biggest season ever.

1 9 2 7

Show Boat: A New Kind of Musical

Imagine it's 1927—Broadway's biggest year ever. Things are still going well (the crash is two years away), but you are hard-pressed to see even a fraction of the 270 plays that have recently opened on Broadway. Still, you have seen a lot of dandy musicals: *Padlocks of 1927*, with nightclub hostess Texas Guinan; the collegiate *Good News!*, which reminded you of your days playing varsity football for Dartmouth; George M. Cohan still going strong in *The Merry Malones.* Florenz Ziegfeld did very well by you: you were particularly thrilled by the live ostrich that carried Claire Luce across a jungle-like set alive with cobras, tigers, and flamingos in the *Ziegfeld Follies* of 1927.

Imagine then your shock and surprise on the night of December 27. You had heard about this new Ziegfeld production called *Show Boat,* a musical based on—of all things—a novel by Edna Ferber. The critics had loved the show when it was in tryouts in Pittsburgh, and you hurried off to buy tickets for opening night at a steep $5.50 apiece. You should have known something was up from the minute the orchestra struck up that brooding overture, which sounded like opera but with minstrel sounds—banjos and a lot of humming in the background. And then, when the curtain rises, instead of chorus girls and boys singing some cheerful nonsense over the rustle of latecomers, there's a stage full of powerful-looking black men singing, "Niggers all work on de Mississippi, Niggers all work while de white folks play—Loadin' up boats wid de bales of cotton, Gittin' no rest till de Judgment Day." For the next three hours, you and everyone around you watches dumbstruck as this musical charts the lives of three generations of a show business family and broaches the Big Questions of American life—race relations, family strife, alcoholism, miscegenation—with a load of beautiful songs, including many that will become standards: "Ol' Man River," "Bill," "Make Believe," "Can't Help Lovin' Dat Man," "You Are Love." No one applauds; no one knows what to do or say. When the curtain falls, everyone leaves silently. The next day's reviews pronounce the show the greatest musical of all time, but you are just a little confused.

Your reaction would not have been an unlikely one to America's first serious work of musical theater. As Ethan Mordden wrote in an extensive *New Yorker* piece on conductor and director John McGlinn's definitive 1988 recording (EMI), *Show Boat* was and "remains the Great American Musical—the one that forced the strategic advance from variety show to narrative as the structural basis in the composition of the musical." There was plenty of reason to have been surprised; little in the work of the composer, Jerome Kern (of the light and sophisticated comedies *Very Good Eddie* and *Sally*), or the librettist, Oscar Hammerstein II (of such romantic shows as *The Desert Song* and *Tickle Me*), gave a clue to such artistic ambition. Ziegfeld was himself dismayed: after pouring tons of money into one of his most lavish productions, he was sure he had a catastrophe on his hands. (Of particular concern to him were the lack of chorus girls and sprightly dance numbers to show them off.)

This is not to say, however, that *Show Boat* was not entertaining. *Show Boat* is primarily about entertainment and how it keeps us afloat on the very surface of the muddy, unchanging realities of the New World, symbolized by the great flowing waters of the Mississippi. That Ol' Man River—and the flight to escape it through music, dance, and the illusion of the theater—is presented by Kern and Hammerstein as the great equalizer, the medium through which a viciously segregated society becomes fluid, melds, civilizes itself. The plot—"the essential backstager," as Mordden wrote—is powerfully simple in its construction. Cap'n Andy Hawks and his shrewish wife, Parthy, operate a showboat that brings melodrama and comedy to various Southern cities along the Mississippi around 1890. They are assisted by two black helpers, Joe and his wife, Queenie, and a small company of actors, including the husband-and-wife team of leading players, Steve Baker and Julie La Verne. In one starkly explosive scene, it is revealed that the white-appearing Julie had a black mother. In order to escape arrest for miscegenation—which is a crime in the State of Mississippi—the all-white Steve cuts his wife's finger and sucks the wound, so that he can honestly claim to have black blood in him as well. Nonetheless, they are advised to leave the showboat for a very uncertain future. Meanwhile, the Hawks's young daughter, Magnolia, marries river gambler Gaylord Ravenal, but the marriage falters after they move to Chicago, and Magnolia is left to

Variety, January 4, 1928.

Wednesday, January 4, 1928

PLAYS ON BROADWAY

SHOW BOAT

Florenz Ziegfeld production of Edna Ferber's novel, musicalized by Jerome Kern (score) and Oscar Hammerstein II (libretto). Settings by Joseph Urban, dances by Sammy Lee, dialog staged by Zeke Calvan, costumes by John Harkrider, musical direction by Victor Baravalle, and $5.50 top by Mr. and Mrs. Public. In two acts and 18 scenes. Opened Dec. 27 at the Ziegfeld, New York.

Windy	Alan Campbell
Queenie	Aunt Jemima
Steve	Charles Ellis
Pete	Bert Chapman
Parthy Ann Hawks	Edna May Oliver
Cap'n Andy	Charles Winninger
Ellie	Eva Puck
Frank	Sammy White
Rubber Face	Francis X. Mahoney
Julie	Helen Morgan

ping, rich with plot and character, it's almost a pity the Edna Ferber novel wasn't dramatized "straight," sans the musical setting.

But, musicalized and Ziegfeldized, it's a worthy, sturdy entertainment. It has everything, and tops everything ever done before by Ziegfeld. It has story, music, production, casting and consistent entertainment from the 8.30 to 11.30 curtains, and is a show which defies fidgeting as the conventional zero hour of theatre curtain time approaches. One forgets the clock.

The principals are Norma Terris, Eva Puck and Sammy White, Howard Marsh, Charles Winninger, fend for herself and her baby. She is saved when she auditions for a part in a night-club revue that she has, unwittingly, been handed by the now alcohol-ravaged Julie who, after seeing Magnolia, goes off and is never seen again. Years later Magnolia and her daughter are stars of the stage, and the entire family is reunited.

Show Boat was a milestone that transcended its importance in Broadway theater; as a true melting pot of Afro-American, Anglo-Saxon, Central European, and Jewish American influences, it was also a harbinger of the future of popular American culture. Until *Show Boat* musicals were segregated into two very different veins: passionate Viennese-style operetta and musical comedy. The former was epitomized by shows like *The Student Prince* and *The Merry Widow;* the latter encompassed farcical romances, urbane or plebeian, by Rodgers and Hart, George and Ira Gershwin, Vincent Youmans, and Kern himself. The songs for these shows were as luminescent as their books were usually trite and tiresomely frivolous. At the same time there was a great black presence on Broadway in all-black revues and very popular book shows such as Eubie Blake's *Shuffle Along.* Gershwin and others had been influenced by black music and had incorporated it into their own work. But it took the sophisticated and liberal instincts of Kern and Hammerstein to merge these various musical strains—operetta and black spirituals, musical-comedy patter and old standards, folk music and ragtime—into one magnificent whole, a tale of America that uses the various forms of popular culture (melodrama, vaudeville, Hollywood movies) as plot markers.

This fusion comes to life most miraculously in the Act I, Scene II, song, "Can't Help Lovin' Dat Man." First sung as a slow, lilting ballad, this blues number is, when played in uptempo fashion, as layered textually as any other moment in musical theater history. In the kitchen of the showboat, Magnolia, Queenie, and Julie discuss Magnolia's infatuation with a handsome man she has spotted on the wharf (Gaylord). Julie warns her that he might turn out to be "just a no-account river feller" but then admits that "once a girl likes you starts to love a man, she don't stop so easy." Julie starts to sing the song but is interrupted by Queenie, who is surprised to hear a white person sing what she knows to be a distinctly black folk ballad. "What's so funny about that?" Julie responds fiercely, with an expression of terror on her face, and defiantly returns to the verse. Both Queenie and Joe, who has just walked in, join Julie, while Magnolia gets into the joyous spirit by doing a black shuffle dance.

In ten glorious minutes Kern and Hammerstein offer, in the simple form of a smartly re-created folk ballad, a chilling foreboding of Julie's tragic future and the whole premise of Magnolia's love not only for Ravenal but for Julie, Queenie, and the multiracial milieu into which she was brought up. Considered from a broader perspective still, it is a statement of love for a true American art form. It is the moment when you can actually hear the future of Broadway being born.

SCOTT BALDINGER

Torch singer Helen Morgan made "Bill" one of *Show Boat*'s most rousing numbers.

Monster Madness

In darkened movie theaters across the country on the auspicious date of Friday the 13th, February 1931, audiences shivered in their seats as they watched an eerie new "talking film" called *Dracula,* starring an unknown actor with the vaguely sinister name Bela Lugosi. Advance word had alerted audiences to the film's weird and terrifying premise: the tale of a vampire who escapes the inevitability of death by sucking the blood of beautiful young women. Advertised as "The Strangest Love Story of All" (to capitalize on its Valentine's Day weekend opening), the film was shot in a stark monochrome and filled with ghoulish images of cobweb-strewn castles and foggy crypts. Nurses were stationed in some theaters to be on hand should any of the patrons faint in terror.

Near the end of the picture, the character Dr. Van Helsing took out a crucifix and held it up to the evil vampire, who flung his cloak over his face to avoid the powerful force generated by the Christian symbol. At the initial showing at the Roxy Theatre in New York, the audience suddenly burst into loud applause, cheering on the doctor as Good triumphed over Evil. Much to everyone's surprise, Universal Pictures, which had been on the verge of bankruptcy, had a huge hit on its hands. The film proceeded to break movie house records, becoming the number one box office draw of the year.

Today, it is hard to imagine the effect that *Dracula* had on the moviegoing public of 1931. The film's special effects seem gimmicky and unconvincing, Lugosi's ham acting seems ludicrous even by the standards of the early talkies, and the tortured script leaves a lot of plot twists unresolved. But American audiences, struggling through the severest depression the country had ever experienced, had never seen anything like it before and were entranced by its mysterious glamour and gruesome mood. Lugosi's portrait of a decadent European aristocrat who rises from his casket every night to prey on virtuous young women struck a chord with viewers who had survived a stock market crash and were coming to grips with the after-effects of massive waves of immigration.

Eschewing fangs and elegantly attired in white tie and tails, Lugosi made Count Dracula almost human, acting more like one of those charming Continental playboys who haunted gambling casinos than a devilish fiend with a thirst for blood.

FACING PAGE

Creature Features: Universal Pictures became Hollywood's "house of horror" with the 1931 surprise box office hits *Dracula,* starring Bela Lugosi, and *Frankenstein,* featuring Boris Karloff. Karloff went on to star in three *Frankenstein* sequels, including the 1935 smash *The Bride of Frankenstein,* with Elsa Lanchester.

Makeup maestro Jack Pierce examined cadavers to get the most chilling effect for the monster in *Frankenstein*.

Instead of being repugnant, Lugosi made vampirism chic. The director, Tod Browning, used expressionistic cinematographic techniques then popular in Germany—skewed angles, black and white contrasts, shadows and fog—to great effect, transforming Dracula's castle into a Poe-like realm of perverse beauty.

When Mordaunt Hall, the *New York Times* film reviewer, wrote that Browning's picture "succeeds in its Grand Guignol intentions," he could only describe the film as a "mystery," since the term "horror film" had not yet been invented. True, in silent films, John Barrymore had succeeded in capturing the horrific essence of *Dr. Jekyll and Mr. Hyde* (1920), and the legendary Lon Chaney, "the man of a thousand faces," had made a series of scary pictures—*The Hunchback of Notre Dame* (1923), *The Phantom of the Opera* (1925), and *London after Midnight* (1927), in which he played a policeman masquerading as a vampire (Chaney had, in fact, been offered the part of Dracula, but he died before the film went into production). But *Dracula* was the first Hollywood picture especially designed to frighten and shock audiences by making the monster himself the focus of dramatic interest. As a result, a cult of personality developed around the Count Dracula character. Lugosi received mountains of fan mail in care of Universal and became so identified as the personification of evil that Disney's animators used his face as the model for the devil in *Fantasia*.

Universal capitalized on the public's newfound fascination with the grotesque by rushing into production a film version of Mary Shelley's classic nineteenth-century novel *Frankenstein*. The studio had owned the film rights (of a play version by Peggy Webling) for twelve years but had feared to produce it because of its grim subject matter. The surprise success of *Dracula,* however, suddenly made it possible. The story of a mad scientist who creates a monster from severed parts of cadavers had been filmed twice before—first in 1910 by Thomas Edison (the film, unfortunately, is lost) and again in 1915 as *Life Without a Soul*—but this new talking version (a mere seventy minutes long) written by John Balderston (who penned the popular Broadway play on which *Dracula* was based) was going to be different. Smelling a hit, Universal pulled out all the stops. Bette Davis and Leslie Howard were slated to star, with Lugosi playing the monster, but the studio had second thoughts, realizing that Davis was destined for greatness in more dramatic roles. When British director James Whale was signed on, he chose Colin Clive and Mae Clarke. Lugosi, fresh from his success as the count, refused to play a nonspeaking role, so Whale opted for a relatively unknown British actor who went by the name Boris Karloff. The rest, as they say in B movies, is history.

Opening at the start of the Christmas season in December 1931, and released in a print tinted a ghoulish green which made the monster look more like a walking corpse, *Frankenstein* proved to be an even bigger smash than *Dracula,* mostly because of Karloff's riveting performance. Listed only as "?" in the opening credits, he imbued the creature with a tremendous sense of pathos and a mime-like intensity. Karloff was aided by Jack Pierce's inventive makeup work (he examined cadavers to get the right effect) and a costume that weighed forty-five pounds. The effect was so frightening that when waiting around the set, Karloff often wore a handkerchief over his face so as not to offend the crew.

Frankenstein marks the first time a studio promoted a movie by actually telling people to stay away. In fact, a scene was added to the beginning of the film in which a doctor instructs audience members to leave the theater at once if they do not feel they have the stomach to view what comes next. Indeed, many people were not prepared for the violence and horror and complained about the film's lack of morality. English critics cautioned that *Frankenstein* was a "freak picture, rated intense" that "cannot be judged by ordinary standards of entertainment" and should not be seen by "children and sensitive women." Other commentators were outraged by three scenes in particular which they felt went beyond common decency. In the climactic laboratory scene, Dr. Henry Frankenstein witnesses the first signs of life in the creature and shouts the now famous words, "It's alive! It's alive!" Immediately following that statement, he added, "Now I know what it feels like to be God!" That line was cut after protests, as was the scene in which the monster kills the troublesome hunchbacked dwarf (played by Dwight Frye, who portrayed Renfield in *Dracula*). But it was the notorious flower scene in which the monster throws Mary, a young village girl, into a lake, drowning her, that incited the loudest uproar. The scene was cut entirely until the movie was released on video. Even now, its more violent moments take place offscreen.

Frankenstein was also one of the first movies to film two different endings, to be selected depending on how the audience responded. After a preview in which Henry was flung off a burning windmill and killed by the monster, audiences left disappointed. The studio opted for a happier ending in which Frankenstein survives (a voice-over was added in which a villager shouts, "He's alive!", providing a dramatic counterpoint to the earlier scene in the laboratory). Apparently audiences in 1931 did not think the doctor should be punished for trying to play God after all.

Whereas *Dracula* had been a romantic thriller, *Frankenstein* went further, romanticizing and humanizing the predicament of a monster attacked on all sides by belligerent villagers. As a symbol of the tortured loner, *Frankenstein* touched American audiences on a deep psychological level. Soon Karloff as Frankenstein (the monster was often called by its creator's name) developed his own fan club. On Halloween, American kids eagerly took to the streets dressed as their favorite monster, sporting shortened sleeves, fiendish makeup, and bolts on their necks.

Universal helped solidify its reputation as the house of horror by releasing a succession of sequels starring Boris Karloff. *The Bride of Frankenstein,* in many ways a superior film, appeared in 1935 (also directed by James Whale), *Son of Frankenstein* in 1939, and *House of Frankenstein* in 1944. Ironically, Lugosi, who had originally turned down the role, gave in and portrayed the monster in *The Ghost of Frankenstein* in 1942. Eager to repeat its success, Universal also invented other horror

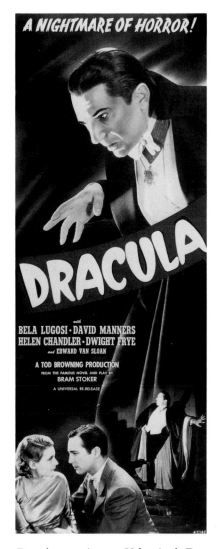

Dracula, opening on Valentine's Day weekend, was billed as "The Strangest Love Story of All."

heroes. *The Mummy* (1932; also Boris Karloff) led to a series of popular sequels, as did *The Wolf Man* (1941; starring Lon Chaney, Jr.). By the end of the forties, the genre began to run out of steam and deteriorated into low comedy in pictures like *Abbott and Costello Meet Frankenstein* (1948), in which all the Universal monsters teamed up to wreak havoc.

After the Second World War, the novelty of seeing fiends like Dracula and Frankenstein on the screen was wearing thin. The atrocities of the Holocaust and the explosion of the atom bomb significantly altered the way in which American audiences reacted to horror. Instead of humanized monsters, audiences craved more mystery and a greater threat of peril. Now the monsters were less sympathetic (*The Creature from the Black Lagoon;* 1954) or alien creatures (*Invasion of the Body Snatchers;* 1956), representing a species that was more advanced, more intelligent, and infinitely more cruel. Seeking out enemies from beyond our own planet was a soothing notion after the devastating revelations of man's inhumanity to man in World War II. Once the hydrogen bomb was detonated, it became apparent that world destruction was not just an idea, but a possibility, and the spate of horror films from the fifties exploited this fear.

Ironically, *Frankenstein* and *Dracula* came back into vogue in the late fifties. Hammer Films in England came up with the notion of remaking the horror classics in color, winning over a new generation of fanatics by spilling buckets of bright red "blood" and showing realistically sharp fangs. The series, starring Christopher Lee as Dracula and Peter Cushing as Frankenstein, helped revive Britain's lagging film industry. The release of Universal's famous horror movies on television also spawned a new generation of monster flicks and opened the door to questions about the suitability of showing them to young, impressionable audiences.

It was not until *Psycho* (1960), Alfred Hitchcock's masterpiece, that a horror movie created the same kind of sensation as had the original *Dracula* and *Frankenstein*. Using low-budget techniques, Hitchcock delved into the mind of a mentally deranged serial killer who murders patrons at his motel. Like *Dracula* and *Frankenstein, Psycho* is remarkable for its Gothic effects (Norman Bates's bizarre house, the stuffed animals of prey). It similarly set off a stream of sequels and imitators such as *Maniac* (1963), *Deranged* (1974), and *Halloween* (1978), culminating (or deteriorating, depending on your point of view) in the set-piece style murder sprees of films such as *Friday the 13th* (1980) and *A Nightmare on Elm Street* (1984).

During the sixties and seventies, Hollywood and television also trotted out several new and different retellings of the old standards, and not all of these ventures were pure schlock. Roman Polanski offered his interpretation of horror with *The Fearless Vampire Killers* in 1967. Esteemed author Christopher Isherwood wrote a 1972 television version of *Frankenstein* starring Michael Sarrazin and James Mason which emphasized the story's homoerotic elements. Andy Warhol, working with director Paul Morrissey, produced two of the most gruesome remakes in 1974, including the 3-D

The recent success of *Bram Stoker's Dracula* (1992), a particularly bloody version of the original directed by Francis Ford Coppola and starring Winona Ryder and Gary Oldman, proves that vampires never really die after all.

FACING PAGE

Cape Fear: Count Dracula, with his continental manners and ghoulish charm, made vampirism chic.

Bela Lugosi as Count Dracula, about to seduce costar Mae Clark, was Hollywood's smoothest lady killer.

version *Andy Warhol's Frankenstein* that included close-ups of entrails pouring out of the monster's torn abdomen. Mel Brooks had all of America rolling in the aisles that same year with his monstrous parody *Young Frankenstein,* and Michael Jackson later had a lot of fun spoofing the Wolf Man in his best-selling video *Thriller* (1982).

After more than a hundred movies about vampires, it is understandable that a figure like Dracula would also become the subject of many comedies. What is surprising is how entertaining some of them have been. George Hamilton scored a hit producing and starring in the inventive *Love at First Bite* (1979), while *Blacula* (1972) cornered a burgeoning black exploitation market. The less successful *Vamp* (1986) served as a vehicle for sultry disco singer Grace Jones.

In 1978, actor Frank Langella offered a suave update of the original play (the same one that Lugosi had done on Broadway). The Broadway production featured sets by Edward Gorey and was soon turned into a stylized romantic thriller by John Badham. Frankenstein also had his day on Broadway in an ill-fated 1981 production featuring special effects by techno-wizard Bran Ferren (*Altered States*). The show closed after just one night, costing its investors $2 million and making it the most catastrophic flop in Broadway history. Dracula fared better recently when director Francis Ford Coppola returned to the original novel and wove a powerful film which rejoiced in bloodletting. His *Bram Stoker's Dracula* (1992) is a phantasmagorical vision of sexual invincibility and immortality in the age of AIDS.

Today, faced with such sophisticated and technically brilliant horror entertainment as *Alien* (1979) and *The Silence of the Lambs* (1991), audiences remain glued to their seats (or couches), some shivering in fear, others laughing until their sides hurt. Gone are the gimmicky promotional gags, the elaborate warnings, the hired nurses. Gone too are the hammy acting and clumsy special effects of films like *Dracula* and *Frankenstein.* But the legacy of the terrifying spell they cast over sixty years ago will always—like the monsters themselves—live on.

BROOKS PETERS

Star Crazy

During the Hollywood premiere on April 16, 1932, of MGM's much-anticipated, much-talked-about film *Grand Hotel,* fans sat mesmerized as that great celluloid beauty, Greta Garbo, first uttered the now immortal words, "I want to be alone." No doubt some of the less awestruck members of the audience were amused by the line's implications. For *Grand Hotel* was not just another specially designed vehicle for Hollywood's legendary "sphinx," but the first major studio drama to boast an all-star cast of some of the country's brightest stars. Far from being alone, Garbo was forced to share the bill—and the screen—with the likes of John Barrymore and his equally talented brother Lionel (fresh from winning the Oscar as best actor in *A Free Soul*), the larger-than-life Wallace Beery, and the tough-talking, moxie-filled Joan Crawford. Metro-Goldwyn-Mayer, known as the studio with "more stars than there are in heaven," had crammed the movie with quite a few thoroughbreds from its illustrious stables, a daring and inspired innovation that would revolutionize the way movies were produced for years to come.

Prior to *Grand Hotel,* of course, there had been films featuring more than one star. Since the advent of talkies, film producers had been loading their pictures with Broadway and vaudeville headliners. Movies like *Hollywood Revue* of 1929, *King of Jazz* (1930), and *Paramount on Parade* (1930) piled on celebrities to attract larger audiences, but these pictures were nothing more than artfully contrived amusements built around lavish skits and revue numbers. There was no sense of a team of actors working together as an ensemble to create a heightened sense of drama.

Irving Thalberg, "the boy genius" of Hollywood and MGM's production chief, hit upon a new and compelling idea. Why not design a dramatic presentation that would allow him to use his biggest box office draws in a single film so that each would act to his or her greatest ability and bring in fans eager to see their respective favorite personalities? It was an innovative formula that would have been—and still is—impossible in the theater since it would be too expensive to stage or maintain.

On the set of Hollywood's first multi-star blockbuster, *Grand Hotel,* ambitious Joan Crawford held her own. She once laced into the scene-stealing Barrymores: "Remember, boys, the American public would rather have one look at my back than watch both your faces for an hour."

But in the make-believe world of cinema it would be simple to accomplish and easy to market around the globe. The conceit promised record revenues, especially during a debilitating Depression that was keeping audiences away from the movie palaces. By giving the American public, always in the mood for a bargain, more bang for its buck, a film company with MGM's clout could steal audiences away from its competitors. All Thalberg had to do was find the perfect story.

The answer proved to be Vicki Baum's best-selling German novel *Menschen im Hotel,* known in its English translation as *Grand Hotel*. Set in Berlin in the Roaring Twenties, the book details the sagas of five lonely guests who come to the hotel to escape their sorrows and invent new lives. Produced as a hit play in Berlin, Budapest, Prague, Rome, London, Paris, and on Broadway, *Grand Hotel* captured the heart and imagination of a generation coming to grips with the end of a devastating world war. Thalberg wisely saw it as a story made for the screen and bought the film rights for a mere $13,500.

Thalberg then set about selecting his stars. As Grusinskaya, a Russian prima ballerina who is past her prime (the part had been played by the late Eugenie Leontovich on Broadway), Thalberg knew he had to choose his number one box office star, Greta Garbo. Elusive, yet strangely regal, the acclaimed Swedish actress would bring a level of worldly sophistication and European glamour to the role that no American star could. As her lover, Baron von Geiger, a down-on-his-luck nobleman with a penchant for gambling and cat burglary, John Barrymore was a natural choice, being universally regarded as "America's greatest living actor." Surprisingly, the two screen legends had never played opposite each other before, and the love scenes between them promised to provide a huge box office bonanza. But Thalberg wanted to go beyond conventional casting tricks and added fuel to the fire by handpicking Joan Crawford as Flaemmchen, an ambitious stenographer who knows that her greatest asset is certainly not her speed at taking dictation. Casting the saucy, wise-cracking Crawford alongside the goddess Garbo was a coup; no studio had risked putting two leading ladies in a single film. To round off the celebrity register, Thalberg brought in affable Wallace Beery, playing against type as the ruthless industrialist, Preysing, and Lionel Barrymore as Klingelein, a lowly accountant who dreams of the good life while preparing to die of a terminal illness. Two other name actors, Lewis Stone as the mysterious Herr Doktor and Jean Hersholt as the bell captain whose wife is expecting a child, were thrown in for good measure. To make sure that everything went smoothly on the set, Thalberg picked as his director Edmund Goulding, who was known in the industry for his talent in handling temperamental stars.

Long before the film went into production, MGM turned on the publicity machine, spewing out reams of copy that gave new meaning to the word "hyperbole." Promotions heralded "The Greatest Cast of All Time," "The Greatest Cast in Stage or Screen History!" "The Sensation of the Century!", but behind the scenes the harsh realities of the star system were taking their toll. Salaries had to be negoti-

The Greatest Cast in Stage or Screen History

GRAND HOTEL

GRETA GARBO
JOHN BARRYMORE
JOAN CRAWFORD
WALLACE BEERY

ated (Garbo was paid the most at $68,000; Lionel Barrymore, the least at $25,000). Not all of the studio's stars were thrilled about sharing billing with their peers. Greta Garbo was notorious for being difficult with directors, and she always insisted on top billing. The actress was also peeved that her choice for a costar, John Gilbert, had been turned down by MGM. No doubt, too, she was concerned about the effects on her career of playing the downbeat role of an aging star who contemplates suicide. And how would she come off on-screen opposite John Barrymore, "the Great Profile?" The brazen Crawford posed a problem, too, since she was quickly becoming one of MGM's hottest tickets and had a reputation for stealing scenes. Crawford did not help matters by constantly playing Marlene Dietrich (Garbo's rival at Paramount) records in her dressing room at a loud volume.

It was left to director Goulding to try to patch over everyone's tattered nerves. He adroitly overcame one obstacle by separating Garbo and Crawford on the set at all times. In fact, they never appear together on the screen. Even a publicity still was doctored to make it look as if the two had posed together. This careful separation probably spurred each actress on to outdo the other, and how fortunate for the viewers, since both stars gave astonishing performances. Indeed, everyone did. Even today, *Grand Hotel* stands out as a sterling example of ensemble acting. The melodramatic plot may be a bit timeworn, the dialogue somewhat mawkish, but it remains an Art Deco marvel—a classic for all time.

The response to *Grand Hotel* was overwhelming and unprecedented. While some critics groused about "the disconnected and episodic plot" and "rather familiar characters," no one complained about the all-star cast. Each performer was singled out for praise, including Raffaela Ottiano, Grusinskaya's maid, the sole player kept on from the original Broadway cast. But the biggest raves came from the crowds lining up around the block outside the country's movie houses. Thalberg had wisely postponed the general release until months after the premiere, thereby generating an impressive amount of word of mouth. Produced for $695,000, *Grand Hotel* earned $2,594,000 domestically in its first year of release. The film went on to win the Oscar for best picture—a tribute to the foresight of Hollywood's "boy genius."

Grand Hotel had a life after Thalberg as well. The film was remade in 1945 in color as *Weekend at the Waldorf*—sort of a Waldorf salad starring Ginger Rogers, Lana Turner, Walter Pidgeon, Van Johnson, and Edward Arnold that did not quite have the magic of the earlier version. A musical called *At the Grand* starring Paul Muni was presented in Los Angeles in the fifties but never made it to New York. Then a new musical, *Grand Hotel,* did make it to Broadway in 1989 and won the best director Tony for Tommy Tune. The show might have run longer if the producers had cast household names of the caliber of the original film's—but it managed to make a star out of Michael Jeter, who danced up a storm as Klingelein, and won him the Tony for best actor.

Flush with *Grand Hotel*'s extraordinary success in 1932, MGM raced into production a 1933 film version of the equally popular hit Broadway comedy *Dinner at Eight* by George S. Kaufman and Edna Ferber. Once again the all-star cast boasted the Barrymore brothers and Wallace Beery, but this time the boys were pitted against such formidable screen presences as Jean Harlow, Billie Burke, and Marie Dressler. Jumping on the bandwagon, Paramount released *If I Had a Million* (1932) starring Gary Cooper, George Raft, W. C. Fields, Charles Laughton, and Jack Oakie. Another film with a stellar cast was Max Reinhardt's Warner Bros. rendition of Shakespeare's *Midsummer Night's Dream* (1935) featuring James Cagney, Dick Powell, Olivia de Havilland, Mickey Rooney, and Joe E. Brown.

The all-star movie returned to its roots in the 1940s as a vehicle for studios to showcase their best-known stars in lavish musical spectaculars. *Star Spangled Rhythm* (1942) featured a litany of celebrities that promised, in a twist on MGM's famous motto, "more stars than there are in the American flag." The highly successful *Ziegfeld Follies* (1946) boasted Fred Astaire, Judy Garland, Gene Kelly, Lena Horne, Fanny Brice, and Red Skelton, and is considered by some to be the best of the star-crazy musical films. In the 1950s and 1960s, Hollywood displayed its most popular celebs in adventures like *Around the World in Eighty Days* (1956) and *How the West Was Won* (1962); costume epics like *Quo Vadis* (1951), *Spartacus* (1960), and *Cleopatra* (1963); and large-scale comedies like *It's a Mad, Mad, Mad, Mad World* (1963, which seemed to be a spoof of every Hollywood cliché, including the all-star gimmick), *Cat Ballou* (1965), and *Casino Royale* (1967).

During the seventies, Hollywood cashed in on all-star pics in a big way, promoting large-scale disaster flicks that showcased famous faces in less-than-glamorous situations. *Airport* (1970) launched the genre (yet another "comeback" for Gloria Swanson), followed by *The Poseidon Adventure* (1972), *Earthquake* (1974), and *The Towering Inferno* (1974). This type of heavy-hitter was parodied in the disaster comedy *The Big Bus* (1976). Beginning with *Tootsie* (1982), smaller, less overblown projects teamed versatile actors and actresses in films with down-to-earth themes: *The Big Chill* (1983), *Crimes of the Heart* (1986), *Steel Magnolias* (1989), and *Fried Green Tomatoes* (1991). But every now and then a film like *Clash of the Titans* (1981) would rear its celebrity-laden head and guarantee an even wider global market. The all-star formula spilled over into television as well, in wildly successful series like "Love, American Style" and "The Love Boat" on which troupes of aging Hollywood legends made cameo appearances.

The latest signs from Hollywood show that the all-star pic is coming back for an encore. Taking a cue from Reinhardt's classic *Midsummer Night's Dream,* the Samuel Goldwyn Company recently released a new all-star production of Shakespeare's *Much Ado about Nothing* featuring some of today's brightest names in pictures: Emma Thompson, Kenneth Branagh, Denzel Washington, Keanu Reeves, and Michael Keaton. Can an all-star version of Tommy Tune's musical *Grand Hotel* be far off?

J. SPENCER BECK

When Will Hays was named to head Hollywood's watchdog agency, the Motion Picture Producers and Distributors of America (MPPDA), in 1922, he did little to shackle the movie industry for another twelve years.

FACING PAGE

Hollywood Babylon: A year after silent film star Roscoe "Fatty" Arbuckle, *opposite,* was implicated in the 1921 rape and murder of actress Virginia Rappe, postmaster-general Will Hays was appointed to raise the moral standards in Hollywood.

1 9 3 4

Babylon Bridled: The Hays Code

Over fifty years before the Moral Majority, Dan Quayle, and other self-appointed guardians of family values campaigned against Hollywood, there was a similiar movement in America that might very well have put an end to the movies as we know them.

In the early twenties, the resourceful businessmen who had survived the ruthless competition of the burgeoning film industry, turning it into one of the country's biggest, faced a phenomenon they had never anticipated. Just when their estimated annual box office take was reaching half a billion dollars a year, the world's first mass audience began to turn on them. The reasons were complex, volatile, and not entirely rational: the very picture of a splendidly profligate life-style represented in particular by Gloria Swanson in films such as *Male and Female,* coupled with reports of the huge salaries accrued by favorite stars, bred resentment. The very same titles that packed in audiences to the hundreds of quickly made, sensational dramas Hollywood was churning out to fill the voracious need for new product (*Shocking Night, Their Mutual Child, Luring Lips, Plaything of Broadway, Her Purchase Price*) gave the impression that the industry was peddling rampant immorality. But the most incendiary ingredient to the rising well of unease over this vital new art form was not on the screen but behind it—the behavior of the film community itself.

A tragic event crystallized these concerns. In 1921, "Fatty" Arbuckle, one of Hollywood's biggest (in both senses of the word) and most beloved stars, was charged with the manslaughter of starlet Virginia Rappe, following a night of bacchanalian drinking and sexual assault in his San Francisco hotel room. The first two trials resulted in hung juries. In the third round, Arbuckle was acquitted on grounds of insufficient evidence, but his career was nonetheless destroyed. Moreover, the reputation of the film community as a debauched group of misfits hell-bent on destroying the morals of America seemed all but proven to the public. Calls for a crackdown on the industry came not only from religious zealots and reformers, but from the general populace as well. Politicians chimed in accordingly. In Congress, one senator gave a speech that was indicative of this attitude:

> Hollywood is a colony of these people where debauchery, riotous living, drunkenness, ribaldry, dissipation, and free love seem to be conspicuous. Many of these stars, it is reported, were formerly bartenders, butcher boys, sopers, variety actors,

and actresses, who may have earned ten or twenty dollars a week. Some of them are now paid, it is said, salaries of something like five thousand dollars a month or more, and they do not know what to do with their wealth…except to spend it on riotous living, dissipation, and high rolling. These are some of the characters from whom the young people of today are deriving a large part of their education, views of life and character forming habits. From these sources our young people gain much of their views of life, inspiration, and education. Rather a poor source, is it not? It looks as if censorship is needed, does it not?"

From the vantage point of people like this senator, the former fur, glove, and jewelry merchants who were responsible for the movies were incapable of handling the problem themselves. Censorship bills were introduced in thirty-six states; the banking community refused to lend producers money for their upcoming films; and numerous states and localities banned movies outright. In 1923, a congressman named Upshaw introduced a bill to create a Federal Motion Picture Commission, which provided for inspection of scenarios and for government supervisors to assist producers and directors.

Faced with what amounted to a government and business shutdown, the leaders of the industry turned to Will Hays, President Harding's postmaster general and a noted Republican Party leader from Indiana. Together they formed the Motion Picture Producers and Distributors of America (MPPDA), which, with Hays at the helm, promised to raise the moral and artistic quality of movies. Hays was chosen not so much because he was known as a stalwart moralist, but because of his political and banking connections; by turning Hays into the overseer of the movie industry, the producers got respectability, power, and clout in one fell swoop. For

Cecil B. De Mille's pre–Hays Code *The Sign of the Cross* featured a lesbian love dance, assorted gorings and impalings, and almost all of Claudette Colbert's exposed breasts in an infamous milk-bath scene. A restored version is now available.

example, on February 24, 1922, *Variety* reported, "Film loans are at zero." Within three months after Hays took office that year, the film companies' credit with the banks was reestablished.

With Hays in charge, the governmental, religious, and civic organizations clamoring for censorship were almost completely quelled, but it was not until 1934 that Hays could convince his fellow members of the MPPDA that the organization's very specific code of ethics, mapped out clearly in a charter written over the preceding years, be strictly applied to every film produced and released in this country. The advent of sound in the late twenties had let loose another volley of concern over morality, what with the increasing popularity of crime melodramas, racy romantic comedies, and incendiary performers such as Mae West, who brought from the raucous Manhattan stage her own brand of sexually obsessed innuendo. In an uproar over the licentiousness of sound films, the Catholic church formed the Legion of Decency in 1934, which added the element of boycott to its arsenal of tactics.

Religious groups across the country joined the campaign, and it seemed as if a repeat of 1922 was imminent. The Hays code, as it had become known, was swiftly turned into iron law, and succeeded in quelling the clamor for censorship once again. "Mankind," the code said, "has always recognized the importance of entertainment and its values in rebuilding the bodies and soul of human beings…it has distinguished between entertainment which tends to improve the race, and entertainment which tends to degrade human beings, or to lower their standards of life and living."

Prior to 1934, few Hollywood filmmakers were aware of the production code, which had been drafted in 1927. After 1934, with Hays's tough Roman Catholic associate, Joseph Breen, also overseeing, no one could avoid it. The code was breathtaking in its completeness, prohibiting obscenity, profanity, nudity, "sex perversion," lustful kissing, and reference to venereal diseases. Adultery "must not be explicitly treated, or justified, or presented attractively." The code was not solely concerned with sex and violence, but covered everything from illegal drug traffic to white slavery to miscegenation, forbidding presentation of all of these. The prohibitions were biblical in tone—"revenge in modern times shall not be justified"; "methods of crime shall not be explicitly presented"; "the sanctity of the institution of marriage and the home shall be upheld"—and were enforced with biblical certainty.

One noteworthy comparison of pre- and post-code productions actually had something to do with the Bible. Cecil B. De Mille, who had made such enjoyable trouble for the industry with his silent films, had broken into sound with all of his engines humming. *The Sign of the Cross,* his hugely entertaining 1932 drama about persecuted Christians in Nero's Rome, is pretty saucy stuff, even by today's standards. De Mille's clever tactic was to glory vicariously in sex and violence, while condemning it through moralist messages. In this wonderfully acted epic, we can see a very unsubtle lesbian love dance; almost all of Claudette Colbert's breasts in a famous milk bath scene (in which she impatiently commands a female friend to take off her clothes and jump in); and a shockingly explicit Coliseum sequence that includes the decapitation of a pygmy by an Amazon, lions devouring Christians, and gorings, impalings, and other ghastly goings-on. By contrast, De Mille's next religious epic, *The Crusades,* made three years after *The Sign* and one year after the imposition of the Hays Code, was about as clean as you can get. In 1944, a Hays-approved *Sign of the Cross* was rereleased with over fifteen minutes cut from the original.

Self-regulation proved to be at least as intrusive and insidious to the filmmaking process as government censorship. Breen's office reviewed and approved shooting scripts and the finished films; nothing could slip by it, no one could supersede it without the possibility of being fined a huge sum, opening up the possibility of a massive Legion of Decency boycott, and even being thrown out of the parent MPPDA. Once in a blue moon, an independent or rogue producer like Howard Hughes (over the salacious use of Jane Russell in *The Outlaw* in 1943) would ignore the office's remonstrations and get away with it—at least temporarily (*The Outlaw* was quickly recalled). The writer-director Preston Sturges was probably the only nonproducer who managed to ride consistently roughshod over the office, perhaps because his brilliantly clever use of the language confused the enemy; in 1944, with *The Miracle of Morgan's Creek* (in which a young woman gives birth to quintuplets after being impregnated by a soldier whose name she has trouble remembering), Sturges, the critic James Agee wrote at the time, "raped the Hays Office in its sleep." Hardly anyone else did until producer-director Otto Preminger, who battled the office over the words "virgin" and "pregnant" in his 1953 adaptation of the stage comedy *The Moon Is Blue* (he went ahead and released the film without the seal of approval). But substantial change did not come until 1966, when, according to film critic Ephraim Katz, "pressure of social change, Supreme Court decisions concerning obscenity, and civil liberties groups brought a sweeping revision in the code."

The industry's long-lived and much vaunted self-regulation continues to this day with the rating system, put into effect in 1968, which classifies films according to their suitability for viewing by the young. The same pressures that forced the Hays Office into being are very much present today, affecting the content of film and television in subtle but equally insidious ways. In 1993, a planned rerelease of Sam Peckinpah's western *The Wild Bunch* was thwarted when the ratings board gave it an NC-17 rating, although there was no significant difference from the original 1969 R-rated version. The fact that it is regarded by many to be one of the great American films of the sixties mattered little to a board that routinely gives carte blanche to the Arnold Schwarzeneggers and Sylvester Stallones of the film world.

SCOTT BALDINGER

FACING PAGE

How West Was Lost: Thanks largely to the Hays Code, Mae West's career took a nosedive after 1935. The master of the double entendre, forced to rewrite her scripts and tone down her image, made only a few lackluster films in the late '30s before her outrageous comeback at the age of seventy-eight in *Myra Breckinridge*.

Labor Pains on Broadway

Not two minutes into the first scene of *Waiting for Lefty*'s electrifying debut, a verbal lightning bolt hit the audience. Ecstatic applause and shouts of fellowship ensued. It was Sunday night, January 5, 1935, and the Group Theatre was presenting Clifford Odets's new play at the Old Civic Repertory Theatre on Fourteenth Street in Manhattan as part of a low-profile evening of one-acts to benefit *New Theatre* magazine. The Group Theatre actors, who had just recently introduced the psychoanalytic "method" technique of acting to America, imbued their characters with such raw, honest emotion that the members of the audience saw their wives, their husbands, and themselves on stage. This was their plight, written, for the first time, in their language. Line after line packed an explosive dramatic punch. Never had realism of this sort been achieved in America. The audience responded so passionately that the actors were no longer acting. Actors and audience experienced a mystical sense of communion, each carrying the other on a wave of shared exultancy.

While audiences thirty blocks north on Broadway clapped politely at highfalutin drawing room comedies, *Waiting for Lefty*'s audience spontaneously roared, "Strike! Strike!" at the close of the play. Their applause earthquaked through the auditorium for forty-five minutes, and in unprecedented fashion, they stormed the stage Bastille-style to congratulate and thank the actors. It was their show now. Odets had made his point. Theater could help people by showing the disparity between what they were and what they could be. And Odets, with his talent for capturing the cadences of America's downtrodden, could spearhead the new social awareness of the fervent 1930s by revealing that "the genius of the human race is mongrelized."

When the weeping cast persuaded Odets to take a bow, the audience gathered round deliriously to embrace the playwright who had captured their anger, aspirations, and unhappiness so vividly. Odets was so rattled that he later threw up back-

FACING PAGE

American Revolution: The Group Theatre brought hard-core realism and social criticism to the Broadway stage of the 1930s. But it wasn't until their production of Clifford Odets' *Waiting for Lefty* that a revolution occurred, forcing American theater to face the music once and for all.

Playwright Clifford Odets was only twenty-eight years old when his *Waiting for Lefty* stormed Broadway.

stage and then burst into tears. Years later, he remembered that on that night "you saw theater in its truest essence. Suddenly the proscenium arch of the theater vanished and the audience and actors were at one with each other."

In the thick of the Depression, when the Group Theatre was on the verge of financial and spiritual collapse (as it would be many times in its brief, ten-year life), Clifford Odets approached its troika of artistic directors about the possibility of staging one of his plays. Odets, who had quit school by age fifteen and attempted suicide three times by twenty-five, had found his way into the group in 1934 as a minor actor. He dreamed of becoming the resident playwright the founders envisioned when they drafted their mission statement of writing socially impassioned plays which would capture the discontent of America's working class. But Odets was rebuffed. "You don't seem to understand, Cliff," Lee Strasberg, one of the ruling three told him, "we don't like your plays." The actors, however, were so exasperated by Strasberg's dictatorial tendencies that they resolved to do an informal reading of an Odets play anyway. Odets had allies among the other card-carrying communists in the group, but his most influential booster was Harold Clurman, who with Cheryl Crawford rounded out the artistic team.

Odets told Clurman about his idea to write a play in the agitprop style—where the stage is used as a propagandistic soapbox for social causes—about the recent New York City taxi drivers' strike. With Clurman's vote of confidence, Odets holed up in Manhattan's Bellevue Hotel for three days and nights and cranked out *Waiting for Lefty*.

The play uses a taxi driver's meeting, called to resolve the question of whether to strike, as a forum to explore the hard-core deprivations of the poor at the hands of greedy bosses. A corrupt racketeering leader endeavors to convince the unionists that this is no time to strike. The administration in Washington, he says, is taking care of the working man, but objections come from the actors planted in the audience and from the unionists onstage. In the ensuing arguments for a strike, the lights fade out then come up focused on each man's particular story. One man's wife tells him that they are so poor, their children do not know what grapefruit look like. "My God Joe," she tells him, "the world is supposed to be for all of us." Another man had been an up-and-coming surgeon but was forced out of his job because he is a Jew and because the unqualified son of a senator needed his position. Yet another cabbie is shown in an achingly poignant embrace with his lover as they face their financial inability to wed and make a life together. "You and me," he tells her, "we never even had a room to sit in somewhere."

For the first time, the theater gave voice to an entire generation who cried out, not only for higher wages, but for a better life. It was the first successful American stage production to make the lives of ordinary Joes and Ednas into the stuff of art. Harold Clurman wrote that *Waiting for Lefty* was "the birth cry of the thirties. Our youth had found its voice. It was a call to join the good fight for a greater measure of life in a world free of economic fear, falsehood, and craven servitude to stupidity and greed."

Waiting for Lefty revolutionized the whole notion of what theater is and could be. The group's hypothesis proved true: a theatrical performance could be a riveting dialogue between actor and audience that could effect change. A play could have a soul. If every actor onstage developed a complete and truthful inner life, theater would mean something in the lives of everyone involved. As one reviewer from *Time* magazine wrote, "In every Odets play, regardless of its theme or its worth, at least once or twice during the evening every spectator feels that a fire hose has been turned on his body, that a fist has connected with his chin."

There was only one critic present at *Lefty*'s off-the-beaten-track debut, and his paper, the *Morning Telegraph,* scooped even *Variety* with its review. Word of this spectacular event spread like wildfire. After a month of sold-out benefits, the Group Theatre moved *Lefty* uptown to Broadway and added another play—*Till the Day I Die*—to complete the bill. Odets was an overnight success, the Group Theatre an international one.

The group would go on to produce twenty-three productions in total, including *House of Connelly, Success Story, Men in White,* and Odets's plays *Awake and Sing!, Paradise Lost,* and *Golden Boy,* before, hobbled by economic woes and political infighting, it was forced to disband in 1941. But, in its brief, ten-year run, it revolutionized the American theater. Its legacy includes the belief in the efficacy of social plays; the idea of the acting ensemble and the permanent company, which later helped to engender the regional theater movement; and the quest, in the face of enormous financial obstacles, to keep artistic ideals intact. The Group Theatre can also be credited with the development of a truly American acting technique. If you go to a New York City acting class today, from the Neighborhood Playhouse to the Stella Adler Conservatory to the Acting Studio, the teaching philosophy is directly descended from it. Our post-studio days brand of stars, from Robert De Niro to Joanne Woodward, from Paul Newman to Marlon Brando, are all part of the group legacy, as are the movies of Elia Kazan, the plays of Arthur Miller and Tennessee Williams, and the work of the Steppenwolf Company in Chicago.

When Harold Clurman died in 1980, his obituary in the *New York Times* quoted him as once having said, "Our means and our ends were in fundamental contradiction…while we tried to maintain a true theater policy artistically, we proceeded economically on a show-business basis." Clurman had earlier recommended that America view its theaters as it views its libraries, ballet companies, and museums. Fifty years later, this has not happened. But the Group Theatre's most enduring contribution is an ideal—yet unattained perhaps, but still worth fighting for: the theater as a spiritual and creative home for artists and audience, a community that creates the cathartic bridges between the stage and real life.

MICHELLE CONLIN

WAITING FOR LEFTY

Melodrama in one act, presented at the Longacre, by the Group Theatre, as part of double bill; written by Clifford Odets; staged by Cheryl Crawford. $1.65 top.

Joe	Lewis Leverett
Edna	Ruth Nelson
Miller	Gerrit Kraber
Fayette	Russell Collins
Irv	Walter Coy
Florrie	Paula Miller
Sid	Herbert Ratner
Clayton	Bob Lewis
Agate Keller	Elia Kazan
Henchman	Abner Biberman
Secretary	Dorothy Patten
Actor	William Chailee
Dr. Barnes	Roman Bohnen
Dr. Benjamin	Clifford Odets
A Man	George Heller

Voices—Sam Roland, Lee J. Cobb, Wendell Keith Phillips, Harry Stone, Bernard Zanville.

Two one-act plays constitute this bill by the Group Theatre, which also is occupying the Belasco currently with 'Awake and Sing,' a full length play. These one-acters are frankly propaganda and doubtful of more than limited appeal. Low admission scale indicates the type of patronage aimed at.

Both the short pieces are protest plays. As preachments they have unquestioned power, but as drama neither measures up.

Clifford Odets, a young author-actor wrote both these short pieces as well as the full length 'Sing.' His lines ring true as the language of the actual people whom his characters portray. Audiences may be somewhat shocked with the authenticity of some of the dialog, because Odets doesn't hold back when driving home a point.

'Waiting for Lefty,' based on New York's taxi driver strike of last season, contains considerable that is or was true and the characters speak it with conviction. There is no lighter side.

Scene is a hall with the committee on chairs stretched across the stage. The walking delegate opposes a strike. He and others address the audience, supposed to be attending the meeting and out front, too, there are players, some of whom go upon the stage, others being referred to in the program as voices.

Charging the delegate with siding with the bosses, if not in their pay, the drivers are finally worked up to vote for a 'strike,' just after word comes that the absent, fiery 'Lefty' was found murdered behind a car barn. A series of episodes enacted in overhead spotlights, while the committee sits in shadow, explain the men's predicament.

One taxi driver brings home $1.04 to show for his day's work. He is lashed by his bitter wife, who tells him that their two children were put to sleep so that they wouldn't cry for food, and that the rent is overdue. Then she threatens to leave him. Coming to a bare home, the furniture having been taken away by the installment man, the driver rushes to the meeting determined that the only way he can save his home and better his wage is to strike.

Variety, April 3, 1935.

Bette Davis' performance opposite Humphrey Bogart in Warner Bros.' *Dark Victory,* nominated for three Academy Awards, was the actress's personal favorite.

FACING PAGE

There's No Place Like Hollywood: An enduring classic that grew in popularity with its regular screenings on television beginning in the 1950s, MGM's *The Wizard of Oz* was nominated for five Academy Awards in 1939, winning for Best Original Music Score and Best Song ("Over the Rainbow").

1 9 3 9

Hooray for Hollywood!

In 1989, on its fiftieth anniversary, the year 1939 was celebrated at any number of festivals, museums, and film retrospectives as the greatest in the history of Hollywood. By common consent, there were at least fifteen great, enduring classics released that year, and there were some fifty more that were at least notable—pictures that still have reputations today. This was the studio system at its best.

In fact, a case could persuasively be made that 1939 represented the apotheosis of Hollywood's golden age. Having survived the Great Depression, the big studios and American cinema stood unchallenged as supreme in the world. Story lines were as yet undisturbed by thoughts of war, stars and writers were kept firmly in their places, the threat of "genius" had not yet been unleashed in the person of Orson Welles, and movies were still by far the cheapest form of entertainment around.

The factory was running at full tilt. *Variety* reviewed a staggering 474 American-made motion pictures in 1939. Of these, 341 were produced by the seven major Hollywood studios—Columbia, MGM, Paramount, RKO, 20th Century-Fox, Universal, and Warner Bros.—all of which released nearly one film per week that year. Close on their heels were the two leading B-picture combines, Republic and Monogram, which respectively ground out forty-eight and thirty-six films. United Artists, functioning principally as the distributor of Samuel Goldwyn's productions, handled fifteen films. Otherwise, independent features scarcely made a dent in the lineup, as fourteen little companies with forgotten names such as Syndicate, Merit, and Scienart distributed the remaining thirty-four releases.

Very important were B westerns, of which fifty-five were made during the year, or nearly twelve percent of all the pictures produced. These staples of Saturday matinees, double bills, and small-town theaters were the bread and butter for several of the studios, and it should not be forgotten that there were nearly as many of these turned out as there were memorable movies. But the year was top-heavy with gems, films that rank among the best by some of the most talented directors and writers ever to work in the business, titles that are always mentioned among the most popular pictures of all time.

When Vivien Leigh, shown here with *Gone With the Wind*'s producer, David Selznick, *left,* director George Cukor, *right,* and cast members Olivia de Havilland and Leslie Howard, signed the contract to play Scarlett O'Hara, Hollywood's most famous "what if" was finally settled.

MGM's *Gone With the Wind* won an unprecedented eight Academy Awards in 1939, prompting Oscar emcee Bob Hope to quip, "What a wonderful thing, this benefit for David Selznick."

Leading the list, of course, is *Gone with the Wind,* considered by many to be Hollywood's most memorable contribution to celluloid. Released at Christmastime, David O. Selznick's Civil War epic outspent, outran, and outgrossed any film made previously, carting off a wagon load of Oscars (prompting master of ceremonies Bob Hope to quip on Oscar night, "What a wonderful thing, this benefit for David Selznick") and making Vivien Leigh a star. As if that were not enough, that film's director, Victor Fleming, was the man behind the camera on the second most famous film of 1939, *The Wizard of Oz.* Acclaimed but not wildly successful in its initial release, the Judy Garland musical became a confirmed classic only in the 1950s, with its regular Easter showings on television.

Greater, really, than either of these perennials were several decidedly well-made films that have stood the test of time as popular art at its best. Ernst Lubitsch's *Ninotchka* was publicized (and is largely remembered) as the film in which Greta Garbo laughed, but the political humor of its script by Charles Brackett, Billy Wilder, and Walter Reisch remains as sharp as ever, the Lubitsch touch never in more delicious evidence.

Howard Hawks's *Only Angels Have Wings* could not have been more compressed, intense, or atmospheric in its detailing of humorous grace under pressure among a group of flyers in the Andes. Cary Grant was indelible getting his cigarettes lit by everyone else in the cast, and the picture put Rita Hayworth on the map. After years in the B-movie desert, John Wayne also became a star that year thanks to John Ford's *Stagecoach.* Throughout the 1930s, the western had been a disreputable genre that few serious filmmakers touched, but Ford single-handedly legitimized it with his masterful treatment of Dudley Nichols's *Grand Hotel*-like script and an all-star cast. The oater was back.

Ford reached a bit further back into history for *Young Mr. Lincoln,* a moving evocation of the future president's early years, dominated by Henry Fonda's unforgettable lead performance. Touching more closely on contemporary politics was Frank Capra's *Mr. Smith Goes to Washington,* in which James Stewart's green congressman took on the fat-cat establishment in Sidney Buchman's spirited script.

The year produced at least three romantic classics: Leo McCarey's *Love Affair,* with Charles Boyer and Irene Dunne as the maturely star-crossed lovers; Edmund Goulding's *Dark Victory,* featuring the immortal Bette Davis in the actress's own favorite role; and William Wyler's *Wuthering Heights,* starring Merle Oberon and Laurence Olivier as Cathy and Heathcliff. All delivered genuine emotion and good cries on a very refined level, as did Sam Wood's adaptation of James Hilton's novel *Goodbye, Mr. Chips,* for which star Robert Donat won just about the only Oscar that did not go to *Gone with the Wind.*

For adventure, there was George Stevens's *Gunga Din,* with Cary Grant, Douglas Fairbanks, Jr., and Victor McLaglen romping through colonial India. Sophisticated comedy was well represented by Mitchell Leisen's *Midnight,* with

So outlandish was the Oscar competition in 1939 that quite a few memorable films, such as MGM's all-star *The Women,* featuring Rosalind Russell, Joan Crawford, Norma Shearer, and Paulette Goddard, weren't even nominated.

Claudette Colbert and Don Ameche, and George Cukor's *The Women,* with its all-star cast headed by Norma Shearer, Joan Crawford, Rosalind Russell, and Paulette Goddard parading through Clare Boothe's catty Broadway success. And the gangster genre closed out the decade with a bang with Raoul Walsh's *The Roaring Twenties,* in which James Cagney got to gun down Humphrey Bogart before being finished off himself on the snowy courthouse steps.

These were the highlights, the classics that have endured undiminished through the decades. But there were so many more films that may not be shown all the time anymore, but which contributed to the high standards of the era or featured elements—performances, stories, music, sophistication, style—that remain etched in the memory of those who saw them and are still worth a look: Marlene Dietrich's comeback in *Destry Rides Again;* Ingrid Bergman's auspicious debut in *Intermezzo* and William Holden's in *Golden Boy* with Barbara Stanwyck; Astaire and Rogers's last dance together (until 1949) in *The Story of Vernon and Irene Castle;* Charles Laughton's unforgettable performance in William Dieterles's powerful rendition of *The Hunchback of Notre Dame;* the dazzling, Oscar-winning special effects in *The Rains Came*—and the list goes on and on.

Of course, not all of the nearly five hundred films released in 1939 were top drawer. Every week saw the release of the likes of *Song of the Buckaroo, Should a Girl Marry?, Three Texas Steers, Cowboy Quarterback, Torchy Blane Runs for Mayor,* or *Burn 'Em up O'Connor.* As always, most films were made to turn a buck, to fill the distribution pipeline and the thousands of theaters owned by the studios, and are hardly worth remembering today. But even these throwaways do little to diminish a year unparalleled in Hollywood history.

TODD MCCARTHY

United Artists' *Stagecoach* propelled veteran "B" actor John Wayne (pictured here with costar Claire Trevor) to superstardom overnight and legitimized the Western as a format for serious filmmaking.

Bad Guys and Dolls on Broadway

"Can you draw sweet water from a foul well?" That was *New York Times* drama critic Brooks Atkinson's reaction to Richard Rodgers and Lorenz Hart's scabrous 1940 musical *Pal Joey,* which charted the desperate career maneuvers and guileless womanizing of a lowlife nightclub MC. Although Joey Evans would be musical comedy's first antihero, such doubt never entered the minds of the collaborators, having assumed the readiness of 1940 audiences to, as Rodgers later stated, allow "musical comedy to get out of its cradle and start standing on its own feet, looking at the facts of life." Despite favorable reactions from other critics at the time, the emotionally unstable Hart was so upset by Atkinson's review that, upon hearing it at a cast party at his own home, he burst into tears and went into his bedroom for the night.

Lyricist Hart and composer Rodgers were not mistaken to have taken such a leap, however. The public proved to be more in tune with the creators' aspirations than Atkinson (who finally came around when the show was revived eleven years later); *Joey* proved to be another commercial success for the team, which had been bringing their own lustrous brand of caustic and tuneful urbanity to Broadway musical comedies for over twenty years. The period from 1936 to 1942—encompassing the penultimate *Pal Joey* and including their next and last show together, *By Jupiter*—was especially fruitful, including such popular hits as *On Your Toes, I Married an Angel, The Boys from Syracuse,* and *Too Many Girls.* Their output was all the more remarkable considering it corresponded with Hart's tragic, alcoholic decline—a downward spiral prompted by guilt about his homosexuality and disgust with his physical shortcomings that led to his death in 1943 at the age of forty-eight. (Though Hart's problems had made collaboration almost impossible for the businesslike Rodgers, the composer, while having engaged Oscar Hammerstein II to write the book for what was later to be called *Oklahoma!,* virtually pleaded with Hart to write the lyrics. Hart scornfully declined working on what he considered a piece of unworkable corn).

FACING PAGE

A Leg Up: Not only did Richard Rodgers' and Lorenz Hart's gritty Broadway hit *Pal Joey* introduce musical comedy's first anti-hero, it made twenty-eight-year-old Gene Kelly a star.

Variety, January 1, 1941.

Hart's acquaintance with the seamier side of urban life made him something of a kindred spirit with writer John O'Hara, whose epistolary sketches in the *New Yorker* formed the basis for the book of *Pal Joey*. It was O'Hara's own idea to turn the stories into a musical. Five minutes after receiving a cabled proposition from the author, Rodgers and Hart enthusiastically agreed to undertake the project. O'Hara wrote the book but quickly ceded the material over to director George Abbott, who revised it throughout out-of-town tryouts. For the part of Joey, Rodgers and Hart picked a young actor they had seen the previous year in William Saroyan's *Time of Your Life;* in addition to everything else it did to the musical theater, *Pal Joey* made that actor—Gene Kelly—a star.

The heel that O'Hara, Rodgers, and Hart created—while possibly the "hollow, self-serving, two-timing twerp" that Gerald Bordmann called him in his comprehensive guide *American Musical Theatre*—was not an embodiment of pure evil. Joey is rather a realistic depiction of a type of undereducated yet ambitious, lower-class entertainer that O'Hara and Hart had run across in their many travels: attractive and more than a little talented, he is completely lacking in character but never quite clever enough to get ahead of the game. Perfectly willing to become the gigolo of a middle-aged, high-society "mouse" willing to sponsor his dream of owning his own nightclub, he is too stupid to resist flagrantly displaying his contempt for her—to the point that she gives up on him before he can really cash in on her largess. Joey's desperate yet sloppy career maneuvers, while far from admirable, were not beyond the understanding of Depression-era audiences. In this way Joey is not so much an antihero as a kind of cynical, literary depiction of the common man. Such a realistic portrait had never been seen in the American musical theater before. Although complex male figures would later appear in Broadway musicals—the roustabout Billy Bigelow in Rodgers and Hammerstein's *Carousel,* the MC symbolic of overcorrupt society in *Cabaret,* the ambiguous Bobby of *Company,* and the engineer in *Miss Saigon* among them—relatively few have presented so clear-eyed an account of the male ego.

What also made *Pal Joey* notable at the time, apart from its clear literary aspirations, was its pungently sarcastic view of sex, unblinking in its presentation of bought love and all the other undignified measures men and women take once they are "Bewitched." The chagrined sexual cynicism of Hart's lyrics to that song—as well as to "Den of Iniquity," "That Terrific Rainbow," "I Could Right a Book," "Zip," and "Plant You Now, Dig You Later"—are as heartfelt as his successor's future ballads about meadows and corn and the joys of the Oklahoma plains.

SCOTT BALDINGER

Rodgers and Hammerstein: Oh, What Beautiful Musicals

In 1953, composer Richard Rodgers, *right,* and lyricist Oscar Hammerstein celebrated their tenth anniversary as Broadway's most celebrated duo.

On March 11, 1943, a stinging cold wind blew into New Haven, Connecticut, from the east, causing those heading into the Shubert Theatre for a preview of a new "musical play" entitled *Away We Go!* to wonder if it had really been worth coming all the way up to this out-of-the-way college town just for a tryout of an unknown show that did not even boast any stars.

The behind-the-scenes talent had been the big lure. Composer Richard Rodgers and lyricist Oscar Hammerstein II were teaming up for the first time. Rouben Mamoulian, best known for having directed *Porgy and Bess,* was working closely with choreographer Agnes de Mille, whose artful rendition of *Rodeo* had been the talk of New York. Yet the so-called "smart money," well-heeled Broadway angels who had come up to see if this new show had hit potential, were skeptical about a musical based on Lynn Riggs's folk play *Green Grow the Lilacs,* which had been merely a succès d'estime on Broadway back in 1931. And there was speculation that the pairing of Rodgers and Hammerstein was less than ideal. Rodgers, famous for light, sophisticated songs, had just broken up with his longtime collaborator, Lorenz Hart (whose bouts with drinking and depression had landed him in a sanitarium), while Hammerstein, who had followed his work on Jerome Kern's popular *Show Boat* (1927) with a string of flops, was considered all but washed up. The prospects looked bleak indeed.

The curtain rose on a practically bare stage. An old woman sat on a farmhouse porch, churning butter. A boy in cowboy duds strolled on, singing about "a bright golden haze on the meadow" and corn "as high as an elephant's eye." The simple scene was a far cry from the usual theater fare featuring long-legged beauties dancing up a storm and a rousing chorus number introducing the show's headlining star. Toward the end of the first act, a time when the ensemble customarily launched

Variety, March 17, 1943.

FACING PAGE

The Heartland and Soul of America: Although veteran theatrical producer Mike Todd walked out of *Oklahoma!*'s premiere (commenting, "No legs. No laughs. No chance!"), the musical went on to break all previous box-office records and launched the career of Broadway's most successful composer-lyricist team ever.

into its biggest, most energetic number, the show slipped into an extended dream sequence in which dancers substituting for the romantic leads led a highly stylized ballet. During the intermission, Mike Todd, the well-known Broadway producer, left the theater saying, "No legs, no laughs, no chance!"

That comment would live on in infamy as one of the faultiest predictions in show business history, because the musical, renamed *Oklahoma!* during its subsequent Boston tryout, went on to become the biggest Broadway musical of its day, breaking all previous box office records and launching the career of what would become Broadway's most successful composer/lyricist team ever. The radical notion of mingling ballet, folk drama, musical comedy, and operatic songs into a seamless whole worked beautifully to create a magical theatrical event. The colorfully designed sets came alive with a refreshing sense of charm and honest-to-goodness joy. As the *New York Times* said fifty years later, honoring its anniversary, "*Oklahoma!* was a musical with body, not bodies." It ran an astonishing five years, nine weeks, on Broadway, for a total of 2,212 performances. A ten-year road tour carried its heartfelt, all-American message to audiences as far away as Europe, South Africa, and the Pacific. Produced for a mere $83,000, *Oklahoma!* went on to become, in *Variety*'s words, "the biggest moneymaker in modern legit history." The 1955 film version starring Gordon MacRae and introducing Shirley Jones was also a hit, earning $10 million. But the show did more than bring in the bucks (20 million tickets sold in its first ten years, and an eventual gross that topped $100 million); it completely resuscitated the Great White Way, breathing new life into a moribund industry desperate for good news during a harsh and dispiriting Second World War. By laying the groundwork for a revolution in contemporary musical theater, *Oklahoma!* broadened the scope of entertainment, appealing to the hoi polloi in America's heartland as well as to the nabobs in-the-know on the East Coast.

Oklahoma! set a new standard because it was conceived as a musical play rather than as a traditional musical comedy. The Broadway musical had become a predictable endeavor in which an evening's entertainment was written around a personality who had the draw of an Ethel Merman or Gertrude Lawrence. The song and dance routines were routinely designed to amuse, but rarely to challenge. Rodgers and Hart had mastered the genre with hits like *The Boys from Syracuse, Babes In Arms, On Your Toes,* and the remarkable *Pal Joey* (the first musical to make the bad guy the hero). Each of these shows spawned a string of highly hummable pop tunes. But Rodgers and Hammerstein, in tandem with Theresa Helburn of the Theatre Guild, who first proposed musicalizing Riggs's folk drama, were in search of a new kind of show in which the songs would carry out in musical terms what used to be accomplished through dialogue and exposition. For instance, a song like "Oh, What a Beautiful Mornin'" did more than celebrate the dawn of a wonderful day; it reflected the hero's bright-eyed innocence and pleasurable anticipation in taking the heroine to the box social later that evening. It also mirrored the mood of

the country two years into the war, feeling its horizons expanding, its manifest destiny calling. As exemplified in the wide-open spaces of Oklahoma, America was on the brink of becoming the world's greatest superpower. That is a lot for a song to carry on its shoulders (and Rodgers and Hammerstein never intended the show to tackle such grandiose themes), but every musical number in *Oklahoma!* worked on several layers to convey and further the dramatic message of the play. On this score, *Oklahoma!* was even more like an opera than its musical antecedent *Show Boat*.

When it opened at the St. James Theatre in New York on March 31, 1943, critics were punch-drunk with praise, calling *Oklahoma!* "the stuff of which legends are made," "triumphantly blended," "one of the finest musical scores any musical play ever had," "really different, beautifully different," "like a fresh shower." Brooks Atkinson of the *Times* claimed that the production "raised the artistic level of the Broadway musical stage to a point where it had to be taken seriously as literature." A show that did not boast any stars suddenly had more than its share: Alfred Drake, Celeste Holm, and Howard Da Silva (who went on to star as Benjamin Franklin in *1776*). *Oklahoma!* would also gain recognition as being the first musical "to get away with murder," since the hero's accidental killing of his romantic rival was a shocking occurence at the time.

The gargantuan success of *Oklahoma!* made Rodgers and Hammerstein immensely rich and tremendously influential in the theater. One observer likened them to General Motors. But neither lost his sense of humor. Shortly after it was clear that *Oklahoma!* would break all existing records (which would stand until *My Fair Lady*), Hammerstein placed an ad in *Variety* in which he listed his many previous flops. The headline read: "I've done it before. I can do it again."

With the exception of *Pipe Dream,* an ill-fated musical starring opera singer Helen Traubel and based on John Steinbeck's *Cannery Row,* Rodgers and Hammerstein succeeded in avoiding financial failure for the rest of their brilliant career together. They followed *Oklahoma!* with *State Fair* (1945), a musical written directly for the Hollywood screen, then wowed the critics again with the daring and inspiring stage musical *Carousel* (1945), which set even higher standards for dramatic integrity. The songs "If I Loved You," "Soliloquy," and "You'll Never Walk Alone" were truly operatic in style but helped broaden the scope of what audiences expected in the theater—foreshadowing the innovative works of musical writers like Leonard Bernstein, Arthur Laurents, and Stephen Sondheim. Rodgers and Hammerstein next collaborated on *Allegro* (1947), a complex musical about a society doctor who yearns to return to his small town roots. Less known than their bigger hits, *Allegro* was directed by Agnes de Mille, who used choreography and movement to create a new type of theater that broke away from traditional conceptions of staging and narrative. *Allegro* was unusual in its use of a Greek chorus to comment on what was happening onstage. Ethan Mordden, in his *Rodgers & Hammerstein,* calls it "the first 'concept musical'...written around a unique and thematically explanatory staging plan...[that]

shattered every rule in the musical-comedy handbook." *Allegro* was also responsible for introducing audiences to the vivacious Lisa Kirk (later to appear on Broadway in *Kiss Me, Kate*), who was so enthusiastic about putting over her song "The Gentleman Is a Dope" that during one tryout she actually fell into the orchestra.

In 1949 Rodgers and Hammerstein unveiled their next smash hit, *South Pacific,* based on James Michener's popular collection of war stories *Tales of the South Pacific.* Starring Mary Martin and international opera sensation Ezio Pinza, the show ran for 1,925 performances and went on to win the Pulitzer Prize for drama. It broke ground by confronting racism and rekindled romance by celebrating the notion of love-at-first-sight in the operatic "Some Enchanted Evening." Two years later the duo cast their eyes on southeast Asia for source material, writing and producing a musical based on the novel *Anna and the King of Siam* by Margaret Langdon. Considered by many to be Rodgers and Hammerstein's finest work, *The King and I* starred the ever-glamorous Gertrude Lawrence (who unfortunately died during its run) and featured Yul Brynner (who also died during a revival). Brynner won an Oscar for Best Actor in the 1956 movie version costarring Deborah Kerr. The team's next big hit was *Flower Drum Song* (1958), which tackled San Francisco's changing Chinatown, an unsual subject for a Broadway musical—but that, in itself, was a Rodgers and Hammerstein trademark. Running for 600 performances, the musical made a star of Pat Suzuki, who stopped the show with the saucy apologia of sexist stereotypes "I Enjoy Being a Girl." But it was *The Sound of Music* (1959), their last show together (Hammerstein died the following year), that became Rodgers and Hammerstein's most successful endeavor and one of the most lucrative musicals of all time—especially in its film version (1965) starring Julie Andrews, which broke box office records. While some critics have derided *The Sound of Music,* one even calling it "a work almost entirely devoid of artistic merit," primarily because of its sentimentality and occasionally banal lyrics, there is no denying that its portrait of a family bravely escaping the Nazis had a profound impact on a new generation of musical-comedy audiences.

After his partner's death, Rodgers struggled to write another show to rival his earlier successes, but without Hammerstein as an anchor, he came up short. Rodgers and Hammerstein was a hard act to follow. Hammerstein's characters exuded a giddy optimism that looked at life and its problems in simplistic, yet practical terms. Tackling territorial frictions in the Old West, Rodgers and Hammerstein sang: "The Farmer and the Cowman Should Be Friends." Fighting racism, they argued: "You've Got to Be Taught." Combating personal fear, they offered: "Whistle a Happy Tune." The sweetness may seem one-dimensional and a bit shallow by today's standards, but these sentiments laid the foundation for a revolution in musical-comedy writing and, in more general terms, songwriting, wherein sincerity and honesty triumphed over glibness and make-believe.

BROOKS PETERS

Operettas' Popularity Gets New Impetus By 'Oklahoma' Smash

There is further proof that the operetta form of musical show is still, and probably will continue to be, part of Broadway's theatre fare. Latest clincher is 'Oklahoma,' which was received enthusiastically at its St. James opening last Wednesday (31). Since then the line at the box-office has been continuous.

Theatre Guild, which produced the show, prefers to classify 'Oklahoma' as a musical play, but it is operetta as much as 'Rose Marie' and more so than 'Show Boat,' Broadwayites predicting that the new show will attain popularity equal to those standouts.

'Rosalinda,' at the 44th Street, is the first operetta clicker this season, after a somewhat hesitant start. It is on the same block as 'Oklahoma' but has gained such impetus that its engagement should not be affected by the new show, there being no performance similarities. The 44th Street is opening its boxoffice on Sundays though there is no performance of 'Rosalinda' on that day. Management's problem is to find an air-cooled theatre, there being no conditioning equipment in the present spot and none can be obtained for the balance of the war.

Broadway's musicals have been holding up strongly but there is some question whether the previous high grossers will not be affected by the new arrivals. Last week saw the debut, too, of the newest 'Ziegfeld Follies,' Winter Garden, which will doubtlessly go into the gross leadership.

Variety, April 7, 1943.

Hollywood on the Riviera

The beach stretching along the blue Mediterranean was primed for a cardboard reconstruction of Notre Dame Cathedral to promote the opening night's screening of William Dieterle's *Hunchback of Notre Dame* starring Charles Laughton. MGM had sent a special "steamship of stars." Tyrone Power, Gary Cooper, Norma Shearer and George Raft, Charles Boyer, Douglas Fairbanks, and Mae West had been ensconced in their ocean-view hotel rooms for a week, partying with the duke and duchess of Windsor and, in general, dazzling the growing crowds. *The Wizard of Oz, Only Angels Have Wings, Stanley and Livingstone,* and *Bachelor Mother* were all waiting to be screened. It was September 1, 1939, and Hollywood had come to the Riviera for the first Cannes International Film Festival.

But German troops marching into Poland that same morning sent shock waves through France. *The Hunchback of Notre Dame* was shown and the festival abruptly cancelled. On September 3 France declared war on Germany.

While Hitler's invasion cut short the first Cannes Film Festival, the overt Fascist politics of the Venice Film Festival had been the catalyst for the creation of the French event in the first place. Benito Mussolini appreciated the propaganda value of film. He poured money into the state-run film industry to increase production while imposing a hefty tax on the dubbing of foreign films to discourage their distribution.

The Venice Film Festival began in 1932 as an adjunct to the already established Venice Fine Arts Festival. The political overtones of the Venice Biennale became omnipresent by 1935, when Italy won four of the eleven awards and Hitler's Minister of Information Joseph Goebbels arrived to claim the top two prizes Germany shared with Italy. Two years later festival officials protested the Venice jury awarding France's entry, Jean Renoir's *Grand Illusion,* the top prize, primarily because the ending featured a German sentry refusing to shoot an escaping French prisoner. In 1938 the British and American members of the jury resigned when the winners were announced, because the grand prize, the Mussolini Cup, was shared

And God Created Women: Brigitte Bardot and Kim Novak were at the height of their careers when they posed for the paparazzi at the 1956 Cannes Film Festival.

by a German "documentary," Leni Riefenstahl's *Olympiad,* and an Italian entry, Luciano Serra's *Airman.* The winning Italian film was directed by none other than Il Duce's eldest son, Vittorio, and written by Roberto Rossellini.

The French delegation also left in disgust. While Venice had initiated the concept of celebrating filmmaking as an art, it had clearly lost sight of its goal. "We dreamed of an event where countries could be assured of total equality and total equity," recalled Robert Favre Le Bret, who would become the Cannes Festival's first director general. Historian Philippe Erlanger, then head of Action Artistique Française, spearheaded an organizational committee to create an alternative festival in Europe; legendary cinematographer Louis Lumière served as the president. In spite of expressed fears that a rival event would make Mussolini "unhappy," the French government agreed to underwrite a "more objective" film festival. Several cities competed, including Lucerne, Switzerland, and Ostend, Belgium, but the final choice came down to Cannes on the Mediterranean or Biarritz on the Atlantic. When the Cannes town fathers promised to build a permanent "film palace" for the festival, it was selected as the official site. Less than a year after the Venice walkout, Minister of the Interior Albert Sarrault and Minister of Education Jean Zay signed a contract with the City of Cannes.

With the war finally over in 1945, the green light was given by the French government to host another Cannes Festival. Dr. Picaud, the mayor of Cannes, organized the community to restore parks and cultivate gardens. Gambling in glamorous surroundings returned with a vengeance the next summer, when the bombed-out Palm Beach Casino was restored to its former glory.

Opening on September 20, 1946, the second attempt was an immediate success. The Cannes International Film Festival was heralded not only as a major film event, but as a general announcement to the world that the Riviera was again welcoming tourists. The programs promoted sun and palm trees with a tag line that read: "The finest films in the world presented in the finest setting in the world."

The ritual of a grand opening night gala began with the 1946 festival. A "parade of flowers" was led by a procession of torches at dusk as the crowds gathered along the resort's famed beachfront boulevard, the Croisette. Floats from the nineteen participating countries were interspersed with marching bands, including the 9th Regiment of Senegalese. The entry from the Soviet Union featured hundreds of white doves, which proceeded to perch in the palm trees. The American float depicted a gigantic vase of carnations made out of celluloid film stock, complete with MGM, Paramount, and RKO logos. After the parade all the lights in town were dimmed, and fireworks exploded over the Mediterranean. The first lights to be turned back on were in the gardens of the Grand Hotel, the backdrop for a huge party celebrating the festival, with decorations provided by the painter Jean-Gabriel Domergue. Grace Moore of New York's Metropolitan Opera entertained with a repertoire of arias, ending with a rousing rendition of the "Marseillaise."

Glitches cursed many of the plans, however. One of the chartered trains bringing participants broke down in the French countryside, and films were held at the Italian border because of a strike by customs officials. (Roberto Rossellini avoided that problem by carrying the reels of *Rome, Open City* in his suitcase.) The opening film was Yuli Raizman's *Berlin,* a documentary from the Soviet Union. The screening was a catastrophe, interrupted several times when the film snapped and again when the power failed. But no one could blame partisan politics, since reels of Alfred Hitchcock's *Notorious* were shown in the wrong order later that same evening.

The American entries included *Gilda, Anna and the King of Siam,* and *Rhapsody in Blue,* ignoring the rule requiring at least half the films submitted to be new and unreleased. America emphasized the glamorous musicals and star vehicles that had proved commercially successful at home primarily because European tariff laws at the time severely restricted the number of visas given to American movies. The presentation of films at the festival meant free access to the French market over and above the limit. So movies that were popular with the masses, rather than the judges, were the priority, and their stars were often sent along with them. Among the crowd at Cannes, Hollywood was criticized, as it would be in years to come, for not including more films that reflected everyday life in the States. As one pundit commented to a studio envoy, "You Americans like only extravagant films of your big cities, or the personal problems of your odd or abnormal citizens."

All films were shown in the non-air-conditioned Municipal Casino; the promised Palace of Festivals would not be dedicated until the following year. Screenings began at two in the afternoon and went through until seven in the evening. After a two-hour break, they began again at nine and ran continuously until two in the morning. American films were almost always scheduled as the final screening of the night, the promoters knowing full well that these were the most likely to keep the viewers in their seats. However, the end result was that most people simply did not manage to stay awake that long. They slept through the showings, either in their theater seats or back in their hotel rooms.

The Americans took it in stride until the Soviets announced that their major festival party, featuring large quantities of free vodka and caviar, was slated at the same time as the screening for *Wonder Man,* starring Danny Kaye. The jurors were called on to deliberate over the dispute, and it was decided that no films would be shown that night. *Wonder Man* was rescheduled.

The 1946 jury was composed of a single representative from each of the nineteen countries submitting films. One of the few restraints was that no juror could have a direct role in the film industry. French writer Georges Huisman was president of the jury, and Iris Barry, director of the Film Department of the Museum of Modern Art in New York, was the American representative. They were called on not only to judge the films, but to arbitrate conflicts over rules and schedules. In the interest of international peace, a prize was awarded to the best film from each country.

The festival-goers already represented the wide variety that would add to the event's allure in future years. "All sorts of people were there ranging from diplomatists [sic]...through invalid millionaires and crooks of gold, down to plain film folks on the make," reported A. T. Byrne in the *Irish Times* that year. Some things never change. In fact, the description of the 1946 festival by another reporter could have been written this past year: "Here the streets are so jammed that one would think one is still in Paris. The shops are full of stuff at astronomical prices, and the casino is the meeting point of the journalists with their demands and communiqués. On the Croisette it is a constant parade of cars. It's the rendezvous of stars and celebrities, a whole world, half-naked and tanned to a perfect crisp."

Peace was still new, and with glaring economic pressures, many European countries faced more immediate concerns than cinema. The Soviets did not participate in 1947, supposedly due to both lack of films and claims of capitalist treachery. The English stayed home too, still rebuilding from the war. There was no festival in 1948. And while the devout gathered again in 1949, they had to wait until 1951 for the festival to become truly annual without interruption.

The first few festivals were held in September or October because the French were attempting to extend the summer tourist season. Elsa Maxwell, hostess *extraordinaire* and self-appointed expert in almost all fields, pointed out in *Variety* that if the festival were held in April instead of "tired September, worn out by summer tourists, we could have priority on better pictures." Her rationale was that the so-called "better" films had already been shown at festivals in Brussels, Locarno, and Venice. In 1951 the Cannes Festival was moved up to April and has been held in April or May ever since.

"The jury also changed at some point in the fifties," says *Le Monde*'s Daniele Heymann. "The first years, very much in keeping with the spirit of the festival, it was something totally diplomatic. There were writers, politicians, Begums, Cocteau, and Maurois. After a point, the festival became itself—a film festival—and the jury became a jury of filmmakers and journalists."

In those early days, the festival was akin to "going to a super-bistro to get together with pals," recalls French journalist France Roche, who has covered it since 1946. Cannes was still a very small town, the Croisette a one-way street, and groves of trees stood where high-rise apartments overlook the Mediterranean today. Participants numbered in the hundreds, compared to the thirty thousand who now invade every spring.

"It was like a vacation," says Vincent Canby of the *New York Times*. "Everything was in the old Palais a block from the Carlton [Hotel]. And everything was on such a scale that anybody could come in and figure out what was happening in half a day. In fact, almost all the 'names' would stay at the Carlton. If you went on the beach at the Carlton, you could do the entire job in that small area."

Despite its increasing commercialism over the years, Cannes is still the place for aspiring actresses like Madonna to see and be seen.

The festival quickly established itself as a place to see and be seen, and to this day that is one of its most enduring attributes. It was a glamorous reflection of the industry, calculated to be so. When French actress Simone Sylva threw off her bikini top and wrapped her arms around a startled Robert Mitchum at the 1954 festival, the photos hit the wires, and the international definition of Cannes was permanently sealed. That alluring combination of sex and cinema has also resulted in some of Hollywood's most famous pairings: Rita Hayworth met Aly Khan in Cannes; Olivia de Havilland met her second husband, Pierre Galante, at the 1953 festival. And the 1955 festival introduced Melina Mercouri to Jules Dassin and, of course, Grace Kelly to Prince Rainier.

Overall, the changes that have occurred reflect the fluctuations in the industry as a whole. The first years of the festival coincided with the last years of the golden age of the studios. Foreign delegations had enormous means and, diplomatically, the festival represented a rare and important forum for international propaganda. The economic crisis that has pervaded the film industry for the past several years has brought many changes. There are more and more coproductions, and occasionally a film is shown that was originally made for television. There is an increase in films coming from independent producers. Every year the tug-of-war for attention between star-studded, big-budget movies and small "art" films plays itself out. But, as director Lindsay Anderson points out, "The French have always had an extraordinary talent for combining commercial preoccupations with cultural interests."

There is no question, though, that if artistic concerns were ever primary, they are no longer. The official creation of the film marketplace in the early sixties has grown to the point that over a thousand films are screened in a fortnight. Rights to films are bought and sold, country by country, and deals for presales, video deals, and ancillary rights can turn a treatment into a product in record time. But it is still the films in competition that command the media attention that defines Cannes to the outside world.

The ebbs and flows in the financing, production, and distribution of films have always been mirrored annually at Cannes. The trade papers frequently use the festival to "take the temperature" of the business, and oftentimes the reports read as if Cannes were the cause of a soft market, rather than the reflection of one. Year after year articles cite expectations of huge sales and then tell tales of disappointment. Yet Cannes continues to provide the big "*trampolino* to stardom," as Sophia Loren says, not just for actors, but for films as well. Ever since Rossellini's *Open City,* Cannes has put the spotlight on films that might otherwise have never seen the inside of American theaters: *Wages of Fear, 400 Blows,* and *Cinema Paradiso* all sold distribution rights at Cannes.

The death of the Cannes Film Festival has been predicted with regularity, beginning the day after the first festival closed. But it has proved the prognosticators wrong time and time again, remaining the premier international film festival, the place to see and be seen. Cannes has been called the annual crossroads for the entire international film industry and now almost demands participation. For the major American studios, who can make up to seventy percent of their total film revenues from overseas markets, Cannes is the primary business convention of the year. For actors, the festival provides instant international media exposure. For independent producers, Cannes brings together an unprecedented number of distributors and other film festival programmers. For critics, it provides the finest sampling of international films in the finest theaters, as well as access to interviews, press conferences, and quotable quotes that will serve them throughout the coming year. For theater owners and programmers from other festivals, Cannes is the ultimate screening room. For agents and publicists, it has the highest per capita concentration of future clients. And for directors, Cannes provides access to working producers and studio heads on an informal and equal basis.

Today, with over four hundred film festivals scheduled annually, Cannes reigns supreme in large part because of its ability to evolve to meet the needs of the industry it reflects, serves, and occasionally even leads. There may no longer be "steamships of stars," but participants and voyeurs alike continue to invade the Côte d'Azur every spring, not just for deals to be made, but for the relationships that are cemented, the contacts that are created, and the overall sense of knowing that, for those two weeks at least, they are at the financial and social center of the international film industry.

CARI BEAUCHAMP AND HENRI BÉHAR

Playing Monopoly in Movieland

On July 20, 1938, Thurman Arnold, head of the antitrust division of the United States Justice Department, walked into the Federal District Court of Southern New York and filed suit against the five major studios—Paramount, Loews (MGM), RKO, Warner Bros., and 20th Century-Fox—that owned theaters; three then minors—Columbia, Universal, and United Artists—that did not; and 133 film executives. All were charged with acting in restraint of trade. With the possible exception of the Nixon administration's suit against Bell Telephone in the 1970s, the suit against the Hollywood studios would eventually constitute the largest antitrust legislation in the past fifty years and mark the beginning of the end of the studio system itself.

The government's suit, brought under provisions of the Sherman Antitrust Act, eventually forced the studios to divest their theaters (whence they came and which included the nearly two hundred premium first-run sites in the top thirty-five cities) and to stop selling pictures conditionally. But that's not the whole story.

It was President Franklin Roosevelt's own National Industrial Recovery Act of 1933, rushed into being as part of the arsenal to roll back the Depression, that set aside the antitrust laws and effectively sanctioned the studios' methods of doing business in the first place. The government wanted to help big business get back on its feet: what was good for the studios, after all, was good for America.

To comply with the NIRA, the industry had filed the requisite "code of fair competition" documents that spelled out the very trade practices that both served studio bottom lines and made life hard for independent exhibitors. These trade practices involved "block booking," by which better movies were sold on the agreement that an exhibitor also buy a studio's lesser ones; "blind selling," which required exhibitors to agree to play the block sight unseen; and the establishment of "clearances," which gave favored exhibitors a monopoly on showing films in a given geographical area for a set period of time.

Because the studios supplied their own first-run theaters with A pictures and muscled competitors into the fold or out of the business, the Hollywood monopoly was ripe for reform. While FDR bought business time to jump start a recovery, the Supreme Court ruled the NIRA unconstitutional in 1935. In a split second, Hollywood was vulnerable for doing what made America great: restraining trade in one era before getting busted for it in another.

This must have seemed unfair to the studio chiefs, who saw America as a place where, if the gentiles of Wall Street and Harvard Yard had not exactly invited them to knock back martinis and cut them in on partnerships and ambassadorial posts, had at least let them run the scrap business that cinema was when they found it in the teens. This, however, was true only until the fundamentalists were able to scare Congress into believing that millions found most pictures either immoral or amoral.

In the face of the slightest pressure, Hollywood has always fallen over dead when it comes to standing up for the content of its pictures. It has never wanted to risk losing the franchise. This is not the place to detail blow-by-thud descriptions of the Legion of Decency, the Motion Picture Producers and Distributors of America (now the MPAA), the Hays and later the Breen Office, and the rearguard action that was the MPPDA's Production Code. Suffice it to say that the climate of blame ran strong, and that Hollywood ran scared. Lurking beneath the impulse to regulate the industry lay the desire to control the content of its production. If only the government would break the practices of block booking and blind selling, the local exhibitor could exercise responsible choice of suitable material—or else.

During the mid to late 1930s, a series of unsuccessful bills were introduced in Congress to regulate the trade practices of the film industry, including one that would declare it a public utility. In 1939, the Senate's Interstate Commerce Committee held hearings on one of those bills, and twenty-nine civic and educational groups testified to what was indisputably true: the independent exhibitor had little or no control over what he showed. The assumption, of course, was that, given a chance, an independent exhibitor would show Christ thinking up the Sermon on the Mount and admonishing ethnic youth to go to school. The reality was that the independent exhibitor wanted to show what the studios sold their own theaters. The Senate reported the bill out and sent it to the House. MPPDA president Will Hays swung into action and convinced Congress to back off, that the industry had the moral issue in hand.

The Justice Department was another matter, however. Having sent federal agents into small towns to investigate exhibitor complaints, by 1938 it well understood the antitrust link to control of content. Justice would have had to have been deaf, dumb, and blind not to know that regulating Hollywood's business practices would "sell" to the public. After Arnold filed suit, Will Hays went to see FDR on July 25, 1938, but Roosevelt punted back to Justice.

On November 20, 1940, the five major companies agreed to a moderate decree that did not require divestiture of theaters and, with respect to the various sales

FACING PAGE

Variety, **November 20, 1940:** Eight years before the United States Justice Department forced the big studios to sell their theaters, a moderate decree called for higher production standards.

VARIETY

Published Weekly at 154 West 46th Street, New York, N. Y., by Variety, Inc. Annual subscription, $10. Single copies 25 cents.
Entered as Second-class matter December 22, 1905, at the Post Office at New York, N. Y., under the act of March 3, 1879.

NO. 11   NEW YORK, WEDNESDAY, NOVEMBER 20, 1940

LLYWOOD'S TALENT G

) Earmarked for Television
opment; H. Hughes' $2,000,000

shington, Nov. 19.
pital investment of
elevision was an-
turday (16) by the
ications Commission.
m represented as
orations having ap-
e FCC for television
pparently includes
d either for equip-
n service or, in the
S. Philco. Don Lee,
ly have installations,
udgets to continue
owmanship experi-

w grants are to the
ons Division of the
, which has set aside
tions at Los Angeles
sco. The establish-
R. Hughes 'proposes
program production
cooperation with
ions of Hollywood,'
Commish.
es ventures will con-
studio lighting ef-
vement of television
eras, and synchron-
test transmission of
of lines between 421
e different types of
gnals and try FM for
mpanying the pic-
ained In both Cali-

Colonna Rides Handlebars
From $50 to $2,500 Week

Hollywood, Nov. 19.
Motor cars have crowded bicycles
off the roads but handlebars are still
going strong. Jerry Colonna's
sweeping mustache has pedalled
along the financial track from $50
to $2,500 a week in a few years.

Once a trombone tooter at half-a-
century per week, Colonna is solo-
ing his wind chimes at $5,000 for a
fortnight at the downtown Paramount
theatre, plus a percentage over a
certain figure. He leaped into prominence on the Bob Hope air show
after two years of comparative ob-
scurity under a Warner contract.

HAYS' POWWOW
ON SPICY GAB
IN PIX

Tabbed one of Will Hays' regular

DIRECT RESULT OF
CONSENT DECREE

Ethics Frowned On As Stu-
dios Reach Out for Crea-
tive People—Decree Cues
Plants to Improve Quality
or Else

AGENTS' BONANZA

By BOB MOAK
Hollywood, Nov. 19.
Picture production today is in the
throes of the most far-reaching revolution ever to rattle the foundations
of the Hollywood lots. Dwarfing, in
comparison, even the wholesale
housecleaning that came on the heels
of England's declaration of war on
Hitlerism in September, 1939, this
latest reshuffling of studio personnel
threatens to remove from the pic-
ture-making scene scores of familiar
producer, director and writer faces.

Behind the turmoil, which has
jitter-infected everyone from the
biggest of the plant bigs down to
members of the labor gangs, is the
loud and firm demand by home office
heads that the general quality level
of pictures be lifted without further
delay. In addition, the eastern

Theatre Guild-NBC Radio
Also Belasco and Pl

Bromfield Drops Idea
Of Becoming an Actor

Cleveland, Nov. 19.
Because of an over-abundance of
work, Louis Bromfield is dropping
his original intentions of taking a
role in his new play, 'Here Today,
Gone Tomorrow,' which is being
preemed Dec. 3-4 by community
players of Mansfield, O.

Novelist, who lives on a farm
nearby, had hoped to do a Sinclair
Lewis by playing himself in the
comedy-drama, on which his manager, George Hawkins, collabed.
Bromfield, however, will act as co-
director on the Mansfield production,
cooperating with Helen Bacon,
group's director, and collaborator
Hawkins.

ASCAP TANGLE
ENDS PATRIOTIC
TIEUP

Closer
legitimate
casting is
growing
reported
Theatre
Broadcast
cently 're
its plays
players,
The Thea
added sev
to its roa
the new
sible rev
but as a
find a wh

Edward
School a
tion) bac
Theatre (
a bearin
within th

Meantin
David Be
into a p
Leer has
ciates in
there is
Playwrig
was first
ago by J
can.

Drama
casting is
the impe

practices, mostly froze everything in place. That decree lasted for three years, but in August 1944, Justice filed an amendment calling for expanded regulation and complete divestiture. The Supreme Court decided first against Paramount in the landmark Paramount Consent Decree of 1948. Over the course of the next several years, the other major studios agreed to sell their theaters and, along with the three minor studios, to cease selling movies in any way but "theater by theater, without discrimination and solely on the merits."

For years afterward, the "distributors"—for now they were called that rather than "studios"—sold movies "solely on the merits" to competing theater owners. But never underestimate the powers that be in Hollywood. "The merits" soon became part of a sham bidding process conducted by the film companies' general sales managers, who determined which theater best served a given picture. By the 1970s, Hollywood had sharply reduced production, treated the big circuits preferentially, and passed along the escalating risk of high-cost productions to exhibitors by making them cough up advances and guarantees on films sight unseen and sometimes even before some films made it into production. Theater owners constantly petitioned Justice, but the attorney in charge of decrees enforcement, Maurice Silverman, never found persuasive any evidence of ongoing collusion. Exhibitors filed fruitless suits in the court of Judge Edmund S. Palmieri for the Southern District of New York, which oversaw the Decrees. Nothing changed, except that Hollywood had been freed from having to feed its theaters.

Hollywood came full circle, however, with the arrival of the Reagan administration in 1980. The home video market was in its infancy. The name of the once and future game has always been who controls first-run theaters, for the hoopla surrounding first-run inevitably determines later want-to-see. On the cusp of video's massive penetration of the American home, first-run was key. When, in 1984, Columbia Pictures bought the tiny fourteen-screen Walter Reade circuit and essentially reintegrated production, distribution, and exhibition, you could have heard a lizard clear its tonsils in the film industry. What would Attorney General Ed Meese do? Of course, he did nothing. Distribution subsequently went on a rampage of chain-gobbling, including Universal Pictures' acquisition of the largest single stake (49 percent) in Cineplex Odeon Theaters of Toronto. (Universal chairman Lew Wasserman and Ronald Reagan had been "joined at the hip" since Reagan's failed film career transmogrified into 1950s TV shill, followed by his long political ascent from "kook" to king.)

By the end of Reagan's two terms, Hollywood was back where it started in 1948. It owned theaters and still struggled with how to feed them. It sold films how and where it pleased. It was still the target of content reformers and hid behind a rating system that virtually everyone attacked for one reason or another. The only thing that has changed since 1948, it seems, is that a lot fewer people go to the movies, and everyone has a theory why.

HARLAN JACOBSON

The Toast of TV

"The Ed Sullivan Show" went on to become television's longest-running variety show, airing every Sunday on CBS for twenty-three years. But on Sunday, June 20, 1948, it was just one of several variety programs either on the air or in the process of being developed. The show was called "Toast of the Town," and the master of ceremonies, Ed Sullivan, was a veteran Broadway columnist and radio commentator—which seemed appropriate, since he had a great face for radio.

On the opening show, which was broadcast from CBS radio's Studio 44, the Maxine Elliot Theatre, Sullivan pulled together an impressive lineup on a whopping budget of $475, a sum which might cover catering for guests these days. Of that amount, $400 was split by the headliners, Dean Martin and Jerry Lewis, who made their television debut. *Variety*'s review was generally optimistic for the show, if not a bit cautious. "Top vaude and nitery talent available for television is going to be at a premium in the very near future. That's undoubtedly the most important conclusion to be drawn," wrote the reviewer. "But with WPIX coming up with two other shows of the same ilk in the near future, it's difficult to determine where all the talent will come from."

It wasn't a problem the first night. Start with Martin and Lewis, who got a rave from the reviewer, with this caveat: "CBS was guilty again of permitting them to give out with some blue material, okay for their nitery work but certainly not for television." Other acts in the opening-night lineup were dancer Kathryn Lee, singer Monica Lewis, pianist Eugene List, fight referee Ruby Goldstein, and Broadway producers Richard Rodgers and Oscar Hammerstein II.

There were plenty of reservations about Sullivan, however. The show was inevitably compared to NBC's "Texaco Star Theatre," presided over by the polished comedian Milton Berle. As *Variety* wrote, "It lacked the sparkle of the Texaco show, chiefly because Sullivan, as an emcee, is a good newspaper columnist. He's affable enough and certainly has enough show-biz know-how to lend authority to his job, but he doesn't have the comedy touch of Milton Berle."

Indeed, it took a while before Sullivan caught on with the network. *Variety* concluded: "'Toast' proved that TV can be as good as the talent it presents. If Sullivan and CBS can continue booking such top acts, the show will be a natural for any prospective sponsor." Still, reports surfaced that CBS shopped the show to

For twenty-three years, New Yorkers lined up around the block to catch the latest acts on "The Toast of the Town," renamed "The Ed Sullivan Show" in 1955. When David Letterman moved his late-night talk show from NBC to CBS in the fall of 1993, the Ed Sullivan Theatre got a new lease on life.

sponsors with Sullivan and, also, without him. They stuck with Sullivan.

He was an odd choice. His delivery was as bad as his posture, and some detractors called him "Stone Face." For a TV pioneer, his style was only imitated by comics, who relentlessly poked fun at him. But he wasn't threatening to his guests and never detracted from what the show was really about: showcasing performers who had something to sell. Nowadays, that line isn't always so clear, as hosts like David Letterman and Arsenio Hall often seem to be bigger stars than their guests.

Sullivan's demeanor and onstage manner changed little on the show, which was finally named after him in 1955. It didn't take that long for performers to begin flocking to him. An appearance on his program could prop up a washed-up performer or establish a new one. He put down scores of challenging shows which came up against him from NBC and ABC. At the same time, Sullivan appeared in such films as *The Czar* and *Mr. Broadway,* both seemingly apt titles for his growing stature in the entertainment business.

Though his manner was stiff, the increasingly popular television host had his strengths. While presiding over the show, he never stopped writing his Broadway column in the *Daily News* and had a reporter's flair for finding new talent—whether human or canine (dog acts were a staple of the program). He was astute at identifying new trends and opening the show to versatile acts. He was one of the first to give a chance to rock and roll, for example.

Soon he was battling bitterly over guests with fellow hosts Milton Berle and Steve Allen, which would make the well-publicized booking battles between modern-day late-night warriors Jay Leno, Arsenio Hall, and David Letterman seem tame by comparison. They all tried to stake claim over Elvis Presley, for one. Although the sneering 21-year-old singer had done prior TV appearances with both Berle and Allen, none of those had the enduring impact of his three appearances on the "Sullivan Show" between 1956 and 1957. Indeed, Sullivan made history showing the pelvic gyrations of Presley, who was paid a reported fee of $50,000 to perform such hits as "Love Me Tender," "Don't Be Cruel," and "Hound Dog."

The show's biggest "discovery," however, was the Beatles. By the early 1960s, the group was huge in Europe but couldn't get arrested in the United States. Then, on February 9, 1964, the mop tops appeared on Sullivan's show to play "All My Loving," "She Loves You," "I Saw Her Standing There," and "I Want to Hold Your Hand." The group became a Stateside sensation as a result, and Sullivan soon had first crack at all the new groups, particularly the British bands which had had trouble selling records in America. This kept his show rolling strong well into the 1960s; but toward the end of the decade, the program was showing its age. Up against hit series like "FBI," the ratings began to falter for the first time, and CBS finally threw in the towel in 1971, the year Sullivan aired his last "really big shew."

America's most beloved master of ceremonies died just three years later.

MICHAEL FLEMING

Fresh from her 1964 success in the Broadway smash *Funny Girl,* Barbra Streisand pays homage to television's legendary showman.

FACING PAGE

Star Maker: He wasn't particularly charming or photogenic, but Ed Sullivan could pick a winner. American audiences were introduced to everyone from Elvis Presley to the Beatles on his popular weekly variety show, which aired from 1948 to 1971.

Cinerama, CinemaScope, and 3-D: The Big Screen Gets Even Bigger

In the years from 1952 to 1954, Hollywood technology was in ferment. The movie business had entered the new decade in a complacent frame of mind, with decades of money-spinning activity behind it, then, like a thief in the night, television began to seize the initiative. Attendance dropped from eighty million per week to around forty-six million in 1952. The Hollywood studios recognized that this new rival had to be tackled—and promptly.

Television possessed a novelty value, bringing sports, comedy, music, news, and drama into the living room with an immediacy that the cinema could not rival. The new medium suffered from two fundamental disadvantages, however: its tiny screen and its monochrome image.

Thanks to the persistence of a few men's vision, Hollywood found the tools it needed to counter the threat of television. The studios hardly ever act in concert, and the crucial gimmicks of the early 1950s—Cinerama, CinemaScope, and 3-D— met with a mixed reception from the majors. Yet a new, more glamorous movie medium emerged from the dust of battle—higher, wider, deeper, and more colorful than ever before. The stars got smaller, but the screens waxed larger.

Each of the innovations that revived the cinema during the 1950s had been available in some form or another for many years. Only the innate conservatism of the major studios prevented them from exploiting inventions as they first appeared. Even Technicolor took its definitive three-color form only in 1932, when Walt Disney painstakingly printed three cells for each frame because the appropriate cameras were not yet available. Yet twenty years earlier, the French company Gaumont had demonstrated a three-color system known as Chronochrome.

The concept of a wide screen goes back to the infancy of the cinema. The Lumière brothers in France projected some of their films on a screen measuring 48 feet tall by 63 feet wide at the Paris Exposition of 1900. Abel Gance filmed his epic, *Napoléon* (1927), with triple-screen projection in mind from the start. Three regular-sized screens were placed side by side in the auditorium, enabling the center screen to be used for the main narrative and the "wings," as it were, for spectacular events and additional images. Twelve years later, at the New York World's Fair, an inventor named Fred Waller lashed together eleven projectors, throwing their images onto a massive curved screen. The war interrupted the development of the concept, and it was not until 1952 that Waller, aided and abetted by Merian C. Cooper (codirector of *King Kong*) and newscaster Lowell Thomas, could launch his patent, by then called Cinerama.

The film *This Is Cinerama!* opened in New York on September 30, 1952. The effect was devastating. The evening began with an innocuous, black-and-white introduction on a small screen. Then, almost without warning, the film expanded to immense proportions (23 feet tall by 64 feet wide) and sucked its audience into the terrors of a roller-coaster ride. This was achieved by filming, and then projecting, three parallel segments of the same scene. The dividing lines oscillated slightly, but they did not detract from the stereoscopic effect.

Box-office results proved healthier than anyone in Hollywood could have imagined. *This Is Cinerama!* soon smashed *Gone with the Wind*'s records in Detroit, and the New York presentation clocked up 2,165 showings over more than two years. *Cinerama Holiday* (1955) attracted equally large audiences, and as late as 1960 the Cinerama Corporation was able to sign a contract with MGM to produce films for initial presentation in Cinerama and general release in CinemaScope. *How the West Was Won* and *The Wonderful World of the Brothers Grimm* made money for the studio, although keen-eyed spectators could distinguish the lines dividing the three images, even on the 'Scope prints.

In cities large and small throughout the United States, Cinerama revived the notion of moviegoing as an "event." As time passed, however, theaters equipped for Cinerama switched to a single-projector system, retaining their huge screens for the more practical 70 mm gauge.

Almost exactly one year after the advent of Cinerama, CinemaScope was introduced with much fanfare when *The Robe* opened in New York (September 16, 1953). Again, the process had been in development for decades. Henri Chrétien, a French technician, had made an unavailing effort to persuade Paramount to acquire his system in 1935. After the war, Britain's J. Arthur Rank purchased an option, but soon abandoned plans to film in wide-screen. On December 18, 1952, Twentieth Century-Fox decided to move ahead and committed all of its 1953 productions to the new formula.

FOLLOWING PAGES

Shot with three adjacent cameras, the roller-coaster ride in *This Is Cinerama!* was the closest cinematic equivalent of actually being there.

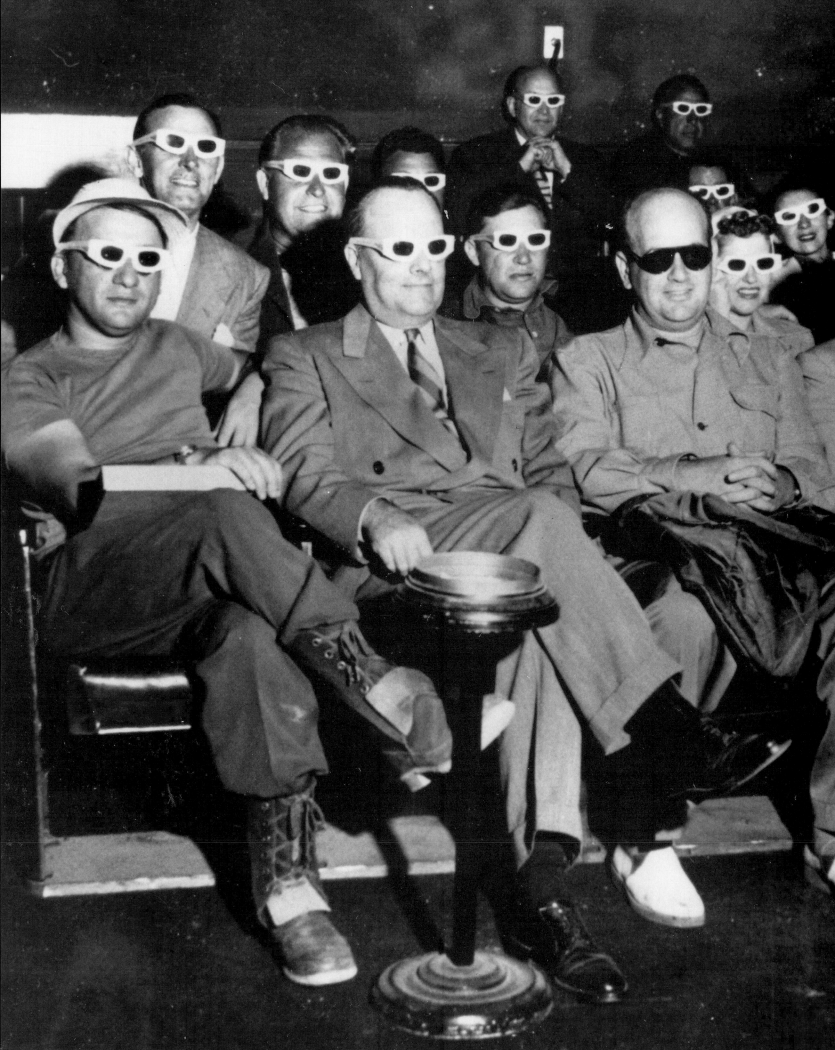

"Its impact on the trade and public must be boffo—in spades," wrote *Variety* when *The Robe* appeared. The spectacular imagery (backed by stereophonic sound) disguised the poverty of Henry Koster's direction, and the public flocked to see the Fox release. Within nine months, some seventy-five films went into production in CinemaScope. All the studios (except RKO, Paramount, and Republic) took out licenses from Fox or worked on developing their own system. Three weeks into principal photography on *A Star Is Born,* Warners panicked and started shooting again, in CinemaScope.

CinemaScope emerged as the most durable and appealing of all the 1950s gimmicks. Its image was two and a half times as wide as it was high (2.66:1), but this ratio was whittled down to 2.55:1 to accommodate four-track magnetic stereophonic sound, and eventually to 2.35:1 as almost all conventional theaters scampered to convert to the process. By mid-1955, more than twenty thousand theaters worldwide were equipped for 'Scope projection.

During shooting, an anamorphic lens on the camera allowed a scene to be filmed in the 'Scope ratio. The image was then squeezed onto 35 mm negative film. Projectors were fitted with a similar anamorphic lens and thus expanded the film out to its original shape onto the screen.

Veteran Hollywood directors reacted with skepticism to the arrival of CinemaScope. Fritz Lang dismissed it as suitable only for filming snakes or funerals. John Ford referred to the wide screen as a huge tennis court, while Rouben Mamoulian, obliged to make his swan song, *Silk Stockings,* in the new process, described it as "the worst shape ever devised."

True, the letter-box format inhibited close-ups, and audiences protested when Fred Astaire and Cyd Charisse had their feet "amputated" during a so-called widescreen presentation of *The Band Wagon.* But thanks to the introduction and gradual perfection of Panavision lenses, the quality and crispness of definition in 'Scope releases endeared the process to filmgoers throughout the world. The use in 1992 of the 2.35:1 format for productions as different as *The Last of the Mohicans* and *A Few Good Men* underlines its appeal even today.

Although it predated the advent of CinemaScope by almost a year, 3-D failed to survive as a commercial medium. The Polaroid Company played a key role in launching 3-D with its lightweight, paper-framed glasses that were required for every viewing. *Bwana Devil* (1952) sparked the 3-D craze. Producer Arch Oboler earned a $500,000 advance against receipts from his distribution deal on *Bwana Devil,* and the picture made enormous profits. The novelty factor accounted for its success, and the 3-D effects were meager (the best being the moment when a native hurls a spear out toward the audience).

Once more, the studios grasped eagerly at this new gimmick, and by early 1953 several 3-D productions were in release, and Polaroid was churning out six million pairs of glasses per week. In Copenhagen, one seventy-four-year-old woman, hav-

FACING PAGE

Vision of the Future?: As television began to make inroads in the 1950s, Hollywood struck back in a big way. Creating the illusion of depth and perspective in screen imagery, the 3-D process was the least successful of the film industry's efforts to woo audiences back to the movie house.

ing seen double for many years, went to watch *Bwana Devil* and, after donning the Polaroids, recovered perfect vision!

House of Wax (1953) legitimized the 3-D process in the eyes of critics as well as audiences. An abundance of special effects—cancan dancers high-kicking into the camera, smoke from a fire coiling out over the spectators' heads, a Ping-Pong ball springing out of the screen—assured the André de Toth film a record gross of about $5 million. *The Charge at Feather River,* inferior in artistic terms, piled on the 3-D effects, with every conceivable object, from tomahawks to sabers to lethal snakes, hurtling from the screen. One character even spit in the audience's face.

Variety's top seven box-office films in January of 1954 illustrated the popularity of the new systems: four in CinemaScope, two in 3-D, and one in Cinerama. Something had to give—and 3-D was the first process to buckle. Universal tried in vain to resuscitate the excitement in 1955 with *Revenge of the Creature,* but although receipts were respectable, the studios abandoned 3-D. Alfred Hitchcock shot *Dial M for Murder* (1954) in three dimensions, even though he knew that it would undoubtedly be released "flat." "It was a nine-day wonder," said Hitchcock sardonically, "and I came in on the ninth day."

The technological turmoil of the early 1950s demonstrated a craving for better quality sound, color, and image among audiences still reluctant to desert their local bijou or drive-in for the primitive comforts of television. Various systems, from the sumptuous, crystalline VistaVision (*White Christmas, One-Eyed Jacks*) to Technirama (70 mm film used for epics like *Spartacus* and *Lawrence of Arabia*), steadily enhanced the depth of field of each scene while facilitating the photographing and projection of their images.

The ne plus ultra, the most spectacular of all visual systems, remains Imax, developed in the early 1970s in Canada and commanding a screen 52 feet high by 64 feet wide. Imax cameras use the world's largest existing film format to print—and project—images horizontally. Whether diving into a volcanic crater, swooping through the Grand Canyon, or plunging the spectator into a Rolling Stones concert, Imax sends audiences awestruck from specially built theaters. With auditoriums being built in Eastern Europe and already well established in cities such as Brussels and Bradford, England, Imax seems likely to outlast such tongue-in-cheek innovations as Sensurround and Smell-O-Vision. And in the home, the dream of interactive television, with the solitary viewer "entering" his personal screen to combat Predator, RoboCop, or Rambo, may yet render all the cinema's efforts obsolete.

PETER COWIE

1954

Long Live the King!

A weary Pvt. Elvis Presley ponders eight weeks of basic training in the spring of 1958.

Early in 1953, Sun Records founder Sam Phillips supposedly remarked: "If I could find a white man who had the Negro sound and the Negro feel, I could make a billion dollars." While Phillips's personal income never reached that ten-figure number, surely the recording and merchandising legacy of Sun's greatest act, Elvis Presley, has long surpassed it.

When a young truck driver named Elvis Aron Presley entered the Memphis Recording Service in the late summer of 1953 to make a private recording of an old Ink Spots number, "My Happiness," no one paid much attention. When, a year later, Sun Records put out Presley's first commercially released single, a version of Arthur "Big Boy" Crudup's "That's All Right, Mamma" backed by the old country favorite "Blue Moon of Kentucky," a legend was born.

That first record combined two of Presley's soon-to-be dominant influences: the easy country stylings of "Blue Moon" with the more raucous, fast blues swing of "That's All Right." And the latter tune set the stage for Presley's—and rock and roll's—meteoric ascent. While the kid from Tupelo, Mississippi, may not have invented rock and roll, he freed it from its underground status, once and for all.

Sun's next few Presley releases—"Good Rockin' Tonight," "Mystery Train"— were enough to land the young singer on the Grand Ole Opry radio show in September 1954, although his singularly passionate style was a bit too much for the hat-and-fiddles crowd. A month later, however, as the Hillbilly Cat and the Blue Moon Boys (guitarist Scotty Moore and bassist Bill Black), he blew away the listeners of the "Louisiana Hayride" show, winning a one-year contract to play every weekend. There wasn't much money, but the exposure to a national audience was invaluable.

From there it was a dizzying ride to the top. "Baby, Let's Play House," released by Sun in April 1955, hit the Top 10 on the country chart, catching the attention of former carny barker "Colonel" Tom Parker. Parker (real name: Andreas van Kuijk), a figure of some controversy in the Presley mythos, nevertheless negotiated a major recording contract with RCA Records and representation with the William Morris Agency, establishing a firm launching pad for the fast-rising star. By now, the teenage thirst for rock and roll was increasingly exponentially, and Presley was persuaded to rock along with them. The immediate result was a string of wildly popular and historically significant recordings: "Heartbreak Hotel," "Hound Dog," and "Don't Be Cruel."

Elvis's insistent, provocative way with a lyric, combined with his bad-boy good looks and hip-swiveling high-stepping, was now being held up by some communities as yet another example of the link between rock and roll and juvenile delinquency. Following a particularly gyrating appearance on "The Milton Berle Show," the singer was condemned by the PTA. During his third "Ed Sullivan Show" appearance in January 1957, he was filmed only from the waist up.

Nevertheless, teenage Presley passion could not be curbed, and Hollywood was the next entertainment beacon to beckon. Independent producer Hal Wallis signed him to a three-picture deal, with the first being *The Reno Brothers,* a Civil War drama top-lining Robert Wagner and Jeffrey Hunter. Thanks to the inclusion of a particular Presley-sung ballad, the picture was retitled *Love Me Tender* before hitting theaters in 1956. The singer completed several other successful pictures in the following months, including *Loving You* and *Jailhouse Rock* (for which he choreographed the title production number). Outcry about his hard-rocking image, as well as the rebel roles he played in *Jailhouse* and 1958's *King Creole,* continued unabated, however, and Presley seemed fated for a showdown with the establishment.

Then something happened that changed Elvis Presley forever: the United States Army. "Elvis died when he went into the army," Beatle John Lennon would later quip, and indeed when he was formally inducted on March 24, 1958, his career would never be the same. Gone forever was the ducktail; gone too was much of the reckless, rocking passion that marked those early Sun and RCA recordings. Upon his return stateside in 1960, he began recording songs that evidenced a more mature, even laid-back image, including the lushly orchestrated "It's Now or Never" and "Are You Lonesome Tonight?" His appearance on a Frank Sinatra TV special that May was seen largely as a passing of the torch: Elvis was now firmly establishment.

Following that television appearance and a March 25, 1961, benefit concert for a memorial to the *USS Arizona* in Pearl Harbor, Presley would do no more television or live shows until near the end of the decade; if you wanted to see Elvis, you had to go to the bijou. He cranked out twenty-seven films during the 1960s, their titles giving away the profundity of their content—*Kissin' Cousins, Paradise Hawaiian Style, Girls! Girls! Girls!* But every last one of them made money at the box office.

While charges of interchangeability for most of these pictures would not be too far off the mark, Elvis's last three films (all released in 1969) broke the formula. *Charro!* is a western, complete with a score by Hugo Montenegro (who had done *The Good, the Bad and the Ugly*) and a decidedly Clint Eastwood-ian Elvis, with cigar and scruffy beard. *The Trouble with Girls* includes, of all things, a murder subplot. And *A Change of Habit*—probably the strangest Presley film of all—cast the singer as a doctor working in a ghetto and Mary Tyler Moore as one of three nuns working the same turf. Elvis falls for her, and in a montage at the end, Moore is seen trying to decide between Elvis and the church.

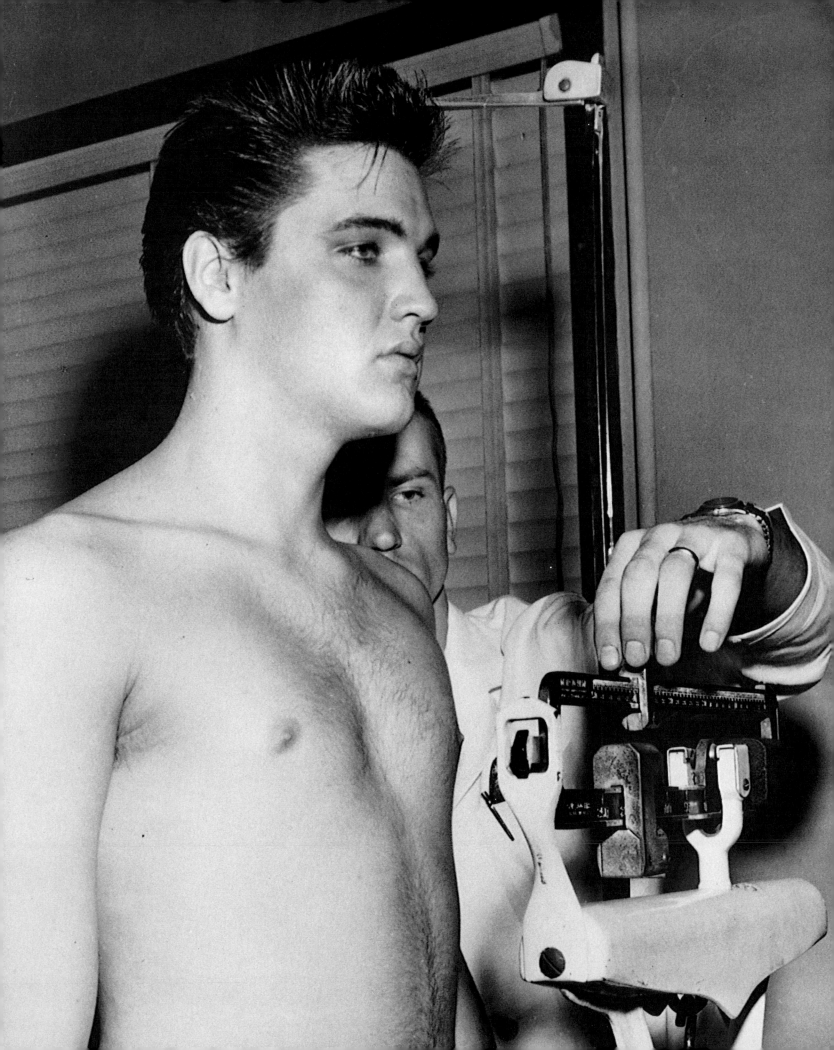

A third distinct period in Presley's career began around this same time, with the December 3, 1968, airing of "Singer Presents Elvis" (later retitled "Elvis—the '68 Comeback Special"). Here, a leather-clad Elvis tore through such hits as "Jailhouse Rock" and "Lawdy, Miss Clawdy," goofing with the band and joking with the audience. His 1969 recordings included "In the Ghetto," "Don't Cry, Daddy," and "Suspicious Minds"—all heavily orchestrated and featuring dramatic vocal performances. Along with a continued penchant for making gospel records, Elvis Presley had firmly entered his fully adult phase.

Throughout the late sixties and early seventies, Presley toured incessantly, trading in the black leather for white, fringed jumpsuits, which, as the singer continued to put on weight, became increasingly gaudy. Richard Strauss's overwrought "Also Sprach Zarathustra" was added as the intro to Elvis's Las Vegas-style concerts, and no small degree of self-parody—intentional as well as not—began to creep in.

By 1973 Presley was spending most of his time at his Memphis mansion, Graceland, along with his dad, Vernon, bodyguards, friends, and assorted hangers-on, all lumped together under the not-so-playful tag "The Memphis Mafia." The singer started acting more erratic, shooting out TV sets when something appeared that he did not like and petitioning for, and receiving, a narcotics agent's badge from President Richard Nixon—hardly a symbol of youthful rebellion. The badge was doubly ironic, since Presley was by now freely abusing drugs, mixing amphetamines and sleeping pills to keep up with his frenetic concert schedule. He was hospitalized several times during the seventies and, on August 16, 1977, he was found dead in his bathroom at Graceland. The official cause of death was cardiac arrhythmia, but more probably it was the various drugs fighting in his system.

Following his death came a perhaps predictable flood of books attempting to explain the who, what, and why of Elvis. Much has been made of the dichotomy of his nature—the devout gospel singer versus the wild rocker and, later, the semi-coherent drug abuser—some even suggesting that this was Presley's tortured psyche's way of "including" his twin brother, Jessie, who was stillborn. Such self-anointed psychologists also note the significant role played by his mother, Gladys, for whom he had recorded "My Happiness" and whose death in 1958 left him devastated.

Along the way, Graceland has become nothing short of a pop-culture mecca, while jokey "sightings" of Elvis are still reported regularly in tabloids. Elvis's status as an icon, secured well before his death, is compounded by his eventual transformation from youthful renegade to a genuine *Citizen Kane*-like character—one who had it all but finally did not know what to do with it or with whom to share it.

But by far, the most important legacy is to be found in the recordings themselves, charting as they do the adolescence (if not the actual birth) of rock and roll music and style. Here, truly, is where one can say, "The king is dead; long live the king."

KEVIN ZIMMERMAN

FACING PAGE

Naked Warrior: "Elvis died when he went into the army," John Lennon would later quip about the singer's induction by Uncle Sam in 1958. The ducktail may have been gone, but Presley's career was far from over.

The Shuberts vs. the Justice Department

In New York City on February 17, 1956, Federal Judge Irving R. Kaufman signed a historic consent decree compelling the Shubert Organization to sell off twelve of its theaters (including four in New York), get out of the booking business, and obtain the government's approval for any future theater purchases. It was the theater world's equivalent to the breakup decades later of Ma Bell, a culmination of ten years of scrutiny by various state and federal agencies, including a six-year investigation by the antitrust division of the Department of Justice.

For well over half a century, control of the commercial theater, including vaudeville and the "legitimate" theater, had been centralized in all-powerful, tightly held companies. The Theatrical Syndicate presided over by Marc Klaw and Abraham Lincoln Erlanger ruled the industry from the end of the nineteenth century through the First World War. But the Syndicate proved no match for the three Shubert brothers—Sam, Lee, and Jacob—who began their empire-building in Syracuse, New York, and by the end of the new century's second decade had supplanted the syndicate (something Sam would not live to see, having died in 1905 from burns received in a gruesome train wreck).

In their heyday, the Shuberts *were* the American theater: they owned and managed the houses, produced the shows that went into them, sold the tickets to those shows, booked their tours, and challenged any critic who might write an unkind review (see "The Shuberts vs. the *New York Times*," page 18). In the 1920s, they owned 30 theaters in New York and nearly 60 in other cities; in addition, they booked some 750 additional theaters. Although the Shuberts lost millions during the Great Depression, they emerged with a consolidated empire and still managed to produce most of the shows that ran on Broadway.

What sustained the company from the very beginning is what continues to sustain it today: having hit musicals play their theaters for long runs. The only thing that has changed is that a profitable run in 1927 could be less than half a year; today a musical must typically run for two years or more to recoup its investment.

The Shuberts were as much about real estate as they were about theater, as they had proved in November 1948 with the single-swoop purchase of the Booth, Broadhurst, Plymouth, and Shubert theaters, along with Shubert Alley, in New York City. The $4 million-plus deal, second in size only to the purchase of the land that became Rockefeller Center, gave Lee and Jacob ownership of the block of theaters between Broadway and Eighth Avenue on West 44th and West 45th streets, bookended by the Manhattan and Astor hotels. By that time, however, their business practices in New York and on the road had piqued the interest of various investigative agencies. A box office scandal in Philadelphia during the run there of *Annie Get Your Gun* revealed just how much cash was flowing under the table from scalpers into the Shubert coffers. The subsequent publicity also showed how ruthlessly and completely Lee and Jacob controlled the theater.

A near decade on the defensive took its toll on an organization that was already fractured by intra-family rivalries and illness. By the time of the consent decree, the Shuberts had all but stopped producing. Over the following years, the organization was essentially taken over by Gerald Schoenfeld, a lawyer who had represented the company during the Justice Department investigation, and his friend Bernard B. Jacobs, also an attorney. Their takeover was completed in 1973, with Schoenfeld assuming the title of chairman and Jacobs, president; now Schoenfeld and Jacobs are universally called "the Shuberts."

Under the two lawyers, the Shubert Organization became a subsidiary of the Sam S. Shubert Foundation, which had been established in 1948. The move gave the company tax advantages that infuriated its competitors. But the foundation has also become a major source of underwriting for nonprofit theaters, which have in turn becomes crucial suppliers of Broadway shows. Moreover, the company returned to producing. And while the Shuberts remain the most powerful and sometimes feared force in the commercial theater, the company has been responsible for updating business practices with computerized box offices, credit card ticket sales, and mass marketing of shows.

Judge Kaufman's consent decree inadvertently set all of those changes in motion. While the nature of the Shuberts' impact on the theater world changed as a result, it was the simultaneous advent of the nonprofit theater, on the one hand, and television on the other, that did far more to change the nature of the commerical theater. The Justice Department implicitly recognized that fact in October 1981, when it terminated Judge Kaufman's restrictions, twenty-five years after the signing of the consent decree.

JEREMY GERARD

Shuberts Stripped I
In U.S. Decree; N

By HOBE MORRISON

As generally expected, the Government's anti-trust suit against the Shuberts, Marcus Heiman and the United Booking Office has been settled by consent decree. The agreement does not, as some mistakenly suppose, involve the destruction or breakup of the Shubert theatrical empire.

The Shuberts must divest themselves of 12 theatres in six cities, including four in New York. They are enjoined from various monopolistic and discriminatory prac-

Variety, February 22, 1956.

Nixon vs. Kennedy: The Political Power of TV, Part One

On the evening of September 26, 1960, in Chicago, the opening statements of the first televised presidential debate in American history were to begin at 8:30. But when TV director-producer Don Hewitt looked into the control room monitors, he knew that nothing either candidate said was likely to matter.

"[Richard] Nixon looked terrible," Hewitt recalls. The Republican candidate was battling a virus and had lost so much weight that his shirt was too large. The vice president was also in physical pain from having banged his knee on a car door the previous day. John F. Kennedy, who had napped before the debate, showed up tanned and rested—"like an Adonis," Hewitt says—and declined makeup. As a result, Nixon, who had appeared before the carpenters' union that afternoon, also felt he had to refuse makeup (he used only a light coat of Lazy Shave to conceal his five o'clock shadow).

When Hewitt saw the disparity between the two candidates on camera—Nixon's suit even contrasted poorly with the set—he called over CBS president Frank Stanton and asked what they could, or should, do. Stanton turned to Nixon adviser Ted Rogers and asked, "Are you satisfied with the way your candidate looks?" Rogers said, "Yeah, he looks fine to me." Stanton told Hewitt that giving advice at that point would be interfering.

"It never dawned on [Nixon] that this was a key to the election; he thought it was just another campaign appearance," Hewitt says. "I met with Jack Kennedy beforehand, and he wanted to know everything—where to stand, which way to face—I never [saw] Nixon." When the debate started, Sandy Vanocur, one of the journalists asking questions that night, was struck by the fact that Nixon was always looking at Kennedy, while Kennedy looked out at the audience—and the camera.

For those who listened to the debate on radio, there was no clear victor—both candidates held their own in the discussion of the issues. But for the seventy-five million Americans who watched on TV, Nixon—sweating, slouching, and with no makeup—was no match for the vigorous and virile-looking Massachusetts senator.

FACING PAGE

Screen Test: Richard Nixon's poor performance in the first televised Presidential debate may or may not have cost him the election, but television had changed American politics forever.

(In retrospect, Kennedy's triumph was supremely ironic, since he spent much of his political life hiding physical ailments—chronic back problems and Addison's disease—which frequently required heavy medication.)

The Kennedy camp had hoped that the debate would "let people know he was a viable alternative," says Ted Sorenson, the adviser in charge of debate preparation. "He still needed to generate enthusiasm within his own party."

They got more then they bargained for. "The debate created a palpable sense of excitement," says political columnist David Broder, who was covering the Kennedy campaign. "Not only cold you see the difference in the size of crowds, but you could also feel the difference—these people felt they knew Kennedy." Sorenson recalls that the "phenomenon known as jumpers"—women who stood at the side of the road, jumping up and down and screaming—started immediately after the debate.

There were three other debates that fall. Nixon wore makeup and looked healthier, but it was too late. "Nixon did very well in the three debates following that, but the first debate was the defining one," Vanocur says. The debates averaged 67 million viewers and, as Theodore White wrote in *The Making of the President,* gave voters "a tribal sense of participation." The election results included a record-high voter turnout and, of course, a victory for Kennedy.

A Roper survey revealed that 57 percent of the voters said the TV debates influenced their choice. The crucial statistic the survey uncovered was that six percent said they based their final decision on the debates—of those four million votes, three million were for Kennedy. In an election where the candidates were separated by only 112,000 popular votes, that first debate may have provided the margin of victory. In fact, Hewitt recounts a scene from 1964, when he was sitting backstage at the Republican National Convention in San Francisco as Nixon prepared to introduce Barry Goldwater. Frances Arvold was applying makeup to Nixon's face—an assignment she was supposed to have done before that first debate in 1960. "I said to him, 'You know, if you had let Frances do that four years ago, then Barry Goldwater would be introducing *you,*" Hewitt says. "He said to me, 'You're probably right.' He admitted it right there."

The 1960 debate was not only a success for Kennedy; it also marked a turning point for television's role in the election process. Only ten years earlier, the debate's impact would have been minimal: in 1950, only 11 percent of American homes had TV sets; by 1960, that figure had skyrocketed to 88 percent. "The debate secured television's position in politics," Broder says. Television eventually "institutionalized the debates as the centerpiece of the campaign," with each side building strategies around these spectacles.

That transformation was to take another sixteen years, however. While television's role in the politics of the 1960s was undeniable—images of the Vietnam War on the evening news sparked the antiwar movement and helped knock Lyndon

Johnson out of the 1968 race—there were no televised debates in 1964, 1968, or 1972. The 1960 debate had taken place only because Frank Stanton and others convinced Congress to suspend temporarily the FCC ruling that guaranteed equal time to all candidates (the ruling would have forced the networks to invite the fourteen other legally declared candidates).

It was not until 1976 that the FCC reinterpreted its ruling, stating that debates conducted by an independent organization, like the League of Women Voters, were news events the networks could cover without offering equal time. Although most politicians and journalists say none of the debates in the five presidential campaigns since then has decided an election, in four of the races, the debates were crucial.

The first such crucial moment came in 1976, with Jimmy Carter taking on President Gerald Ford. In the second debate, Ford inexplicably declared that "there is no Soviet dominance of Eastern Europe and there never will be under a Ford Administration." He went on to say that Poland was "independent" and "autonomous." Ford might very well have lost anyway—the Republicans were the party of Watergate, and Ford had pardoned Richard Nixon—but his verbal gaffe received so much attention (including a front-page story in the *New York Times* devoted exclusively to those comments) that he was put on the defensive, and Carter gained considerable momentum.

In 1980, the Iran hostage situation and faltering economy probably doomed President Carter's reelection bid, but the debates sealed his defeat. First, Carter refused to participate in the September 22 debate which included independent candidate John Anderson. While Anderson did not gain much from the exposure, Carter was criticized and Republican Ronald Reagan's ratings soared. Meanwhile, Carter continually attacked Reagan as a "dangerous hawk," who could not be trusted with America's nuclear arsenal. But in the second debate, on October 28, Carter's blows were deftly deflected by Reagan's performance: the actor-politician appeared calm and reassuring, casually quipping, "There you go again," after one of Carter's verbal assaults.

Of course, after two terms of Ronald Reagan, it seemed that to succeed in the television age, a likable TV persona was essential—not just for the campaign, but also for the presidency. In 1988, the handlers for Democrat Michael Dukakis were so concerned about their candidate's inability to project warmth on-screen that he was forced to make statements like "I think I'm a reasonably likable guy" in his first debate with Vice President George Bush. But any hope of overcoming Dukakis's image problem evaporated in the second debate when CNN's Bernard Shaw asked the Massachusetts governor, "If Kitty Dukakis were raped and murdered, would you favor an irrevocable death penalty for the killer?" Dukakis gave a lengthy answer with no trace of genuine human emotion. He failed to mention his wife, digressing instead to stress that Massachusetts "had the lowest murder rate of any industrial state." By the time he finished rambling about drug education and "getting youngsters to get away from drugs," the debate was lost.

For Don Hewitt, the incredible significance placed on picking a winner and a loser in the debates is a grave concern. His concern echoes that of many people who see TV's influence on presidential elections as potentially dangerous. "We are picking Mr. America," he says.

Vanocur disagrees. While it is unfortunate that voters place too much emphasis on style over substance, "TV is only an instrument," he says. "Dukakis could have taken Bernie Shaw's question and knocked it right out of the park. But he didn't." Sorenson adds that, while he has long been "disappointed by the quality of the questioning," the debates are valuable to the public precisely because the candidate has to "answer questions with no assistant whispering in his ear."

The 1992 presidential campaign was perhaps the greatest indication yet of the increasing power of television in our political process. In an unusual campaign featuring a strong independent candidate, the debates clearly played a critical role. Although Ross Perot already had the nation's attention via his appearances on TV talk shows, the debates placed him on the same stage as the two major-party candidates, granting him instant legitimacy. However, while Perot's energetic debate performances won voters over, the confused showing by his vice presidential choice, Admiral James Stockdale, disrupted his momentum.

Meanwhile, Bill Clinton benefited in much the same way as Kennedy did in 1960: the three presidential debates averaged sixty-six million viewers, and Clinton let people know that he was both presidential and like them. While George Bush was caught checking his watch, Clinton proved to be a television natural. This was especially apparent in the last variation on the "debate," when ordinary citizens asked the questions. Clinton looked like an Oprah-in-training, walking around, connecting personally with each questioner. On the other hand, when Bush was asked how the country's economic problems affected him personally, he looked like a kid who had not done his homework, answering helplessly that he didn't "get" the question.

The 1992 debate with citizen questioners received near-universal acclaim—the public was part of the process, and the questions stuck to the issues—but many people still feel the debates could be improved, says ABC news veteran Hal Bruno, who moderated the 1992 vice presidential debate. Although politicians prefer a panel of journalists to dilute the potential for tough follow-up questions, Bruno says, "The single moderator format is the best."

But for all the criticisms of the scheduling and format of the debates, Bruno adds, "They make good use of this powerful medium." In response to the public's hunger for them, he confirms, "We are seeing them more and more on the local level," ensuring that television's influence on the American political process will continue to grow.

STUART MILLER

1962

The Rise of the Hollywood Agent

In the summer of 1962, Jules Stein and Lew Wasserman formalized a decision they had made earlier, one that would have enormous repercussions in the entertainment industy. The company they ran, MCA (Music Corporation of America)—the most powerful talent agency in show business—would be getting out of that business to concentrate on television and feature-film production.

It was a delicious Hollywood irony: the agency business had made MCA so powerful that Stein and Wasserman could afford to abandon it. Or, put another way, the decision symbolized how far the role of agents had come in Hollywood, from the image of the perpetually hustling, fast-talking "ten percenter" to a ruthlessly efficient, smoothly run, multimillion dollar company which struck fear into the hearts of movie studios, television networks, actors, actresses, and competitors.

The decision to leave agenting was not entirely voluntary. MCA's exemption from a Screen Actors Guild ruling that a talent agency could not simultaneously be a producer was about to expire, and the federal government had filed a civil antitrust suit against MCA, charging its talent agency with restraint of trade. At the same time, Stein and Wasserman were in the process of acquiring Decca Records, which owned Universal Pictures, one of Hollywood's major studios. Decca's shareholders had accepted MCA's stock-swap offer, and Stein and Wasserman hoped to spin off the talent agency as a separate company. But the Justice Department blocked the Decca takeover and spin-off with a temporary restraining order, forcing MCA's hand. The short, gregarious Stein, MCA's founder and chairman, and the tall, taciturn Wasserman, the company's president, huddled with high-priced lawyers and brainstormed their dilemma day after day in the firm's Beverly Hills office, restaurants, and each other's home.

Agenting had made the company, but production was driving it, and the prospect of owning a major movie studio's production, marketing, and distribution systems was too tempting to pass up. "I felt our organization was capable of earning more than ten percent," Wasserman explained twenty-three years later, "and that we could do better on the other side of the table."

"The actual death of MCA," *Variety* reported, "occurred in such a prosaic, offhand fashion it was like the funeral of a long-forgotten star of yesterday."

Agent of Change: By the time MCA chief Lew Wasserman won the coveted Jean Hersholt Humanitarian Award at the 1974 Oscars ceremony, agents were no longer shoot-from-the-hip ten-percenters but the new Hollywood moguls.

On the warm Monday morning of July 23 in Los Angeles, California, lawyers for MCA and the Justice Department waited for Judge William C. Mathes to finish work on another case. Then they quietly slipped into his sparse federal courtroom and obtained his signature on a stipulation agreement that spelled out the terms for the dissolution of MCA's talent agency. "MCA deeply regrets that circumstances beyond its control," Wasserman said, "precluded the company from having the opportunity to discontinue its talent agency functions in a more orderly manner."

Two months later, MCA signed a consent decree to a number of government stipulations (such as promising not to reenter the agency business) dictating how it would have to conduct business in the future. The federal government ended its antitrust suit against MCA, allowing its acquisition of Decca and Universal to go forward.

The event was a benchmark in show business history. It both propelled MCA to even greater heights of power, influence, and profitability in the entertainment business (culminating in the six billion dollar sale of the corporation to the Japanese conglomerate Matsushita in 1990) and also marked how important an industry agenting had become—and how influential (and emulated) MCA's business methods in the field would prove to be.

To be sure, MCA was hardly the first or only talent agency in Hollywood. Agents like Abe Lastfogel, Charlie Feldman, Leland Hayward, and Ted Ashley were all legendary power brokers. Agencies like William Morris, General Artists, and Famous Artists commanded respect and wielded influence. What made MCA so important was its large-scale organization, planning, efficiency, and "take-no-prisoners" negotiating skills, aided by the detailed legal and financial knowledge it exerted in its field. Simply put, it truly was run like a modern corporation.

MCA was tough from the start. Founder Julius Caesar Stein was born in 1896 and put himself through school by playing the violin and saxophone in his own band in and around Chicago. He graduated from the University of Chicago in 1921 as an opthamalogist. One day, his band received two separate offers to play dances on the same night. Stein's group played one date, and he found another band to play the other—for a 20 percent commission. The future Hollywood mogul was in the booking business.

In 1924, Stein gambled he could make more money as a full-time band booker than as an eye doctor. He left his medical practice and founded MCA with William R. "Billy" Goodheart, a hot-tempered pianist who proved to be a hard-driving businessman. Working out of a cramped, two-room office in downtown Chicago, Stein and Goodheart quickly made their mark in the Midwestern music business. They booked dance bands throughout the region and advised them on their careers for a ten percent fee. They persuaded dance hall owners to rotate bands on a regular basis. They insisted MCA be the exclusive agents for the bands—and that owners hire MCA bands exclusively. They also reached a modus vivendi with the pervasive

Chicago mob, led at the time by notorious figures such as Al Capone. And they secured an invaluable alliance with James Petrillo, president of the Chicago local of the American Federation of Musicians. Petrillo later became the AFM's national leader and secured many sweetheart deals for MCA, including granting the agency an exclusive "blanket waiver" to operate as both a talent agency and radio production company.

By the mid-1930s, at the height of the big band era, MCA represented approximately half of the country's top bands, including Harry James, Tommy Dorsey, Artie Shaw, and Guy Lombardo. Radio was king, and thanks to Petrillo's waiver, MCA made a killing by selling the networks a complete package for radio shows, providing bands, singers, writers, directors, and producers (many of whom they also represented).

Success was sweet. The flamboyant Stein drove a Rolls-Royce and bought an estate on the shore of Lake Michigan. Goodheart established MCA as a power in New York, running the agency's office at 43d Street and Broadway. But Hollywood still beckoned.

Stein annointed Lew Wasserman to lead the charge. Born in 1913, Wasserman met Stein in Cleveland, where Wasserman was selling candy in a burlesque house and doing publicity for a nightclub that booked MCA acts. Stein hired him away to write press releases for the company at the end of 1936. Within two years, Wasserman demonstrated a nearly photographic memory, a steel-trap mind for show business details, loyalty, and unquenchable ambition. He was tapped as Stein's protégé and sent to work with him in California.

Musicians were no longer MCA's priority; actors, writers, and directors were— preferably ones with big names. Stein's first triumph was signing Bette Davis. MCA then fattened its roster with other stars by luring them away from other agencies, buying them off or buying out the competition altogether. The culmination was MCA's buyout of the Hayward-Deverich Agency in 1945, adding over three hundred clients to the roster, including a host of screenwriters, playwrights, and actors such as Henry Fonda, Jimmy Stewart, Katharine Hepburn, and Gregory Peck.

The company now had a secure grip on both the music business and Hollywood. Its influence was pervasive. A federal judge who presided over an antitrust case MCA lost in 1946 described the company as "the Octopus…with tentacles reaching out and grasping everything in show business." Stein made himself chairman, moved into a legendary Beverly Hills villa, and turned the day-to-day operations over to Wasserman, the company's new president. MCA's modern era had begun.

Throughout the forties and early fifties, Wasserman dedicated himself to securing and expanding MCA's power. He worked long hours, seven days a week. Despite never having gone to college, he became an expert in financial, business, and legal details. Above all, he was a demanding taskmaster. He instilled an almost militaristic code at the agency. To counter the public image of the flamboyant, fast-talking agent, MCA employees were expected to emulate Wasserman's conservative dress of white shirts, plain dark suits, and narrow ties as well as his conservative behavior and relentless work ethic. Loyalty was demanded, ruthlessness expected. Mistakes were not tolerated. Wasserman was capable of flying into frightening temper tantrums. Once, an agent who was the object of a particularly vicious tongue-lashing fainted. Other agents thought he had suffered a heart attack and rushed over to aid him. When the man revived, Wasserman continued berating him, resuming as if nothing had happened.

Wasserman's business accomplishments mounted. In 1949, he negotiated the first contract for an actor to receive a percentage of a film's gross receipts. The star was client Jimmy Stewart, and the movie was *Winchester '73*. The deal set an important precedent for actors with box office clout and was the catalyst that enabled movie stars' incomes to soar to unprecedented heights. Then, in 1952, Wasserman scored one of MCA's greatest triumphs. He combined his persuasive powers and the company's tradition of working closely with labor unions (and their leaders) to obtain a "blanket waiver" from the Screen Actors Guild (headed by MCA client Ronald Reagan) freeing MCA from the union's prohibition against agents acting simultaneously as producers.

The waiver deal unleashed howls of protest from MCA's rivals and drew the attention of the Justice Department, but often overlooked is the fact that MCA made a significant concession to the union: it agreed to let actors collect residuals each time a property they appeared in was broadcast, considerably enhancing actors' potential incomes.

Waiver in hand, Wasserman began transforming MCA into a production powerhouse. Television sets were becoming a staple in American households, but the movie studios refused to provide programming. MCA moved in to fill the vacuum with a vengeance. A subsidiary, Revue Productions, began grinding out shows, and by the end of the fifties, MCA had sixteen shows on network TV and filled one third of NBC's primetime programming. Wasserman had the foresight to go even beyond the networks, pioneering the concept of syndication, selling MCA's shows and reruns of old shows—and other producers' programs—directly to local stations.

Wasserman also mastered the art of selling a package of MCA-represented talent to movie studios and TV networks. If a buyer wanted one particular talent badly enough, he had to take the others. For television, the company would assemble a writer, director, and actors and sell a show to a network, receiving not just its usual ten percent commission from its clients, but also ten percent of the network's licensing fee plus an additional five percent of revenues from syndication and overseas sales.

By the late 1950s, Wasserman had also begun the company's inevitable push into feature films. In 1958, MCA bought Paramount Pictures's pre-1948 movie

Variety, June 20, 1962.

MCA Takes Over Decca Control In Stock Swap Deal

As expected, Decca shareowners have accepted the Music Corp. of America stock swap merger offer

library for $35 million, and a year later bought Universal Pictures's studio facilities and 367 acres in west Los Angeles surrounding it for $11.2 million. By the time MCA left the agency business in 1962, the Hollywood joke was, "If MCA isn't God, nobody in the company knows it." Wasserman became the consummate insider, making not only entertainment but real-estate deals, acting as Hollywood's wise man to mediate labor disputes, and becoming an increasingly influential player in politics, cultivating his longtime ties to Ronald Reagan as well as to the Democratic Party.

"Lew Wasserman gets what he wants," said Screen Actors Guild president Dana Andrews, "one way or the other. He had enemies all over town, and still does. But people respect him because he has power."

In the 1980s, agent Michael Ovitz of the Creative Artists Agency came closest to re-creating Wasserman's influence. Ovitz too built his agency into a powerhouse, mastered the art of packaging TV shows and movies, and cultivated a reputation for being low-key but extremely well informed, intelligent—and ruthless. Like Wasserman, he too took his agency way beyond agenting, signing deals with Nike to expand into sports marketing and with Coca-Cola to produce advertisements and marketing campaigns.

But agenting was the key to power, and Wasserman wrote the book—or, rather, rewrote it. When he assumed the mantle of studio chief over thirty years ago, he redefined forever the power structure in Hollywood, becoming the natural successor to the first generation of moguls who had transformed that sleepy village half a century earlier.

CHARLES PAIKERT

Only two years after the Fab Four were first introduced to American audiences on "The Ed Sullivan Show," John Lennon could quip: "We're more popular than Jesus Christ right now."

FACING PAGE

The British Invasion: The Beatle frenzy of 1964 was topped off with the release of *A Hard Day's Night,* which garnered two Oscar nominations, for Best Screenplay and Best Musical Score.

1 9 6 4

Beatlemania

Beatlemania was already in full swing in England and much of the rest of Europe when the Fab Four from Liverpool appeared on Ed Sullivan's TV stage for the first time on February 9, 1964. That appearance was the first real shot in the group's short battle to conquer America, effectively laying the groundwork for a revolution in the manner that pop music would be made and presented.

Months of recording and touring to ever-growing audiences and the European success of the group's first album, *Please Please Me* (released the previous year), convinced the Beatles' manager, Brian Epstein, that the time was right to try taking on the United States. A film clip of the Beatles had appeared on "The Jack Paar Program" in January, and America's premiere showman, Sullivan, was convinced to give the British sensations top billing for an unprecedented three consecutive Sunday night shows. Always on the lookout for new international talent, Sullivan told the *New York Times* that, after witnessing a typical Beatles mob scene at London's Heathrow Airport, "I made up my mind that this was the same sort of mass hysteria that had characterized the Elvis Presley days."

"I Want to Hold Your Hand" had hit number one in the States on January 13, resulting in some 50,000 applications for the 720 seats for the February 9 taping, leaving Sullivan hardly any choice but to let the group both open and close the program. What television viewers witnessed that night—in addition to performances of "Twist and Shout," "All My Loving," "She Loves You," and "I Want to Hold Your Hand"—was pandemonium, as girls in the audience screamed, cried, and passed out in the throes of Beatle-zeal, a microcosm of what was beginning to happen around the world. Some 70 million people, or 60 percent of all American TV viewers, had tuned in, with the seeds of countless bands undoubtedly being born before it was over.

"The Ed Sullivan Show" and news conferences surrounding it delivered the boys wholesale to thousands of waiting fans. While some found it hard to discern the differences among the band members due to their similar "mop top" haircuts, the four distinct and witty personalities manifested themselves soon enough (Reporter: "How do you find America?" John Lennon: "Turn left at Greenland"). This resulted in a quick, if rather unfortunate, pigeonholing—John, the smart one; Paul, the cute one; George, the quiet one; Ringo, the cuddly one—that would dog them for the rest of their lives.

Besides firmly establishing the Beatles at the top of the pops—and soon leading directly to their lodging singles in each of the five top slots on the charts for one week, a never-duplicated feat—the Sullivan appearance opened the floodgates for what would soon be termed the "British Invasion": a mad rush by record labels to sign practically anybody with a British accent and a guitar. Some, like the Rolling Stones and the Who, made music of lasting impact, while the great majority—Herman's Hermits, Gerry and the Pacemakers, Chad and Jeremy—had only a couple of bona fide hits before the law of diminishing returns set in. Meanwhile, an invasion of another kind exploded at retail shops around the world, with Beatle boots, lunch boxes, trading cards, and especially Beatle wigs beginning to fly off the shelves. The manufacturer Lowell Toy Group was eventually turning out fifteen thousand wigs a day.

Of far greater importance, though, was the Beatles' impact on how pop and rock records were made. Up until this time, pop music had been primarily a singles market. Albums were reserved for only the most diehard fans and were often padded with cover versions, or songs that were carbon copies of an artist's most recent hit single. With the Beatles, this began to change. For one thing, in Lennon and McCartney (and, to a lesser extent initially, George Harrison), the group had its own songwriters, affording them the relative luxury of not having to rely on outside scribes or their producer to give them their "sound." And, while the Fabs' first couple of albums do show occasional signs of formulaic composing, the McCartney-Lennon team soon began exploring—and then breaking—the boundaries of pop songwriting.

The roots of this experimentation can most clearly be heard on the 1965 album *Help!* Much more than a collection of pop tunes dashed off in support of the band's second feature film, the disc features Lennon's catchy title tune (actually a very real plea for understanding in what was fast becoming a claustrophobic world of celebrity), his Bob Dylan-esque "You've Got to Hide Your Love Away," and McCartney's fragile ballad-for-the-ages, "Yesterday."

Recording artists no longer put out an album a year, but even those who take up to three, or even five, years per album rarely show the swift growth and maturation the Beatles exhibited during their career: the introspective, folkish tone of 1965's *Rubber Soul* giving way to more baroque experimentation on 1966's *Revolver;* the full-blown psychedelia of 1967's *Sgt. Pepper's Lonely Hearts Club Band* followed by the stylistic grab bag of the *White Album.* That the journey from the fresh-faced "I Want to Hold Your Hand" to the majestic epitaph for the sixties, 1970's "Let It Be," took only seven years is nothing short of remarkable.

Meanwhile, the concerts continued to become more and more frenzied, culminating in the band's August 15, 1965, concert at New York's Shea Stadium, where fifty-five thousand people screamed through a multiple-act extravaganza that climaxed with a Beatles set lasting all of twenty minutes. But the grind began to get

On tour in 1965, Paul McCartney called the band's concert at San Francisco's Cow Palace "the wildest of the whole trip." Two weeks earlier, 55,000 hysterical fans had greeted the Beatles at Shea Stadium in New York City.

dangerous, thanks to a pair of 1966 incidents: a perceived snub of Mrs. Ferdinand Marcos caused a near-riot in the Philippines, while Lennon's off-the-cuff remark that "we're more popular than Jesus Christ right now" resulted in "Beatles bonfires" and various threats of bodily harm. Lennon eventually recanted, yet the group effectively ended its live performance days following an August 29, 1966, concert at San Francisco's Candlestick Park.

The Beatles officially broke up almost four years later. The members went on to have varying degrees of independent success, although none consistently produced albums as artistically ground breaking as during their former Fab Four days. For example, Lennon's stark 1970 *Plastic Ono Band* and more forgivable 1971 *Imagine;* McCartney's typically muddy concept disc *Band on the Run* (1973); Harrison's sprawling *All Things Must Pass* (1970); and Ringo Starr's relaxed, radio-ready *Ringo* (1973) are albums generally regarded as each man's singular best, but none is up to the level of even the Beatles' less interesting efforts.

With Lennon's death at the hands of a gun-toting, psychologically disturbed former fan in New York on December 8, 1980, continued rumors of a Beatles reunion were finally ended.

While others have sold more albums and singles, none have equalled the Liverpudlian lads' output for range, daring, or consistent artistic accomplishment. Quite a performance for Ed Sullivan's four "youngsters from England."

KEVIN ZIMMERMAN

TV Crosses Over

In 1950 "Beulah," the first television show to feature an African-American as its main character, premiered on primetime. It was a charming, if completely unprovocative, sitcom about a clever, rotund maid who served a kindly, all-American white family, the Hendersons. That was, after all, 1950, when America was the land of social order, and television—with shows like "The Aldrich Family" and "Toast of the Town"—was meant to be bland and reassuring. "Beulah"'s message was simple and allaying: yes, African-Americans—or, then, "colored people"—were perfectly capable folks, acceptable to the mainstream of American society, but only as servants. On Tuesday, September 17, 1968, sometime between 8:30 and 9 P.M. on NBC stations across the country, the beautiful black actress Diahann Carroll as Julia Baker, woken by Marc Copage playing her young son, Corey, got out of bed in front of millions of viewers to make television history.

In the first episode, "Julia" revealed its heroine was a widowed nurse, living in a plush suburban apartment among friendly white neighbors in a presumably racially integrated section of Los Angeles (Julia's husband, an air force captain, had been killed in Vietnam). On the same episode, Julia searched for employment. When her job application to the in-house clinic of an aerospace firm was rejected by the company's personnel director and token bigot, Julia immediately telephoned Dr. Morton Chegley, the clinic's head, to voice her appeal. During this pivotal conversation, Julia confessed: "I'm colored."

"What color are you?" the gentle doctor asked.

"I'm a Negro."

"Have you always been a Negro, or are you just trying to be fashionable?"

And so she was hired. A fully employed professional, Julia Baker was decidedly several social notches above Beulah or Charlie (the elevator operator on "My Little Margie," 1952 to 1955) or Willie Best (the repairman on "The Stu Erwin Show," 1950 to 1955) or Delilah (the housekeeper on "Father of the Bride," 1961 to 1962) or Louise (the housekeeper on "Make Room for Daddy," 1953 to 1964) or Birdie Lee (the housekeeper on "The Great Gildersleeve," 1955 to 1956). And although

FACING PAGE

Color of Success: Although condemned by some as an unrealistic portrait of African-American life, "Julia" was the first television show starring a black actor playing neither a servant nor an entertainer. The series paved the way for some of television's most successful programming in the 1970s and '80s.

some of the characters in "Amos 'n' Andy" (1951-1953) had respectable jobs, certainly none were professional. With Julia, televison acknowledged for the first time blacks as bona fide members of the middle class.

It should be noted that before "Julia" and even before "Beulah," there had been "The Bob Howard Show," "The Hazel Scott Show," and "The Nat King Cole Show." While Bob Howard, Hazel Scott, and Nat King Cole were not portrayed as servants in white households, they were performers at a time when blacks were already accepted as musicians. Curiously, these artists came and went with their songs; their musical programs exerted little, if any, social impact. Additionally, there were other primetime shows—most notably "I Spy" with Bill Cosby—that featured blacks in non-servile roles, but those roles were supporting in predominantly white programs.

As race and class barriers seemingly were broken with "Julia," violence raged in the streets of America. Merely three years before the premiere, America, also through the television set, caught sight of the miasma of tear gas and thudding police billy clubs that were ubiquitous symbols of social unrest, as African-Americans took to the streets demanding their inalienable but long-deprived civil rights—including what we now regard as basics, like voting privileges and equal access to public places. "We Shall Overcome," the vaulting battle hymn of the civil rights crusade, was still heard, as protesters, both black and white, pressed President Lyndon B. Johnson and his administration for complete equality.

Additionally, reports of abysmal poverty among blacks living in urban squalor appeared daily in newspapers across the nation. Images of socio-economic malaise were beamed directly from crime-ridden ghettos into every American living room. Even with the passage of the Voting Rights Act of 1965 and President Johnson's historic appointment of the great civil rights fighter and jurist Thurgood Marshall, an African-American, to the United States Supreme Court in 1967, the year 1968 would not be one associated with domestic order and peace.

Amid the street violence and social unrest, the National Advisory Commission on Civil Disorders released a ground-breaking report. Its Chapter 15, specifically titled and aimed at "The Media of Mass Communications," urged that "Negroes should appear more frequently in dramatic and comedy series" on primetime television. Reported *Ebony* magazine: "Under pressure, the men who control television belatedly issued a new order of the day: in the CBS version, 'to intensify immediately the portrayal and use and actual number of Negroes.'"

Almost overnight "Julia," whose pilot reportedly had drawn only a lukewarm reaction from the networks' programming executives, was snapped up by NBC. Several sponsors, most visibly General Foods, quickly bid for it. According to a popular Hollywood theory, the show was originally written for a white actress, but famed Hollywood producer Hal Kanter swiftly rescripted it for an African-American upon hearing of the impending commission report. Whatever the case, "Julia," after its first episode, in which there was tension surrounding Nurse Baker's race and her employability in a primarily white firm, went on to portray her life as wholly comfortable. But this portrayal of the day-to-day events of a single, black mother was hardly representative of the lives of millions of other single, black mothers living in the harsh reality of poverty and oppression, not the Hollywood fantasy of liberal middle-class neighborhoods and benevolent bosses. Television viewers needed only to watch the evening news to see that "Julia," not unlike 1950's "Beulah," was but a whitewashed, idealized version of the average African-American life.

Immediately upon previewing the show's pilot, critic Robert Lewis Shayon declared in the April 20, 1968, issue of the venerable *Saturday Review:*

> Though [Julia's] situation might exist in the few interracial neighborhoods which have evolved, it is all a far cry from the bitter realities of Negro life in the urban ghetto, the pit of America's explosion potential. The producers will argue that TV viewers cannot take much more; that this is, in a real sense, the 'opening of a door' to more meaningful representation of Negro family life. A sadder comment is that this is the best that commercial TV can do in the nation's crisis…a sort of adventurous tokenism.

The show's producers offered their rebuttal through their star. "We are dealing with an entertainment medium," Carroll told the Associated Press after the publication of Shayon's critique. " 'Julia' is a drama comedy; it isn't politically oriented. Because I am black that doesn't mean that I have to deal with problems of all black people. That's not my sole responsibility…all TV is divorced from reality…It isn't our business to 'tell it as it is.' Maybe people just don't want to see things like that after they've had a pretty grim day themselves."

Evidently Carroll's emphasis on the sheer entertainment value of television sitcoms was valid: "Julia" made it to the Top 10 in the Nielsen ratings in its first season and remained on the air for three years, until its final episode on May 25, 1971. Throughout the run, however, the controversy surrounding the show's denial of the bitter realities of African-American life increased. Relentlessly refusing to see the show as a mere entertainment vehicle, more and more liberals and militant blacks accused "Julia" of being an instrument of pacification of the oppressive white majority. Later, in her autobiography, *Diahann,* Carroll claimed that she did suggest that her producers make the show more relevant. Unfortunately neither the network nor the producers was capable of introducing more realism into "Julia." Under heavy criticism, she wrote, she walked away from the program after its third season.

The overall failure of "Julia" lay deeply within the system itself. It was the first sitcom to deal exclusively with the life of a black woman, and yet its creators were middle-aged white men—who understandably could never accurately depict the African-American life. Furthermore, Hollywood, despite its affectations, could

JULIA
With Diahann Carroll, Lloyd Nolan, Marc Copage, Lurene Tuttle, Michael Link, Betty Beaird, Allison Mills, Eddie Quillan, Michael Wajacs
Producer: Hal Kanter
Director-Writer: Kanter
30 mins., Tues. 8:30 p.m.
PARTICPATING
NBC-TV, (color)

One of the more dubious benefits in the long hard struggle for civil rights has got to be a situation comedy featuring Negroes. This show biz genre is an embarrassment to the whole human race.

Anyhow, "Julia" is hipper than "Amos n' Andy," and insiders are advising that the series really takes off in spite of that self-conscious opening last week.

No one can fault the high sight values of star Diahann Carroll, and if that posh pad (Watts it ain't, Orange County maybe?) seems a little lavish for an unemployed Negro nurse, remember she inherited $10,000 when her Air Force captain spun in over in Vietnam. Marc Copage as her young son is cute and natural enough in this situation for anyone but W. C. Fields cultists. Vet actor Lloyd Nolan shapes fine as the good but gruff Dr. Chegley. With some substantial scripting, he and Miss Carroll will make an engaging pair.

Everything worked okay in the initialer except the one-dimensional and much too obvious prejudice of the personnel manager where Miss Carroll will work. In matters as sensitive as race relations, even sitcom characters will have to have a little substance. No laughtrack is a plus.   *Bill.*

Variety, September 25, 1968.

hardly peddle anything other than the popular truths or myths that less-than-vanguard Middle America embraced.

Nonetheless, to write "Julia" off as shallow and distorted would be unjust. In spite of its sunny disposition, the show was a landmark in popular culture—one that generously reminded all Americans that the great middle class in their country did not need to be restricted to whites. Says Alan Carter, a television expert and senior writer at *Entertainment Weekly:* "'Julia' made me feel good as I watched it while growing up. It reassured me that, like my own family in Queens [New York], there were other middle-class black folks out there. In a time when there was a lot of racial tension around, the show was sort of an inspiration in that it showed the whites and blacks living among one another and on an equal footing."

As a result of the fury surrounding "Julia," television producers became more sensitive about projecting a fitting black image. There was already one show, in fact, that featured a decidedly more ethnic-looking African-American actor. The "Mod Squad"'s Clarence Williams III, who sported a large afro as one of the show's triumvirate of police detectives, offered a sharp contrast to the slick Diahann Carroll, whose hair was straightened on "Julia."

The next year, the series "Room 222" (1969 to 1974) showcased Lloyd Haynes and Denise Nicholas as dedicated black teachers who helped students, both black and white, deal with the problems of adolescence and the troubles of the times. In the seventies, both "Sanford and Son" and "The Jeffersons" opened to immediate and enormous success with Redd Foxx's and Sherman Hemsley's riotous humor and pointedly black sassy-ness. And shows like "Good Times" and "227" finally dealt more realistically with urban black life.

In the 1980's, the enormous success of such diverse fare as "The Cosby Show" and "In Living Color" signaled the inroads blacks had made in and on television. Curiously, it was NBC, "Julia"'s network almost two decades before, that bought "The Cosby Show" after ABC turned it down. This time around the show was created and overseen by black talents such as Bill Duke, Roy Campanella, Gilbert Moses, and, of course, Bill Cosby himself. The result was a poignant and humorous portrayal of an upper-class black family. The show delicately addressed issues confronted by black America, while drawing the bridge that linked black and white cultures in this country. Despite "Cosby"'s number one rating on the Nielsen chart week after week, pundits again issued Bill Cosby the same charges that Diahann Carroll faced in 1968: "too soft, prettified, unrealistic."

Surely, the lesson to learn in television is that primetime sitcoms are largely about escapism. And why should a show featuring black Americans necessarily be any different? It is only the growth of public conscience that will shepherd commercial television away from the often insipid and rose-tinted views of Hollywood and closer to a more deeply felt reality shared by increasingly astute viewers.

KHOI NGUYEN

Altamont: The Sixties Onstage

Technically, the 1960s ended at midnight on December 31, 1969. The end of the decade of peace, love, and psylocybin actually occurred, however, a few weeks earlier, on December 7, 1969, at a godforsaken outpost called Altamont in Alameda County, California, just beyond the chain-link fences surrounding Dick Carter's decrepit stock car track, seventy miles southwest of San Francisco and a million miles from reality.

Some four hundred thousand very assorted members of the younger generation had gathered there in the dusky, fading twilight of a raw, but otherwise clear winter afternoon. They had come in cars and vans, on motorcycles, on foot and by horseback. A fortunate few even arrived in one of the fourteen helicopters that had been commandeered by the producers for the quick twenty-minute hop from San Francisco International Airport. They gathered there, in a natural valley framed by giant, twenty-foot storm sewers and the naked northern California hills. They had come not just to see the Rolling Stones, the greatest rock and roll band in the world, as well as a few of their local heroes, but to reassure themselves that the sixties, which had begun right here in their own backyard, would be returned to them for safekeeping.

Less than four months earlier, on Max Asgur's little farm near Liberty, New York, nearly half a million people had assembled for the historic four-day Woodstock concert which threatened to relocate the sixties forever to the East Coast. Woodstock had been a great success, an unmitigated triumph over the establishment. A blockbuster movie directed by Michael Wadleigh was already in the works. And Mike Lang, the young genius who is generally credited with having masterminded Woodstock, was basking in the afterglow, with offers to hold concerts, make movies, cut records, perhaps even take over a country or two as the new guru of rock and roll and principal spokesman for everyone under thirty.

Not everyone was buying his bill of goods, however, and down in the Haight and out at the Grateful Dead's place in Novato, the wheels were grinding. There was not much time, but somehow, someway San Francisco was going to fight back, going to reclaim its role as the epicenter of contemporary youth culture. Plans were underway for a no-admission, end-of-the-year/end-of-the-decade concert at Golden Gate Park, where the sit in and the be in had originated—not like the $24.95 four-day ticket which the Woodstock organizers had intended to impose on their concertgoers, before the first wave of kids rolled over the barricades and made a free concert the only practical alternative. All the great Bay Area bands, the bands that had started it all—including the Grateful Dead, Jefferson Airplane, and the Flying Burrito Brothers—would be there and so would, word had it, the only ones not invited to Woodstock, the seminal English group whose "bad boy" image would have clashed outrageously with the feel-good felicity of Woodstock. There was just one small problem. Like a lot of things in San Francisco—and a lot of things in the 1960s—there was no plan, only a lot of idealistic talk and immensely high hopes. Better living through chemistry could make anything possible. The owners of the Ontario Motor Speedway, a slick, well-suited site outside San Francisco, stepped forward and offered their facility—for a price. A stage was erected, light towers were built, a monster outdoor sound system was installed, but then the Dead backed off—and after them, every other band within five hundred miles. Ontario was a rip-off, they said, and admission would be limited to those who could pay. The idea was totally out of sync, they insisted, not only with the times, but with the whole spirit of the thing.

Enter Melvin Belli, defender of the downtrodden, protector of the poor, and San Francisco's quintessential Mr. Fixit. Approached by representatives of the Dead, Belli attempted to intercede with the owners of Ontario but got nowhere. When it became evident that momentum was gathering anyway, and that the Rolling Stones had put their considerable imprint on the project, he decided to go with the flow and issued a call over San Francisco radio for "five hundred young virgins" to assemble in his converted firehouse offices near the docks and "pluck rose petals for the Stones to shower upon the faithful as they brought down the curtain on this historic event." The virgins showed up, several dozen of them at least, as did the radio and television people and hundreds of others, all volunteering to help. When Dick Carter arrived and offered his racetrack, the concert was on.

All of the paraphernalia was somehow hauled down from the Ontario Speedway and trucked overnight out to Altamont. All through the night, nearly a hundred volunteer sound and light technicians reassembled everything, working in temperatures that dipped into the low twenties, laboring until it actually looked like a concert might happen. The moon, ominously, was in Scorpio, but when dawn finally broke, everything was set. Dick Carter had discreetly arranged for a security force of some fifty rent-a-cops, principally to protect his property. The official state and county police took one look at the size of the motley armada rolling down the highway into Alameda County and disappeared for the duration. Not to worry, representatives of the Dead suggested, the Hell's Angels usually provided security at Bay Area concerts and would probably show up to supplement Carter's meager crew.

Almost half a million fans converged on Altamont, California, to pay homage to the "bad boy" of rock 'n' roll, Rolling Stone Mick Jagger.

Nearly two hundred thousand people were in place by seven A.M., when the last of the sound checks was finished and the first of the choppers landed backstage with several of the Burritos, Melvin Belli, his bodyguard, and assorted representatives of the underground media, including several reporters from *Rolling Stone*. (*Rolling Stone* would devote an entire issue to Altamont and win a National Magazine Award in 1970 for its coverage of the concert.) The helicopters kept coming in, banking low as if they were coming in for strafing runs over the crowd, dropping off performers, VIPs, and more media people like loud, busy locusts over South Vietnam's China Beach. An independent film crew had already scattered some forty cameras around the concert site and would eventually shoot nearly two hundred thousand feet of film in the less than eighteen elapsed hours of Altamont.

By mid morning, almost a half million people had settled into position around and in front of the tiny stage. San Francisco radio stations continued to exhort young people up and down the California coast to get down to Altamont. The challenge, if not the necessity, was to ensure that the official crowd count exceeded Woodstock's. A couple of local acts opened the show, then the Burrito Brothers played an extended set. The crowd, grateful to be a part of history, was mellow enough, considering its size and the fact that every known chemical substance was freely available, including hundreds of bottles of LSD-spiked jug wine. The sound men had done their job, however, and not even the incessant helicopters could drown out the music. Suddenly, a cloud of rolling thunder roared over the hills and sliced through the crowd like a switchblade. Bodies parted, a little like the Red Sea, as several hundred Harley Davidson hogs sliced straight through the placid crowd and parked directly in front of the stage, on ground that only seconds before had been occupied by nearly a thousand blissed-out concertgoers. The Angels were armed with brass knuckles, knives, and the leaded pool cues they carried around San Francisco like oversized swagger sticks. Sonny Barger, leader of the Oakland Angels, was there, as were many of his lieutenant counterparts from other Angel contingents. They took their places around the base of the stage and politely apologized to the Burritos for the interruption.

Next up was Jefferson Airplane. Halfway through "White Rabbit," their leader, Marty Balin, leapt off the stage and threw himself into a scuffle between several Angels and a helpless, half-naked young man who was obviously tripping and had inadvertently fallen against one of their bikes. Balin suffered a mild concussion but got himself back up onstage, and Airplane began again. More scuffling occurred at the foot of the stage, but this time it was over almost as soon as it started, the Angels quickly ending the commotion with a few swift blows across the back of another young spectator. Grace Slick tried to intervene. "Everybody's fucking up," she said, not inaccurately. "The Angels are fucking up. All of you people are fucking up. Let's cool out, okay?"

It was okay, apparently, with everybody but the Hell's Angels, some of whom had now climbed up onstage and ringed the performers, with whom they had struck up an uneasy alliance. Bay Area performers were used to them. They were part of the scene and sometimes served a useful purpose as "auxiliary concert security" when none other was available. Someone said the Dead had invited them to Altamont and paid them with over a hundred cases of beer. It was pretty certain that most of the Angels would have flunked a breathalyzer test that day, and more than a few seemed to be pretty far gone on some of the more advanced merchandise so freely available in the crowd. Melvin Belli had been ensconced right there, beside the performers, for most of the day; that had been his agreement with the Rolling Stones, he said, in exchange for his assistance in helping to get the concert off the ground. When he and his bodyguard were rudely shoved off the stage, the crowd sensed that things might be taking an ominous turn.

Meanwhile, Mick Jagger and the other Stones spent much of the afternoon in a trailer backstage. Jagger kept poking his head out from time to time, partly to banter with the pack of reporters who had surrounded the trailer and partly, of course, to take the measure of the crowd. He was hearing all the stories—each new incident, each new thumping by the Angels—spread throughout the crowd like wildfire, although if you were not in the first ten or so rows in front of the stage, you were safe, since there was almost no way anyone could get to you. For most of the crowd, the most threatening aspect of the lengthening afternoon were not rumors of the Angels' brutality, but the continued reports, and obvious evidence, of serious acid tripping.

Finally, as the sun dropped behind the hills and the anticipation had become almost unbearable, the Stones took the stage. Mick Jagger skipped out in a sinister-looking red-and-black satin, ruffled-front shirt, huge, studded, black leather belt, and skin-tight gold velvet trousers, followed by Keith Richards, cool and dispassionate in his red sequined shirt and worn-out jeans. They rushed right into one of their most provocative numbers, "Sympathy for the Devil." Jagger sent the crowd into spasms of ecstasy as he began prancing around the stage, oblivious to the Angels, who were now packed in so close that they were brushing up against him. The other Stones—Richards, Bill Wyman, Charlie Watts, Mick Taylor—were expressionless, playing furiously but without any visible sign of emotion. All of the group's energy seemed to be spewing out of Jagger, his rubber face contorted, his eyes rolled back in their sockets, his mouth stretched wide in an evil, sardonic leer—not quite the devil incarnate, but certainly a performer whose fantasies of himself and his portentous persona were about to be realized. Ominously, he stopped after just a few bars to advise the crowd, "Something very funny always happens when we start this number."

His words were wrapped in little puffs of steam; the temperature had fallen below freezing. Charlie Watts had kept up an insistent drum beat while Jagger spoke, stopping only when it became obvious the Angels were thumping anybody within striking distance. "Brothers and sisters," Richards shouted, "cool out! Cool on down! Or we're not going to play anymore." But he picked up his guitar, and the band was once again roaring through "Sympathy," picking up right where they had broken off.

What happened next came to define the end of a tumultuous, often violent decade. A young black man stood among the hundreds of thousands of middle-class whites, a pretty, blond white girl on his arm. His lime green jacket made him easy to spot, and he had been positioned right up front, near all the action, for at least five hours. Finally tiring, he had leaned against one of the black and chrome hogs parked in front of the stage. Angry words were exchanged. The black man pulled a .38 revolver from his coat pocket. Within an eye blink, three Angels were on him. When the crowd finally backed away, the man was dead, four knife wounds in his back, neck, and face. The avenging Angels melted into the crowd and were never seen again. The Rolling Stones finally saw what had happened and called for a doctor. They finished up their one-song set and beat a hasty retreat to the rear of the stage, as Sonny Barger and several of the other Angels threw the baskets full of rose petals out at the crowd.

Five or six hours later, all the talent had gone, but there were still several thousand debilitated souls sprawled out among the debris that was Altamont. The scene was horrifyingly reminiscent of a scorched battlefield in Vietnam, where many of those at Altamont would soon find themselves. Four people lost their lives that day, including the young black man, whose death was captured on film. Four babies were born to four mothers insensitive enough to have been among the crowd at "Woodstock West." Just as the Rolling Stones had burst upon the stage at Altamont, police and FBI agents were blowing away a small stucco house in the center of Watts in Los Angeles, wiping out most of the active leadership of the Black Panther Party. At Altamont, white sympathizers had been collecting money all day, passing buckets among the crowd for a Panther Legal Defense Fund. Someone even saw several of the Angels dump modest donations into one of those buckets, utterly unaware that the Panthers, for all intents and purposes, no longer existed.

The movie *Woodstock* was released a few months later and went on to win an Academy Award as best feature-length documentary in 1970. *Gimme Shelter,* the Altamont film, was not even nominated and, because of the controversy surrounding the Hell's Angels' on-film stabbing, had difficulty at first even finding a distributor. Today, however, the documentary has been released and rereleased around the world. It has achieved something approaching cult status and serves as an accurate and unforgettable glimpse into the heart of 1960s darkness—the anarchy, the hedonism, and the self-destruction that lurked just under the surface of the most idealistic decade of the twentieth century.

PORTER BIBB

A Supreme Farewell

At 11:54 P.M., on Wednesday, January 14, 1970, the Supremes took the stage at the Frontier Hotel in Las Vegas at a well-publicized event that would mark Diana Ross's final appearance with the group. Playing before an SRO crowd of fifteen hundred, the performance lasted slightly over an hour and a half. The "girls," dressed in matching gold-jewelled black velvet Bob Mackie gowns, delivered their hits and a few standard show tunes in their smooth, well-rehearsed supper-club style. Ross was only twenty-five years old at the time, and she was about to leave the security of the superstar trio in front of which she had pushed herself (literally as well as figuratively) for the past five years. With her charismatic and animated style, she had vocally and visually led the Supremes twelve times to the top of the pop charts, with the black trio becoming the all-time biggest selling girl group and transcending racial barriers with their glamorous appearance and "Crossover" Motown Sound. As the sixties ended, so did the most successful American pop group of the decade.

The Supremes, which had started as a quartet known as the Primettes in the late fifties in Detroit's Brewster Projects, was largely the creation of Berry Gordy, Jr., who had started Motown Records out of a two-room bungalow in Detroit in 1959 with an eight hundred-dollar loan from his family. A former boxer and auto-plant worker, Gordy had already written successful songs for rhythm-and-blues singer Jackie Wilson before deciding to distribute his own product. In the late fifties, R&B artists such as Little Richard appealed mainly to black audiences, while cover versions of their songs by white pop artists like Pat Boone sold in the millions to white audiences. Gordy wanted to make black pop records that would transcend color barriers. The Supremes would be his catalyst.

During the height of Martin Luther King, Jr.'s, ascendancy as a civil rights leader, Motown was making music that was nonthreatening to white audiences. King's nonviolent integrationist message paralleled Motown's ambitious attempts to court and win over the white mainstream. Gordy and his artists created "the Motown Sound…the Sound of Young America" with a roster that began to read like a future *Who's Who* of music legends: Smokey Robinson, Marvin Gaye, Stevie Wonder, Mary Wells, the Temptations, the Four Tops, Gladys Knight, and later Michael Jackson and Lionel Richie. But it was Diana Ross and the Supremes (as the group's name was later lengthened) that would become Gordy's top attraction.

Beginning with 1964's "Where Did Our Love Go," the hit records and popularity of the Supremes began to soar. The trio had five consecutive number-one records, a feat unmatched even by the Beatles, making Ross, along with fellow Supremes Mary Wilson and Florence Ballard, household names overnight. In this pre-video era, the only way for exposure was through live appearances and radio, and soon the group was booked in concerts all over the world, as well as on every major television show. By 1965, Motown Records, led by the Supremes, was dominating the formerly whitewashed pop charts and airwaves.

Wherever the Supremes played, from "The Ed Sullivan Show" (over a dozen times, starting in 1964) to the Copacabana nightclub in New York (beginning in July 1965), they opened the door for other black acts. The group's glamorous appeal crossed not only racial lines but also generational ones. Other black entertainers like Nat King Cole and Ella Fitzgerald had crossed over before, but they played to an older audience. The Supremes sold to the same kids who were buying Beatles and Beach Boys records. James Brown may have been selling millions of discs in the mid-sixties, but his core audience was still black.

The three quickly became role models for black women; talk-show host Oprah Winfrey has stated that she knew she had a chance to make it when she first saw the Supremes on "The Ed Sullivan Show." Always reinventing her already exaggerated look, Diana Ross became a perfect spokesmodel for the fashion trends and fads of mainstream sixties pop culture, with the group endorsing Coca-Cola, Arid Extra-Dry deodorant, and even its own line of Supremes White Bread (not even Michael Jackson can make that claim).

By 1966, there was already talk of Ross leaving the Supremes, as the attention she was getting from the media as well as from Berry Gordy led to jealousies among her singing partners, who were now being overshadowed and pushed further into the background. In fact, after Florence Ballard was fired from the group in 1967 (the singer died of a heart attack while penniless and on welfare in 1976), only Diana's voice was used on the recordings, with studio backup singers standing in for Mary Wilson and Ballard's replacement, Cindy Birdsong.

With their new member, the Supremes climbed to even greater heights, all due to Ross's irresistible appeal. Gordy saw her as the next Barbra Streisand, even rush-releasing a Supremes album of songs from Streisand's debut film, *Funny Girl* (1968), to coincide with the film's release. The public, however, decided that there was only one Streisand, and *Diana Ross & the Supremes Sing and Perform 'Funny Girl'* was their worst charting album ever.

Ross was soon making television appearances without the Supremes, and there

was talk of Motown relocating to Hollywood, where Gordy wanted to branch into film and TV. In the late sixties, the group had two major NBC television specials showcasing Ross, but the trio's record sales were lagging (except for the socially conscious "Love Child"). As the black-power movement gained momentum, the Supremes, with their saccharine image, seemed dated next to more soulful and gritty performers like Aretha Franklin and Sly and the Family Stone. Even veteran R&B acts such as James Brown and Ike and Tina Turner were beginning to get their due "R-E-S-P-E-C-T" from white audiences. By 1969, Gordy decided Ross no longer needed the Supremes, and a solo career was planned.

The night of the "Farewell" performance (as it was billed), the audience sipped drinks named for each of the "girls" (Diana's Delight, Mary's Mystique, Cindy's Sin) and seemed oblivious to the tensions that had reached a boiling point within the group. The three performers were barely speaking to each other, and for Wilson and Birdsong, this "Farewell" was merely publicity to launch Ross's solo career. (The two would, however, continue on into the seventies as the Supremes with newcomer Jean Terrell.) Onstage, the Supremes received plaques, awards, and gold watches from Saks Fifth Avenue, as well as an in-person tribute by one of Nevada's U.S. senators and a telegram from Ed Sullivan, in which he ironically praised the group for making it on sheer talent and without "back-stabbing and hypocrisy."

Fellow celebrities who joined in the festivities included Dick Clark, Steve Allen, Lou Rawls, and Motowners Smokey Robinson and Marvin Gaye. Ross sang "My Man" directly to Berry Gordy, and after a dramatic "The Impossible Dream," the group broke into "Someday We'll Be Together" (originally intended as a Ross solo record), which was number one on the pop charts at the time. During their lengthy rendition of the song, Ross stopped between verses to speak out about bringing "all of our boys home from Vietnam" and "black and white together"—something America's most successful girl group of all time had already accomplished musically during their brief but brilliant recording career.

DAVID HORII

Their saccharine image wearing thin by the late 1960s, Diana Ross left the Supremes at a much-publicized Las Vegas concert on January 14, 1970. With new member Jean Terrell, *center,* the most successful pop group of the '60s stumbled on for another seven years before finally calling it quits.

He Did It His Way

On June 13, 1971, in Los Angeles, Frank Sinatra, a drink in one hand and a cigarette in the other, sat on a stool on the stage of the Music Center, illuminated by only a pin spot. The cigarette smoke enveloped him in ghostly wisps, as the rich, intimate baritone phrased lyrics of heartbreaking, unrequited love. Finally, the single light faded to black, leaving a darkened stage, and on that mournful note, the fifty-five-year-old saloon singer, whom a tearful Rosalind Russell had introduced earlier that evening as "the greatest entertainer of the century," officially retired.

Sinatra's career, which had started with a skinny Italian kid singing for pennies in his family's saloon in Hoboken, New Jersey, spans almost two thousand individual recordings, a hundred albums, fifty-eight movies, and three Academy Awards. His music defined the forties, fifties, and early sixties, and more than any living person, Frank Sinatra has come to represent the American song.

In July 1940, Sinatra's vocal of "I'll Never Smile Again" with Tommy Dorsey's orchestra was number one on the disc chart and radio's "Hit Parade" for two months, selling a million records. In the thirty-one years that followed, he consistently had records in the Top 10. In movies, either on camera or unseen behind the titles, he introduced nine Oscar-nominated songs, of which four won.

From the moment the ex-big band singer stepped onto the stage of New York's Paramount Theater in December 1942, Frank Sinatra dominated show business as no other entertainer had before or has since. Even before the gaunt twenty-seven-year-old in a floppy, polka-dot bow tie crooned a note, a tsunami of hysteria, teenage shrieks, squeals, screams, applause, and cries exploded from the packed audience, walloping bandleader Benny Goodman. "What the hell was that?" he blurted. It was the first wave of a new social phenomenon, whose successive crests carried Elvis Presley and then the Beatles, but never reached the emotional peaks of the breakers that launched Sinatra to superstardom.

Sinatra was a movie star whose roles ranged from unforgettable portrayals in *From Here to Eternity* (for which he won his Oscar as Best Supporting Actor) and *The Man with the Golden Arm* to mercifully forgotten clam-bakes with his pals. A movie producer and the owner of a tremendously successful record company. A radio and then TV star of his own shows. A concert performer whose appearances in Las Vegas casinos and European soccer stadiums were sold-out events. The swain whose flirtations, marriages, affairs, and divorces with the world's most glamorous women were reported by the press with the frenzy of a war. A casino owner. A wise guy whose associations with the Mafia inspired reams of news stories, long FBI files, and best-selling novels, and may have influenced John F. Kennedy's election. The confidant of presidents from Franklin Roosevelt to Ronald Reagan. A philanthropist whose personal contributions and fund-raising for charity approaches a billion dollars and whom in 1993 the Academy of Motion Picture Arts and Sciences awarded the Jean Hersholt Humanitarian Award. The 1971 benefit concert raised $800,000 alone for the Motion Picture and Television Relief Fund.

Sinatra's career has been an American epic. And yet ultimately, through some alchemy of art, that turbulent life always distilled down to the thirty-two throbbing bars of "My Way." The song has become Sinatra's personal anthem, his lyrical bio, and that night twenty-two years ago, it brought the black-tie crowd of Hollywood luminaries at the Music Center to its feet for one of four standing ovations. With the exception of four songs, including his early hit "This Love of Mine," Sinatra did not write the lyrics, but there has never been any doubt in the minds of his audience—whether the squealing bobby-soxers at the Paramount or the middle-aged, mink-clad matrons decades later at the Sands Hotel in Las Vegas—that Sinatra was singing his songs: "All or Nothing at All," "Nancy," "The Lady Is a Tramp," "I've Got You under My Skin," "I Get Along Without You Very Well."

The Voice, with its intimate attention to the lyrics, the emotional power of its phrasing, its delicate shading and long melodic lines, is Sinatra's personal history.

In Hoboken, Sinatra's mother, Dolly, was a Democratic ward leader who could deliver a large block of votes from Little Italy at every election, and her only son, Frankie, sang at political rallies. According to legend, the eighteen-year-old high school dropout and his financée, Nancy Barbato, were watching Bing Crosby on the stage of Loew's Journal Square in Jersey City when Sinatra vowed to become a singer. He entered all the amateur night contests in vaudeville and movie houses between Newark and New York, eventually winning first prize on radio's "Major Bowes' Original Amateur Hour" in 1937. Touring with Bowes, Sinatra was the lead tenor with an instrumental trio, forming the Hoboken Four. When the grueling bus tour reached California three months later, he quit.

Back in Jersey, he played local clubs—sometimes five shows a night—on the shore. By 1939, he was singing on eighteen different local radio shows just for the exposure. (Only WNEW paid him carfare.) He earned fifteen dollars a week as the singing master of ceremonies at the Rustic Cabin, a Jersey roadhouse, and when his salary was raised to thirty-five dollars as band vocalist, he and Nancy married.

Harry James, the trumpeter with Benny Goodman's band, was forming his own group at that time, and the young crooner broadcasting from the Rustic Cabin had the sound he wanted. With Harry James and his orchestra, Sinatra made his first record, "From the Bottom of My Heart," on July 13, 1939.

FACING PAGE

Last Dance: Sinatra, who has made over fifty films, showed a surprising dancing talent in his last MGM musical, *On the Town* (1949), in which he costarred with Gene Kelly.

It was the era of the big bands, and the biggest was Tommy Dorsey's. Six months after joining James, Sinatra received an offer from Dorsey, who was noted for showcasing his vocalists. James magnanimously released Sinatra from his two-year contract.

Sinatra toured and recorded with Dorsey and his vocal group, the Pied Pipers, for three and a half years. Sinatra's voice had matured to a classic baritone, and he closely studied Dorsey's distinctive melodic technique with the trombone to learn how to control a breath for sixteen bars. ("I figured if he could do that phrasing with his horn, I could do it with my voice.")

As a band crooner, the ambitious Sinatra could not go as far as he dreamed. But Dorsey, a sharp businessman, was not as generous as James in releasing the singer from his contract, which specified that he receive a third of all of Sinatra's future earnings.

Sinatra's historic first solo engagement at the Paramount in 1942 broke all of the theater's records. The mass female hysteria at his appearances was an exploding social phenomenon, but it was one primed by his publicist, George Evans, who distributed free tickets to high schools, paid for ambulances to stand outside the theaters to carry off fainting fans, and gave girls five bucks apiece to scream and swoon.

Sinatra also returned to radio in 1942, but this time as the star of "Your Hit Parade" at one thousand dollars a week. Moonlighting from his radio show, the singer became the fashionable attraction at New York's Riobamba Club, where his salary rose to fifteen hundred dollars a week (a hundredfold increase over the Rustic Cabin across the river), before he moved to the Wedgwood Room of the Waldorf-Astoria. Sinatra's success followed the script of a Hollywood movie, and as life imitates art, art began to imitate his life. Writers tailored songs and then movie scripts for him.

Sinatra's solo of "Night and Day" in Columbia's *Reveille with Beverly* ignited the pandemonium of his personal appearances. RKO quickly signed and starred him in *Higher and Higher* and *Step Lively,* two frivolous musical-comedy romances.

In 1943, the MCA agency and Sinatra's lawyers bought out Dorsey's interest for a reported sixty thousand dollars, part of the money coming from the advance on a recording contract with Columbia. The agents, Columbia, and CBS made Dorsey an offer he could not refuse: either release Sinatra from his contract, or Dorsey's own records would not be played on radio. The next year, Sinatra's earnings were estimated at $5,000 to $6,000 a week from radio, $250,000 from motion pictures, and $150,000 in record royalties. Personal appearance tours added as much as $30,000 a week, leaving hordes of sobbing, hysterical teenaged girls in their wake.

In a fireside chat at the White House, President Roosevelt told Sinatra he had "revived the charming art of swooning." But on Columbus Day, 1944, thirty thousand screaming bobby-soxers who could not get into the Paramount Theatre to hear him rioted in Times Square. The New York City Board of Education accused Sinatra of contributing to truancy, saying, "We cannot tolerate young people making a public display of losing control of their emotions."

MGM mogul Louis B. Mayer had no such qualms. He bought the crooner's contract from RKO and costarred him with Gene Kelly and Kathryn Grayson in *Anchors Aweigh* in 1945. Sinatra had entered the galaxy of the golden age of the MGM musical, which culminated for him with *On the Town* in 1949. Off the set, Sinatra's brawling behavior, globe-hopping extramarital affair with Ava Gardner, and verbal and physical punch-outs with the press were making headlines. His openly liberal politics and his stand against the blacklist enraged Senator Joseph McCarthy's supporters and right-wing columnists, who labeled him a pinko.

1950 was a very bad year. Sinatra's squabbles with the studio over being cast only in lightweight musicals and a plummeting box office forced Mayer's hand. MGM formally announced, "Frank Sinatra asked for and received his release from the studio." At Columbia Records, he and Mitch Miller, the director of artists and repertoire, fought over songs and arrangements the singer found gimmicky. With plummeting sales, the company would not even give Sinatra an advance on his next album. Perhaps even worse, the emotional turmoil surrounding his divorce from Nancy, the turbulent, tabloid-hounded romance with Ava, the sleepless nights, and the endless fights cost him his voice. "Sinatra would open his mouth and nothing would come out but a croak," an engineer for Columbia Records at the time recalled. "Usually when a singer is in bad shape, we can help him by extending his notes with an echo chamber. But Sinatra was one of the meanest men we ever worked for, so we engineers and musicians just let him go down."

During a show at the Copacabana in New York in 1952, Sinatra's throat hemorrhaged, and he barely finished the engagement. He was emotionally exhausted and physically ill. At thirty-seven years old, the phenomenon of the forties was written off as washed-up.

Sinatra was soon back to playing nightclubs on the Jersey shore, but the old friends who gave him a job when no one else would were often involved with the mob. Those associations and loyalties would haunt Sinatra throughout his career. He had married Ava Gardner and now flew with her to Africa, where she was filming *Mogambo* with Clark Gable and Grace Kelly. He spent his time reading, notably a best-selling first novel, *From Here to Eternity,* which had a character named Angelo Maggio, a feisty, flamboyant trooper from Little Italy.

"I was determined to land that role," Sinatra remembers. "As soon as Columbia pictures acquired the movie rights, my agent, Abe Lastfogel [at William Morris], camped on the late Harry Cohn's doorstep."

Sinatra had to borrow the money from his wife to fly to Los Angeles to "undergo the humiliation of a screen test" for a supporting role for which the studio had already announced Eli Wallach. Sinatra felt he was born to play Maggio, and his test impressed studio head Cohn and director Fred Zinnemann. The actor was paid only $8,000, compared to the $150,000 a picture he had previously received.

Starring opposite Grace Kelly in *High Society* (1956), Sinatra had previously been nominated for two Oscars, winning once in 1953 as Best Supporting Actor in *From Here to Eternity.*

From Here to Eternity won eight Oscars (including one for Sinatra) in 1953. His voice came back with a maturity, authority, and charm that touched audiences. One could not hear "I'm a Fool to Want You," which he cowrote, and not think of the tortured romance and marriage to one of the world's most beautiful women.

Also in 1953, Sinatra signed with Capitol Records, a seven-year association that would produce many of his swinging trademark recordings like "Young at Heart" and "The Lady Is a Tramp." In movies, he quickly parlayed his Oscar, switching back and forth among musicals, comedies, and intense, often violent dramas, sometimes acting as producer. In 1955 alone, he starred in five films.

The movie star, recording artist, and saloon singer was again earning a million dollars a year. It was the most astonishing comeback in show biz history. The forties phenomenon became the fifties legend. His popularity and income doubled and redoubled to $4 million in 1957, a new high for a show business personality. By 1961, he had been the top recording artist for five years, had made many more movies, was part owner of the Sands Hotel, and, always the saloon singer, he was the top draw on the nightclub circuit.

In the late sixties, Sinatra established his own label, Reprise Records, producing a string of hit albums. When Reprise was incorporated into Warner Bros. Records, he became a major stockholder. He later sold his interest for a reported $27 million.

After that farewell appearance in 1971, Sinatra commented, "Hell, I just quit, that's all. I don't want to put any more makeup on. I don't want to perform anymore. I'm not going to stop living. Maybe I'm going to start living."

Editor's note: Sinatra's 1971 "retirement" ended two years later with the album *Ol' Blue Eyes Is Back* and then the Main Event world tour. In 1983, he was honored by the Kennedy Center for lifetime achievement in the arts. The 1988-1989 Ultimate Event world tour with Liza Minnelli and Sammy Davis, Jr., broke box office records in twenty-nine cities, including a concert in Rio de Janeiro before 175,000 people, the largest audience ever to attend a concert by a soloist. In Tokyo, the tour reached an ultimate one-night gross of $1.8 million at the seven thousand-seat NK Hall, with top tickets at $520.

A two-hour CBS special in December 1990, "Sinatra 75: The Best Is Yet to Come," kicked off a year-long Diamond Jubilee world tour. In 1992, CBS broadcast a five-hour miniseries dramatizing his life. In an interview with its screenwriter, William Mastrosimone, Sinatra, in a rare moment of reflection, noted, "I have had at least five lifetimes."

RICHARD SETLOWE

FACING PAGE

Chairman of the Board: When Frank Sinatra officially "retired" in 1971, the pop, radio, TV, and movie star; director; producer; record-company owner; casino boss; political candidate; and philanthropist had achieved superstardom never before or since matched by another entertainer.

Senator Sam Ervin, who headed the Senate Select Committee to investigate Watergate, wrote after the hearings: "In making it possible for Americans to see and hear and witness, commercial television...performed services of incalculable value to the cause of truth."

FACING PAGE

Daytime Drama: For Nixon co-conspirators like chief aide H. R. Haldeman, the televised Watergate hearings were the "bully pulpit" of public opinion that put him and the others behind bars.

Watergate: The Political Power of TV, Part Two

In 1973, the American public witnessed an unprecedented phenomenon: the credibility of their president and his closest aides unraveling on national television. For two and a half months, from May through July, the country sat riveted as a Senate committee conducted daytime hearings on the cover-up of a break-in at Democratic Party headquarters in Washington's Watergate Hotel, which had taken place the year before. The hearings raised issues that went to the heart of America's democratic process. Had President Richard M. Nixon willfully broken laws to ensure his reelection? And if so, could he be prosecuted like any other citizen accused of a crime? These dire questions hung over the lengthy proceedings like time bombs waiting to explode.

In the end, the televised hearings had a profound effect on the national psyche, forever altering the relationship between the media and the political sphere. They clearly demonstrated the ability of television to act as "the bully pulpit" of modern democracy.

On June 17, 1972, five burglars equipped with electronic bugging devices were caught by police in the Democratic National Committee headquarters in the Watergate Hotel. Protracted investigations by law officers and the *Washington Post* reportorial team of Carl Bernstein and Bob Woodward revealed links between the burglars and the inner sanctums of Nixon's White House—especially an organization set up by aides within the White House known as CREEP (The Committee to Re-Elect the President). As these investigations slowly revealed, CREEP had chosen extralegal methods to help ensure Nixon's success in the 1972 election. These had included smear campaigns against possible Democratic challengers and the creation of a slush fund for various covert operations, including burglaries, wiretapping, and bugging.

By the winter of 1972-1973, various attempts by the White House to ignore,

VARI

Published Weekly at 154 West 46th Street, New York, N.Y. 100
Second Class Postage Paid at New Yo

Vol. 276   No. 1

New York, Wedne

PRESIDENT FORD VI

Pic B.O. Booming As July Grosses Explode By 28%

By A.D. MURPHY

Hollywood, Aug. 13.

SOME THINGS PERFE

By LAR

There's no way of precisely projecting the style and substance of the Ford Administration, of course, but two general conclusions vis-a-vis the Nixon regime seem

stations feel
tightening first.

The econom
effects of Pres
sion might be f

ETY

PRICE 75¢

NEWSPAPER
Second Class P.O. Entry

ariety, Inc. Annual subscription, $30. Single copies, 75 cents.
. and at Additional Mailing Offices.

y, August 14, 1974   34205   56 PAGES

-A-VIS NEWS MEDIA

Y CLEAR EARLY ON

ICHIE

tional belt-
d journalistic
Ford's ascen-
t immediate

news coverage Ford may get,
however, there seems little doubt
that he will be easier on the media
than Nixon. Aside from the fact that
no President for a few years, at

Nixon's Departure Means Comedians Lose Meal Ticket

By FRANK MEYER

Richard Nixon's return to the

ABOVE AND FACING PAGE

Since Watergate, television's role in political debates, such as the Clarence Thomas–Anita Hill hearings, continues to expand.

PREVIOUS PAGES

Variety, **August 14, 1974:** After Watergate, President Ford called a truce with the media.

stonewall, or cover-up the investigation had begun to backfire, inciting the outrage of prosecutors and Congress. A special bipartisan Senate Select Committee was assembled to investigate Watergate. Wrote Theodore H. White in his book *Breach of Faith* about the weeks leading up to the start of the Watergate hearings on May 17, "Whether one passed newsstands at airports, rail stations, subway stations, whether one preferred the morning paper or the evening electronic news—the entire news system was announcing the Greatest Show on Earth."

Senator Sam Ervin of North Carolina was chosen to lead the committee. A feisty seventy-six-year-old with a penchant for quoting the Bible as well as obscure nineteenth-century American poets, Ervin became a central figure in the drama soon to be played out live on national television. With his bulldog face and Southern accent, he came to exemplify the search for the truth beneath the morass of conflicting testimonies and alibis. Indeed, the Watergate hearings became a duel of personalities, transforming abstract conceptions of politics into a concrete struggle between individuals.

The hearings that followed the media buildup did not disappoint the public—in fact, quite the opposite. They offered politics as pure spectacle, a miniseries equal in impact to the highest theater—"the country's most engrossing daytime show," raved *Time* magazine, "an epic whodunit." As the witnesses appeared before the Greek chorus of senatorial interrogators, they seemed to be facing the judgment of history itself. The television coverage provided the public the chance to make up its own mind about who was telling the truth and who was lying.

The hearings culminated in the testimony of John Dean, former counsel to the president, during the week of June 25 to 30. At thirty-two, Dean had the bland, bespectacled look of the prototypical "company man." His banal face quickly became a famous one, as he appeared on the cover of every major current-events magazine and newspaper. Whereas many witnesses before him had seemed to dissemble or claimed not to be able to recall many of the key dates and events (a New York weekly noted that the only knowledge that teenagers would gain from the Watergate hearings would be the phrase: "In retrospect, I have no knowledge whatsoever, at this point in time, to the best of my recollection"), Dean presented his testimony in a calm and clear manner. He began with an up-front admission of guilt, confessing to obstructions of justice, misappropriation of funds, and encouraging the perjury of others to aid the cover-up.

Dean proceeded to recount his own involvement in Watergate step-by-step, from the first time he learned about the break-in two days after it occurred to the intensive role he played in the cover-up. Working with Nixon's two chief aides, Bob Haldeman and John Ehrlichman, Dean became involved in a convoluted network of dealings that included secret payoffs to the families of the burglars, the shredding of sensitive documents, and the coaching of witnesses to lie before the grand jury. To a breathless audience, he testified that he had told Nixon that the

Watergate cover-up was "a cancer growing within the presidency," and that he was not sure it ultimately could be contained. Dean also revealed the existence of a Haldeman-sponsored enemies list which included the names of prominent athletes and entertainers, such as Joe Namath and Paul Newman.

Dean's testimony—and those that followed it—electrified the nation. Over the next weeks, a White House aide revealed that Nixon had taped all of his conversations in the Oval Office. The committee tried to subpoena the tapes but was rebuffed by the White House, which said in essence that the government's legislative branch, Congress, had no jurisdiction over the executive branch, the presidency. Despite this temporary rebuff, the tapes became a powerful symbol of the White House's seemingly endless entanglement in scandal. Magazine covers and posters featured the White House wrapped in reels of tape or a gigantic tape player spinning atop its roof.

Although they had no legal consequences in themselves, the Watergate hearings were a public relations nightmare for Nixon, turning the populace against his presidency virtually overnight and ensuring his eventual downfall. This, in a way, was the point of the entire proceedings, as a commentator noted at the time: "Ervin is running an educational forum and not a court, and he knows it. He is resolute in his belief that there is something magic about truth. The folks after a while get some notion of who is lying and who is not."

The Watergate hearings demonstrated that television's awe-inspiring ability to reach a mass audience could serve a vital democratic purpose. Watergate strengthened the power of the media to affect American society. As Senator Ervin wrote after the hearings, "In making it possible for Americans to see and hear and witness, commercial television, which telecast a substantial part of the committee's public hearings, and public television, which telecast all of them gavel to gavel, performed services of incalculable value to the cause of truth." In the wake of the groundbreaking investigations by the *Washington Post* and other papers, investigative journalists briefly became folk heroes. It was as if the St. George of the media had slain the dragon of a corrupt government.

Since Watergate, the public has seen television's role in politics continue to expand. In 1991, the Senate confirmation hearings of Supreme Court nominee Clarence Thomas galvanized the nation. Although Anita Hill, who had accused Thomas of sexual harrassment, was officially discredited by the congressional panel investigating her claims, she became a powerful symbol of women's disenfranchisement from the political system. In the 1992 general elections that followed the hearings, more women were elected to Congress than ever before. In this instance, as with Watergate, television returned the ultimate power of democratic judgment to the people. In this way, it helped to preserve the always-fragile accord that makes our government work.

DANIEL PINCHBECK

Jaws, which starred Roy Scheider and Lorraine Gary, became Hollywood's top-grossing film until it was surpassed by *Star Wars* in 1977.

Jaws and Hollywood's Killer Instinct

It was news in 1975 when Universal Pictures opened *Jaws,* Steven Spielberg's movie version of the Peter Benchley best-seller (which had grabbed an unusual amount of production publicity), nationwide in a record-breaking 460 theaters Memorial Day weekend. Before the opening, Universal purchased three back-to-back days of saturation TV advertising, which was unheard of in those days and hugely expensive. It was an enormous risk to make 460 prints without knowing in advance that the picture would succeed. But succeed it did. By January of 1976, *Variety* had proclaimed Jaws the new world's rental champ, with a gross of more than $100 million worldwide, surpassing even *The Godfather.* Few understood this at the time, but distribution methods as they had been practiced were doomed to go the way of the dinosaur.

Henry Martin, who was president of Universal Pictures in 1975, recalls, "We had a strong belief in the picture. The advertising—a pre-buy on TV before the opening—matched the plan of release." Martin, advertising-publicity vice president G. Clark Ramsay, and the MCA (parent company of Universal) brass attended a preview of *Jaws* in Costa Mesa, California, before finalizing the plan. "The audience reaction was tremendous," Martin says. "[MCA chief] Lew Wasserman asked me if I wanted to make any changes in the release plan. I said I was satisfied with the decision we had made. He said, 'That's good enough for me.' We were lucky. We called it right. The word of mouth was tremendous."

"*Jaws* had a big impact because it was a piece of pop culture that swept the whole country," says Disney distribution chief Dick Cook. "The fact that it was available in every community heightened the phenomenon. I remember standing in line the first weekend with no clue of what I was going to see, and it was so available that I wanted to see it again immediately. It changed the way people looked at the business."

Even so, *Jaws* rolled out slowly by today's standards. "It was a twelve-week first-run engagement," explains Martin. "Four, four, and four. We didn't get into subsequent runs until several months after the opening. We got up to over six hundred prints at our widest release."

Martin, who retired in 1978, adds, "After a period of time, practically every picture adopted the broad-release concept." He still believes that only the public's clear acceptance of a picture in limited release should justify buying more prints. "If word of mouth calls for more theaters, that's the way to go. You don't have to throw all your eggs into one basket."

It is hard to believe, but in 1975 the Hollywood studios were still releasing movies the old-fashioned way—via word of mouth. Top-of-the-line, star-laden Hollywood movies opened in one theater in New York and played there for several weeks before opening in exclusive engagements in other big cities. After twelve weeks of first-run limited engagements, they would move to second-run mini-multiples in smaller cities and residential neighborhoods. After another six weeks, they would go wider, to sub-run, less desirable theaters. At its widest release, a movie would be playing in perhaps six hundred theaters tops.

When *Jaws* opened, Twentieth Century-Fox executive vice president Tom Sherak was film buyer for a small theater circuit in Baltimore. "*Jaws* was the first time a major movie was allowed to go immediately into small-town America," he recalls. "Ordinarily we would have gotten the film four weeks after its first release. The studios used to be much more watchful over what towns they went into and over print costs."

Back in 1975 the six major studios—Warner Bros., Twentieth Century-Fox, Paramount, United Artists, Columbia, and Universal—were still releasing A and B pictures, and second and sub-runs were often double features. If a picture was good, the idea was to sell it to sophisticated, adult moviegoers first, then slowly, through word of mouth, broaden the audience to include the suburbs and small towns across the country. B pictures, or programmers, which often included westerns and actioners, would go wider earlier in regional release. It was an insult to A-list filmmakers not to open in exclusive, first-run engagements.

A publicity and marketing push was designed to open the picture, then as now. But the promotion departments were poised to capitalize on good reviews and word of mouth, to sustain interest in a picture that was hopefully going to have good "legs" and stay in theaters for months. The focus was on print advertising and targeting the sophisticated, adult core audience in major cities—most importantly, the media center, New York. Studios had the luxury of tailoring ad campaigns to different markets, experimenting until just the right approach worked with potential audiences. Success in one market helped prime exhibition interest in another. TV ads were saved for wider regional breaks, because then, as now, they were expensive. Film prints were considered costly, and the decision about how many to make was a serious one. "It was a kinder, gentler world," recalls Sherak. "Everything was narrower, more specific, quieter. Movies used to have more than one chance to work. The days of one movie playing behind another on a track are over. There is no such thing as sub-run anymore. That's video. Everything has become first-run."

The studios were familiar with buying saturation television advertising on top of a wide release. Maverick filmmaker Tom Laughlin had embarrassed them all by using "four-wall" booking techniques (whereby a distributor would pay a flat rate for the use of a theater), pioneered by Sun International and other religious-film distributors, for the rerelease of *Billy Jack* in 1973 and his subsequent independent wide release of *The Trial of Billy Jack* in 1974. He shocked the studios, who thought they knew what they were doing, by grossing unprecedented sums within a concentrated time frame. "They showed what strong, fast-hitting TV advertising could do," recalls Paramount worldwide distribution chief Barry London. Adds marketing consultant Mike Kaplan, "It was the first time they had done it on this big of a scale."

Martin says Universal was impressed not by four-walling but by saturation TV advertising for movies like Universal's own *Shenandoah,* a Civil War western starring Jimmy Stewart, which used the South and Southwest as pre-launch territories before moving north with "hit" status in 1965. In 1977, Fox's *Smokey and the Bandit,* starring Burt Reynolds, used the same pattern with great success.

Opening a picture all over the country, however, was a novelty. Columbia tried it with *Breakout,* a Charles Bronson actioner, which opened in a remarkable thirteen hundred theaters earlier in May 1975, but the movie boasted no presold elements: Bronson was a bigger star abroad than stateside, and while the studio earmarked $2 million for TV spots, they were spread over the first weeks, not before the opening. The results were weak. Back then, wrote the late Lee Beaupré in a 1978 article in *Film Comment,* most pictures were "virtually unknown quantities the day they opened," and "expensive national TV buys made no sense if the picture was playing few cities, or in one house in a city…Increases in advertising costs and a continuing geographic spread of suburban perimeters have made [exclusive runs] a generally uneconomical method of opening a film in the bigger markets."

After *Jaws* the studios recognized that they could presell a potential blockbuster with saturation advertising ahead of the opening, creating awareness that otherwise would have come only afterward, via word of mouth. But the wide downtown and suburban release was still reserved only for certain big-ticket potential winners on which the majors were willing to spend serious print and ad money. It took some time—and changes in American cities and movie theaters, as well as the influence of several key executives imported from television, including Frank Price, Bob Daly, and Barry Diller, who knew how to presell simple "high-concept" stories to millions of viewers—before the wide release became the norm and not the exception. "When everybody in the business saw *Jaws* do the kind of business it did," says Columbia distribution president Jeff Blake, who was a district manager for

The Mechanics of Hollywood: When *Jaws* opened all over the country in a record-breaking 460 theaters at one time, film distribution methods changed forever—and so did the movies themselves.

Paramount at the time, "they felt differently about the summer. They used to put some saturation product out in the beginning of the summer, but not a major film with an important director. *Jaws* revolutionized that."

When Fox's *Star Wars,* which was to outdo *Jaws* as the most successful movie of all time, opened two summers later in only thirty-two theaters—one or two in each of the major cities—on Wednesday, May 25, 1977, it was *The Deep,* Columbia's successor to *Jaws,* also from a Benchley novel, that had gobbled up many of the best screens. *Star Wars* made more money per screen than any movie in history, widened to over one thousand theaters, and went on to gross its first $100 million faster than any picture before.

For Columbia's Blake, all you have to do is look at the "amazing" difference in the release of the three *Godfather* movies to see "the way distribution has changed," he says. "When *The Godfather* came out on March 15, 1972, it opened in 5 theaters and expanded to 233 the next week," he says. "It never went to more than 500 screens, was still playing at Christmas of that year, and made $133 million. *Godfather II* opened December 12, 1974, in 5 theaters and expanded the next week to 441. It was in 800 theaters at its widest. By the time *Godfather III* opened Christmas Day, 1990, it went out to 1,901 theaters and grossed $6 million in one day. *Godfather II* doubled the runs of the first, while *Godfather III* multiplied it five times."

By 1978 Columbia still had to convince director Alan Parker that it was a good idea to open *Midnight Express* in over eight hundred theaters. "Parker complained that we were trying to make his movie look like everyone else's," recalls Jack Brodsky, who has worked in publicity, marketing, and production. "We said, 'Yes, that's the idea,' and the picture was a big hit." And in 1981 Paramount made an event out of the opening of *Raiders of the Lost Ark* by releasing it in one thousand theaters at once. "It wasn't until 1981 that everything went wide," says *Variety's* A. D. Murphy. "That summer the trades reported on the wide releases every week as bombs or blockbusters."

In order to accommodate changing distribution patterns, exhibition had to change as well. The old "clearances" (whereby owners demanded four to fifteen miles between theaters showing the same picture) were starting to break down, and the downtown first-run pattern began to change as the middle class preferred to see its pictures in the suburbs. As late as Universal's *E.T.* in 1982, which replaced *Star Wars* as the biggest earner of all time, the Los Angeles Cinerama Dome still had the clout to demand a clearance for all of L.A. and Orange County. Universal had its hands tied as *E.T.* broke records all around the country yet was stuck in one lone Southern California theater for three long weeks before it could break out.

When *Jaws* opened, theaters were still big, single-screen houses. As multiplexing slowly began to take hold in the 1980s, that encouraged wider runs, says Sherak. "Once you broke up the theaters, the more runs you had, the more revenue. You'd have more screens, but about the same number of seats. So you have more chances to have hits and failures. The ones that work carry the ones that don't work, which you move down to the smaller screens."

By 1984 the revolution had come full circle. *Beverly Hills Cop* opened in December and in its third week broke the two thousand-screen mark. Increasingly, the studios lengthened the summer and Christmas playing periods, opening big pictures before Memorial Day and before Thanksgiving. The media began to have an impact as wide-release opening weekends became news, first in the summer and at Christmas, then gradually, with consumer reporting by "Entertainment Tonight" and *USA Today,* every weekend. The studios began to engage in opening weekend contests over which picture would be number one, which encouraged booking more and more screens. "Nobody ever knew what movies grossed before," says London. "With every new record there's more pressure to go see the movie. We're getting more people motivated faster and quicker to see a movie than ever before. The cassette has encroached on market repeatability. Consumers know that in six months they can see a movie as many times as they want."

In 1992 *Batman Returns* played over three thousand screens during its record-shattering opening week, but ticket sales declined precipitously in successive weeks. "When you're in over two thousand runs you start to bastardize the movies," explains Sherak. "To this day the first one thousand to twelve hundred runs still account for 85 percent of the life of the movie. Today you have to convince filmmakers not to open their films on too many screens, because they won't want to see them come off the screens in three weeks."

"We've become a year-round business," says Disney distribution president Dick Cook, "with hit after hit in the fall and spring. Communication systems are so rapid now. It is hard to build a movie in today's environment because you feel forced to try to appeal to everyone on some level right from the beginning. Every week the public is assaulted with other ways to spend their money. "

While each studio will argue that it boasts several "platform" successes, released very slowly without any television advertising, like *Driving Miss Daisy, Thelma & Louise,* or *A River Runs Through It,* the fact remains that today the majors are in the blockbuster business, and they lack the flexibility to tailor distribution patterns to individual pictures. "Today six hundred theaters is like a platform," says Brodsky.

Small but only decent movies like *Man in the Moon, Of Mice and Men,* and *Dogfight* do not have the urgency that tells moviegoers they must rush to the theater. "The studios still don't presell a lot of non-name movies," says former *Star Wars* publicity director Charles Lippincott, "which then wipe out instantly. Most of the time they still haven't figured out how to presell. They've lost sight of the integrated plan. Sometimes they're lucky, sometimes they don't have a clue. We really have a picture-of-the-week business."

While the studios respect the kind of orchestrated publicity buildup that brought independent distributor Miramax's *Crying Game,* which featured no star names, to

By January of 1976, *Jaws* was the new world box-office champ, with more than $100 million in theater rentals, and director Steven Spielberg was a star in his own right.

unprecedented awareness for an art film, Sherak insists that the big studios are in a different business. "It's not what they do. They look for home runs. For a studio it takes just as much time to hit a single as a home run. So why try to hit singles when your whole philosophy is built on home runs? Unfortunately, slower, artier films require patience and get lost between the cracks. We've become a fast-food business."

"Everything now is slam, bang, that's it," says Kaplan. "Most movies are gone in two weeks. While Universal did a great job with *Fried Green Tomatoes,* most of the time the only nurturing left is in the art market. If a movie opens to only $5 million, it's an instant flop. Every movie is famous for fifteen minutes."

Unfortunately, this all means that in order to presell a movie to as many Americans as possible, so that it will be the number-one grosser opening weekend, the studios must make commercial, not quality, pictures. Audiences are lured to see a movie not by how good it is, but by how many tickets were sold on Friday night. The way the studios distribute movies dictates the movies they make. "It's depressing at the moment," says producer Laura Ziskin (*Pretty Woman, No Way Out, The Doctor*). "The films the studios are willing to make are shrinking to a narrower and narrower range. They want to make bulletproof movies that reach the broadest possible audience, like TV. The public wants winners. You have one night to make it. You have to be a hit before anyone has seen the film, which takes away the possibility of a film finding an audience."

This shortsighted thinking has forced many adult and female moviegoers— for the studios aim their sights squarely at the young men who flock to see movies like *Wayne's World* opening weekend—to stop going out to movies altogether. They wait to see a movie they have heard good things about on video or cable. What do the Hollywood studios expect? They used to serve steak, and now they are selling hamburger.

ANNE THOMPSON

Chained to the TV

Over 100 million viewers tuned in during the week of January 23, 1977, to watch the gripping saga of Alex Haley's ancestors as they struggled from pre-Revolutionary slavery through post-Civil War Reconstruction. Although other adaptations of best-sellers like Irwin Shaw's *Rich Man, Poor Man* (1976) had preceded "Roots," this was the first miniseries to become a national event and awaken many Americans to the South's peculiar institution. This remains the largest audience ever for a miniseries, and at the time it aired, "Roots" broke the record for the largest audience for *any* TV program.

"Roots" was a watershed in television history for reasons beyond sheer numbers, though, for it was one of the first and only programs to portray African-Americans in a dramatic manner. Its success and that of its sequel, "Roots: The Next Generations" (1979), ensured the survival of the miniseries as a genre. To this day, the network programmer's surest bulwark against viewers tuning into cable or popping a cassette into the VCR remains event television of this kind.

The "Roots" path from pitch meeting to airing was atypical. Courage, nerve, and some foresight were required from the coterie of producers and ABC executives who were willing to gamble on a story that was a "downer" in Hollywood parlance. There was a tremendous amount of resistance at the network to both the length of the story (eight successive nights) as well as the content. Many doubted whether viewers could become emotionally involved in the travails of an African-American family whose center was neither a major sports figure nor an entertainer. Its greatest champion at ABC at the time, Brandon Stoddard, then a senior vice president of miniseries, concurs. "There was great concern about the length," says the executive, "and there was great concern about whether white America would watch."

Stoddard was the first network executive to grasp that the miniseries genre was a natural for sprawling works of popular literature. Haley, whose most famous work hitherto had been *The Autobiography of Malcolm X,* had lunch with Stoddard in 1975 and fascinated him with the story of how he had been tracing his family back to Africa. Thoroughly impressed, the maverick executive bought the rights for the miniseries even before the first chapter of *Roots* was written. Haley would finish a chapter then submit it directly to the network for preproduction.

Although whites comprised the ranks of supporting, rather than lead, characters, it is an indication of the mind-set of most TV executives at the time that the white actors in the series, like Lorne Greene and Ed Asner, were some of the first cast. Nevertheless, for many of the black actors, their work in "Roots" would be tremendous career boosters. LeVar Burton and Louis Gossett, Jr., were among the lesser known cast members who sprung to prominence after the miniseries debuted.

When it came time to cast the sequel, many of the actors involved in the original welcomed the opportunity to reprise their meaty roles. Only Ben Vereen, who played Chicken George, reportedly felt that a reprise would be beneath him. Judging from the popular and critical kudos the sequel received, he could not have been more wrong.

The astounding success of the two series only made the subsequent allegations that Alex Haley had plagiarized ideas and whole passages for his 1976 book all the more disheartening. When Harold Courlander, author of the 1967 novel *The African,* brought suit against him, *Roots'* author admitted to having cribbed over eighty passages. In conversations with close associates, Haley acknowledged that, for him, the book's greatest accomplishment was creating a mythic tie to Africa for a people whose history in America had been one of disconnection. As a myth, *Roots* may well survive the test of time, but as a work of nonfiction, it will forever be tarnished.

While Haley's legacy remains ambiguous, that of "Roots" the miniseries is certain. Even as the market share for network TV declined during the 1980s, minis continued to flourish until the latter part of that decade, when a series of *anni horribli* made these hulking programs development pariahs. Longish movies-of-the-week blurred the distinction between MOWs and miniseries. CBS's broadcast of James A. Michener's *Space* in April 1985 died over five nights, while ABC's "War and Remembrance" crashed and burned during the 1988 November sweeps. That war-torn network even went so far as to establish a moratorium (recently repealed) on any projects over four hours. Prior to CBS's phenomenal success with "Lonesome Dove" in 1988, Gregg Maday, Warner TV's vice president for miniseries, remembers just how bleak the marketplace was. "Eight years ago, you just couldn't sell a miniseries—no way, no how."

After "Lonseome Dove," however, the minis rebounded with a vengeance. During the 1992-1993 season, ABC's "The Jacksons" and CBS's "Queen" both scored high ratings. Oliver Stone, the director of films like *Platoon* and *The Doors,* produced "Wild Palms" (a miniseries based on the eponymous *Details* magazine comic book), and the genre continues to flourish. Big-budget minis based on the legend of King Arthur, Alexandra Ripley's *Scarlet,* and John Updike's *Rabbit* novels are all in the works. "Roots"'s offspring have come of age and appear to be prospering.

JOHN BRODIE

1 9 7 9

Apocalypse Now— Glory, Gory, Hallelujah

For a time, director-screenwriter Francis Ford Coppola reigned as the most powerful filmmaker in the world. In 1972, his *Godfather* won Oscars for best picture, best actor (Marlon Brando), and best adapted-screenplay (shared by Coppola and the book's author, Mario Puzo). Commercially, it was an astounding success, and critics hailed it as a masterpiece of American cinema. In 1974, *The Godfather, Part II* was released to immediate fanfare. It swept the Academy Awards, raking in Oscars for best picture, best director (Coppola), best supporting actor (Robert De Niro), best adapted screenplay (by Coppola and Puzo), best art/set direction, and best original dramatic score. That might well have been the year of Francis Ford Coppola.

Prestige, power, and financial resources in abundance, Coppola, who had moved to San Francisco and formed his own production company, American Zoetrope (later changed to Omni Zoetrope), was poised to create a monument to his much-touted creative genius. *Apocalypse Now,* scripted by a young writer named John Milius, was inspired by Joseph Conrad's mordant 1910 novella *Heart of Darkness.* But instead of setting *Apocalypse Now* in the nineteenth-century Africa of Conrad's novel, Milius placed his story in the searing jungles of Vietnam, whose brutal conflict was resolved only two months after the Academy of Motion Picture Arts and Sciences bestowed their many accolades on Coppola and *Godfather II.*

Heart of Darkness is a classic portrait of one man's psyche in the face of unrelenting savagery—one centered around senseless destruction for greed and the propagation of imperialism. Orson Welles, who had wanted to make it into a film upon his arrival in Hollywood in the late 1930s, eventually abandoned his plan.

Almost forty years later, Coppola began to retool it. In 1976, the director took his crew, family, and a small constellation of Hollywood stars on location to the Philippines, whose military was willing to rent him the materials needed for the

FACING PAGE

Heart of Darkness: Marlon Brando, as the deranged Colonel Kurtz, had a brief but powerful role in Francis Ford Coppola's *Apocalypse Now.* A scathing indictment of U.S. involvement in Vietnam, the film changed forever the way Hollywood looked at war.

movie. That his close friend and former collaborator director George Lucas thought the production was outsized for a foreign location did not deter Coppola from proceeding to create what he hoped would be his legacy. "Francis had me convinced that we were gonna win a Nobel Prize for [*Apocalypse Now*]," recalls Milius today.

From the start, the project was shrouded in mystery, yet rumors of the production's various predicaments, from minor nuisances to major mishaps, began to make their way to Hollywood. Indeed, there were serious problems: the crippling typhoon that destroyed parts of the set and halted filming for weeks; the firing of Harvey Keitel, originally cast in the lead role; and the heart attack and hospitalization of Martin Sheen, Keitel's replacement, to name a few. Studio executives, who had thought the Vietnam War too incendiary a topic and had turned down the project, began to envisage Coppola as the movie world's Don Quixote, undertaking a project that could sabotage everything he had labored to achieve. Predictably, the press launched a fusillade of articles questioning Coppola, his monumental production—and even the director's sanity. A particularly memorable headline blared, "Apocalypse When?", as months rolled into years of moviemaking.

In the spring of 1979, after three years of production and over $30 million spent—most of it in credit guaranteed by Coppola himself—*Apocalypse Now* opened in Cannes to wildly mixed reviews. Most undoubtedly made the director cringe. Financially, it would take Coppola years to recoup his investment, thus making him decidedly less bankable than he had been before the film. Today, in retrospect, *Apocalypse Now,* having been deemed great as well as terrible when it first opened fourteen years ago, brought certain issues of the Vietnam era to the forefront for the first time. It changed forever Hollywood's portrayal of war and America's military might. Heroism was displaced by madness, just cause for war by sheer arrogance, any idealism about war by the gut-wrenching civilian—as well as military—casualties. On a more immediate level, *Apocalypse Now* successfully depicts the traumatic and discombobulating Vietnam experience. Said the director in Cannes, "*Apocalypse Now* is not about Vietnam. It *is* Vietnam."

Moviegoers were exposed to the cold-blooded arrogance and hypocrisy of government—the American Government in this instance—for the first time in the history of war movies. "[Colonel Walter Kurtz]'s out there operating without any decent restraint—totally beyond the pale of any acceptable human conduct…Kurtz is playing God to the natives," a general informs Captain Willard (Martin Sheen) at the outset of the film. Willard's mission is to seek out the mysterious Kurtz (Marlon Brando), who has gone mad and created an evil fiefdom in the Cambodian jungle, and to "terminate [him] with extreme prejudice."

It is, however, not only Kurtz who is operating beyond "decent restraint." The maniacal Colonel Kilgore (Robert Duvall), commander of the helicopter corps, conducts his own raid on a bucolic Viet Cong-controlled village in South Vietnam. The grim disparity between the idyllic pre-raid and horrific post-raid scenes made millions of American moviegoers wonder loudly once again whether the Vietnam War had been just. Additionally, the American forces' encounter with a civilian sampan in the movie, an incident with an outcome not unlike the My Lai massacre, seemed to confirm all reports and rumors of atrocities committed by our troops in Vietnam. Although sentiments against the war had been raging since the 1960s, this was the first instance that an American-made picture addressed the moral horror of Vietnam.

Unlike other Hollywood war films—from 1927's *Wings,* which heroically depicted World War I's air battles and won the first Academy Award for best picture, to 1957's best picture, *Bridge on the River Kwai,* which ultimately illustrated the inner strength of captured men—*Apocalypse Now* never attempts to showcase the bravery of soldiers nor the glory hitherto associated with military might. Unlike director Michael Cimino's epic, *The Deer Hunter,* released a year earlier, *Apocalypse Now* illustrates no necessity for war. In fact, seeing *The Deer Hunter* through the experience of *Apocalypse Now* renders the sacrifices of the former's principal characters totally senseless. If Cimino's film tried to show faith in the United States in its uplifting last scene with the singing of "God Bless America," *Apocalypse Now,* in its closing shot, showed a traumatized Martin Sheen emerging from madness and murder. For the first time, Hollywood directly faced Washington and posed questions concerning the validity of war and the behavior of soldiers in combat. If Cimino's *The Deer Hunter* had brought the Vietnam War home to America, Coppola's *Apocalypse Now* lodged it firmly in the American conscience. Again, for the first time, an American-made war movie made the disconcerting suggestion that our enemies are within.

In the 1980s, director Oliver Stone deftly picked up where *Apocalypse Now* left off. Both his Oscar-winning *Platoon* and *Born on the Fourth of July* capitalized on the former's themes: the U.S. Government's callousness and the lack of moral and political grounds upon which we had waged combat. 1981's *Gallipoli* applauded the heroism of allied forces in the eponymous battle, but laid bare the British command's foolish intractability, which led to the senseless massacre of thousands. Most recently, viewers who saw the Civil War film *Glory* (1991) would be hard-pressed to find true glory in the bloody domestic conflict of the 1860s, one that hitherto had been portrayed largely in heroic terms.

Gone are the times when one could count on coming out of a war film having one's faith in government confirmed. *Apocalypse Now* is indeed Vietnam, for it has allowed Hollywood, as well as the rest of America, to cast doubts—and to assail—traditional righteousness. On a lesser note, *Apocalypse Now* has also proved to be Francis Ford Coppola's own Vietnam.

KHOI NGUYEN

After three years of production in the jungles of the Philippines (prompting one headline to blare: "Apocalypse When?"), *Apocalypse Now* opened at the Cannes Film Festival to wildly mixed reviews.

1 9 8 1

MTV Rocks the Music Industry

In its dozen years of existence, MTV has revolutionized everything from the way men and women relate to each other and the clothes they wear to the style of thirty-second advertising spots and the pace of theatrical-movie editing.

When Warner Amex Satellite Entertainment, a division of Warner Bros. and American Express, started distributing this new advertising-supported cable network called Music Television in the late summer of 1981, however, "no one was certain there was enough money [from advertisers] to support such a service," says Bob Pittman, one of the executives most responsible for inventing MTV and nurturing it through the growing pains of its first five years. As he remembers it, ad agencies dismissed MTV at first because of an iron rule existing at the time, which said that if a service did not deliver a 3-rating average (3 percent of all households with televisions tuned into a given cable station, on average, at any given time) in 70 percent of the country, it was worthless as a vehicle for national advertising. (One indication of the changed thinking along Madison Avenue is that, twelve years later, neither MTV nor any other ad-supported cable network comes anywhere near a 3-rating average or a 70 percent clearance. MTV, reaching about 55 percent of the country, averages less than a 1.)

Back in 1981 it was almost as hard to get cable operators to agree to accept a channel that would draw on a limited stock of only about 250 music videos to fill its entire programming day. "We rushed MTV onto the air by August 1," Pittman says, "because record companies were in the midst of their worst year since the sixties. We wanted to be up and running as an outlet for music videos before the record companies completed their budgeting for 1982. The last thing we needed was cutbacks in new videos—there was no way we could've sustained the network by recycling 250 videos," particularly the dozens that would be less than riveting to the young viewers who would be MTV's target audience.

MTV quickly decided that the only way it could break down cable-operator resistance to its service was to saturate each market with a blizzard of promotion centered on the theme, "I want my MTV." The network enlisted a number of star performers to draw attention to the campaign, among them Pete Townsend, Stevie Nicks, Mick Jagger, Adam Ant, Pat Benatar, the Police, and David Bowie. And

Express Yourself: Covering issues ranging from Madonna's AIDS benefits to 2 Live Crew's censorship lawsuits, MTV has increasingly expanded its role into the political sphere.

THE VARIETY HISTORY OF SHOW BUSINESS
170

MTV's original VJs, Alan Hunter, Martha Quinn, Mark Goodman, Nina Blackwood, and J. J. Jackson, helped launch the cable television station that revolutionized the music business.

hammering home the pitch were MTV's five regular veejays: Nina Blackwood, Mark Goodman, Alan Hunter, J. J. Jackson, and Martha Quinn.

"These were down-and-dirty retail ads," Pittman says, "whose purpose was to get people to bug their cable systems to make MTV available in their markets." Once the cable systems bowed to the clamor of the populace and cleared channel space for MTV, the network's next step was to prove the value of the service by tracking record sales in each market. Pittman remembers that the first "case-study" trade-ad campaign centered on the cable system in Tulsa, Oklahoma. When the system started transmitting MTV, featured was the music video of a two-year-old record called "Video Killed the Record Star" by the Buggles because of the video's surrealistic special effects. The album containing the song suddenly began to move off the shelves of local record stores, and MTV's marketers had a direct cause-and-effect illustration of the sales impact of the network.

As MTV began appearing on cable systems in the larger markets (it became available to most homes receiving cable in New York City in 1982), its lightening-fast editing, bizarre visual imagery, and synthesizer-enhanced rock music started percolating through the pop culture. *Fortune* magazine named the MTV network "product of the year" for 1981. Pittman says the designer Norma Kamali put together an eye-opening MTV-influenced display in a Fifth Avenue department store, substituting TV sets for mannequins. The Paramount movie *Flashdance* became one of the biggest grossing movies of 1983, at least in part because a number of the musical set pieces came off as stunningly stylized imitations of the rock videos that were filling the schedule of the MTV network. And the first hit network prime-time TV series directly influenced by MTV was "Miami Vice," which became a fixture on NBC's Friday night lineup from 1984 through 1989. According to Alex McNeil, author of *Total Television,* "The genesis of the series was a two-word notation made by NBC Entertainment President Brandon Tartikoff: 'MTV cops.'"

Meanwhile, MTV was going through some agonizing growing pains. For example, the network had refused to schedule any Michael Jackson videos during its first year and a half on the assumption that its main audience was white teenagers and young adults who were not interested in music by black performers. Angered by what it considered an unfair policy, CBS Records, which produced Jackson's albums, reportedly threatened to pull all of its performers' videos off the network if MTV did not change its procedures. On March 31, 1983, MTV relented, scheduling the world premiere of Jackson's "Beat It" video from the album *Thriller.* Generating seven Top 10 hits, all of them accompanied by lavishly produced videos, *Thriller* went on to sell over forty million copies, making it the best-selling album of all time.

Going even further, MTV next began to promote theatrical movies featuring rock stars. The network covered the premiere of Prince's first movie, *Purple Rain,* on July 26, 1984, as though it were CNN attending a major Senate hearing on Capitol Hill. It soon became de rigueur for most major theatricals to come out with a video that MTV could schedule to coincide with the movie's release. By January 1, 1985, MTV was slotting videos from three of the four top-grossing movies of that week: *Beverly Hills Cop, Dune,* and *2010.*

To break up the monotony of wall-to-wall videos, MTV soon began tinkering a bit with its schedule. On June 5, 1985, it aired its first comedy series, "The Young Ones," which, in MTV's words, "chronicled the exploits of four lunatic British college students." A month later MTV cablecast its longest production, the seventeen-hour "Live Aid" concert, from two stadiums on two continents. Organized by Bob Geldof, who earmarked the proceeds for African famine relief, the concert featured Mick Jagger, Tina Turner, Paul McCartney, Phil Collins, Duran Duran, Neil Young, Elton John, Sting, U2, and the reunion of Led Zeppelin and The Who, among others.

"Live Aid" was just the beginning of MTV's involvement in the international arena. On March 18, 1987, Australia's Nine Network started transmitting the station. On August 1, 1987, MTV launched the only 24-hour-a-day music video network on the European continent. Called MTV Europe, it kicked off with Elton John switching on the channel from the Roxy Club in Amsterdam. Over the next five years, MTV Europe registered explosive growth, from 1.6 million households at its inception to 40 million in 29 countries by the end of 1992.

Meanwhile, back in the United States, MTV continued the push to vary its schedule, commissioning four new series in 1987: "Club MTV," its first five-day-a-week series, a dance show hosted by the network's newest veejay, Downtown Julie

Brown; "Headbanger's Ball," which focused on heavy-metal music and news; "The Week in Rock," featuring news about music, fashion, and life-styles; and "Remote Control," a goofy quiz show with young contestants answering questions mostly about TV and pop music. "Remote Control" became so popular that it spawned a syndicated version that broadcast stations ran on weekends in 1989 and 1990.

Until 1992 most of MTV's news coverage dealt with the worlds of rock music and pop culture. It had made passes at more serious public-service coverage, such as the late-1986 "Rock against Drugs" campaign, which featured performers urging viewers not to abuse illegal substances, citing their own bad experiences. And in 1988 Stevie Wonder, Frank Zappa, and John Cougar Mellencamp were among the performers taping public-service videos exhorting MTV's audience to register to vote in the presidential election. Then, in 1992, MTV put public service at the very top of its programming agenda, earmarking a seven-figure budget for its "Choose or Lose" campaign to educate young viewers on the issues and candidates in the presidential campaign. The event that catapulted the strategy onto the map of national consciousness was a celebrated hour-long Q-and-A with Governor Bill Clinton and a group of two hundred eighteen- to twenty-four-year-olds on June 16, 1992, with MTV's chief political reporter, Tabitha Soren, twenty-five, as moderator. Clinton handled himself so well that the appearance helped to revitalize his campaign.

At the same time, "The Week in Rock" began moving beyond just news of pop culture to cover "a wide range of social and political subjects," says Tom Wolzein, a media expert with Bernstein Research. "During the presidential campaign, for example, it was about the only place on any channel where a viewer could see interviews with virtually every candidate from virtually every party on the ballot."

Having already created three additional basic cable services—VH-1 (a music video network targeted to twenty-five- to forty-nine-year-old adults), Nickelodeon (a children-oriented channel), and Nick-at-Nite (a network that draws on reruns of old sitcoms)—MTV is planning to split into three separate music networks by the mid-1990s. Each will schedule videos, specials, and series geared to a specific audience.

By programming three music networks, MTV hopes to have as much impact on American culture throughout the 1990s as it did in the 1980s. But most observers are convinced that, although MTV will continue to thrive, it will not be able to recapture the freshness of its original agenda—a program service that tapped into the nervous system of a whole generation of young people, acting as a fever chart of their emotional gyrations.

JOHN DEMPSEY

FACING PAGE

Irish Rebellion: Sinead O'Connor's career—and politics—got a boost from MTV's coverage of the controversial singer.

Andrew Lloyd Webber and the Brits on Broadway

"Jellicles can and Jellicles do." On the evening of October 7, 1982, composer Andrew Lloyd Webber became, with *Cats,* the first man in the history of the musical theater to have three shows running simultaneously both on Broadway and in London's West End. In the decade that followed, he would up that transatlantic total to four and spearhead, with producer Cameron Mackintosh, a British invasion of the Broadway theater that would be as sudden and unexpected as if an army of American actors had hijacked Shakespeare at Stratford-upon-Avon.

A decade later, the signs are that the invasion may well be coming to an end. With *Will Rogers Follies* (1991), *Jelly's Last Jam* (1992), and *Crazy for You* (1992), the native American musical seems reawakened after its ten-year slumber and is again flexing its orchestral and choreographic muscles. All the more reason, then, to examine the eighties phenomenon of the Brits on Broadway: "now and [not quite] forever," to paraphrase *Cats*'s ad slogan.

Lloyd Webber and Mackintosh were not, of course, the first Brits on Broadway, nor was *Cats* even the first Lloyd Webber hit there. Indeed, it might not have been a triumph anywhere. Before the musical based loosely on poems by T. S. Eliot (not the best-known lyricist in the business) opened in London on May 11, 1981, the advance word had been so dispiriting that the composer had to take out an extra mortgage on his home and the production and creative crew all had to take percentages rather than salaries (and have therefore, many of them, become millionaires in the process). A bomb scare that opening night was discounted by the audience on the grounds that the New London Theatre had never yet had a hit.

That night, of course, it did, and the raves were to be repeated seventeen months later in New York. The *Daily News* and the *Post* may have both grumbled that it was "not quite purr-fect," but the *New York Times*'s Frank Rich, later to be considered less than friendly toward the composer, wrote of the "pure theatrical

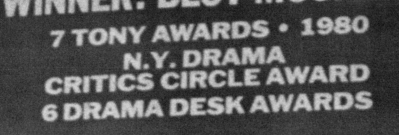

magic" of a show that "transports the audience into a world of complete fantasy which could only exist in the theater and, these day, all too rarely does."

Writers of British musicals had, in fact, been taking Broadway by storm for almost three-quarters of a century before the arrival of Grizabella, "all alone in the moonlight." As far back as 1915, Britons P. G. Wodehouse and Guy Bolton began scoring hit after small-scale hit with the young American composer Jerome Kern, who had himself traveled the other way across the Atlantic to work with them on the grounds that he was more likely to have a prolific stage-musical life in the West End than on Broadway. In subsequent decades Noël Coward, Sandy Wilson, Lionel Bart, and the team of Anthony Newley and Leslie Bricusse all achieved considerable Broadway success with London shows. Before *Cats* Lloyd Webber had, with lyricist Tim Rice, enjoyed a long New York run with *Jesus Christ Superstar,* and their *Evita* and *Joseph and the Amazing Technicolor Dreamcoat* were both still running in October 1982.

What changed with *Cats* was the coming of Cameron Mackintosh, a young British impresario who noticed that all previous West End hits had been brought to America by American managements, from Florenz Ziegfeld to David Merrick. Mackintosh wanted to do it differently, much the way Rodgers and Hammerstein had always done it when their shows played London: he wanted to retain total control over every aspect of production and marketing, from star casting to the logo on the coffee mugs sold at intermission. In that sense, the real significance of *Cats* was that it was the first London score to take the British musical into worldwide marketing. Since then—and all under Mackintosh's management—have come *Les Misérables, The Phantom of the Opera,* and *Miss Saigon.* Significantly, Lloyd Webber scores, such as *Aspects of Love,* that have not been under that management have done noticeably less well at world box offices, whatever their artistic merits.

It was Mackintosh, and his design company, DeWynters, who ensured that the eyes of *Cats,* the waif of *Les Miz,* the mask of *Phantom,* and the helicopter of *Miss Saigon* would stare out at us from identical posters whether in Reykjavík or Rio. From offices a mile or so apart in London, Lloyd Webber and Mackintosh now plan their new shows—sometimes together, sometimes not—surrounded by a small army of accountants, designers, publicists, directors, and choreographers before sending out task forces to set up productions around the world. Even before the hit song comes the logo.

Precisely because of this worldwide commercial success, considerable critical and artistic snobbery still conditions attitudes toward the stage musical in Britain. Several of my colleagues, for example, to this day maintain that the Royal Shakespeare Company should not, under its classical mandate, have gotten involved with the original Mackintosh staging of *Les Miz* at the Barbican in 1985—despite the fact that the show has been pouring $2 million a year into the company's coffers ever since and is perhaps alone responsible for the RSC's economic revival. Despite the fact that there were fifteen playing in the West End in March 1993, roughly one for every two theaters, musicals still do not have their place in the heartland of legitimate theater in Britain.

For just that reason, the Brits are thrilled to be on Broadway. Instead of seeing themselves as an invading army, men like Lloyd Webber and Mackintosh and their artistic teams (choreographer Gillian Lynne, designer John Napier, and director Trevor Nunn principal among them) felt they were at last being allowed into the temple they had previously been able to worship only from afar. Way back in the 1960s, Nunn had begun importing Lynne to Stratford to jazz up his *Comedy of Errors* with a musical finale. Mackintosh had been brought up on the Broadway musical exports to Britain of the 1950s; he began his commercial career with a catastrophic revival of *Anything Goes* before moving on to more successful tours of *Oklahoma!* and *My Fair Lady.* Similarly, Lloyd Webber's schoolboy love had been the movies of Rodgers and Hammerstein. All were united by their passion for the Broadway musical.

Their invasion also came at roughly the same time that Broadway was decimated by a lethal combination of urban decay, spiraling union costs, and some tragically early deaths. The abrupt loss of Gower Champion, Bob Fosse, and Michael Bennett during the 1980s left a choreographic vacuum into which British shows, often heavier on song and scenery than dance, then poured as never before. Not all were by Lloyd Webber or Alain Boublil/Claude-Michel Schönberg (*Les Miz;* actually from Paris via London); one of the longest-running and most highly acclaimed British imports of the decade was a revival of Noel Gay's 1937 *Me and My Girl.* And not all the shows were triumphs. Tim Rice had a rough time with *Chess,* and neither *Song and Dance* nor *Aspects* proved to be a gold mine for Lloyd Webber, while two of his most profitable London hits, *Starlight Express* and *Joseph,* fared rather less well in the United States. But a measure of how things changed in the 1980s for the writers of hit British musicals was the flotation of Lloyd Webber's Really Useful Company on the London Stock Exchange in 1986 at an initial valuation of $70 million—more money than Noël Coward or Cole Porter had made in their musical lifetimes.

What had changed, of course, was world travel and the post-Beatles readiness of the American audio market to accept British chart hits. Ever since *Oklahoma!* had hit postwar London like an earthquake, "smelling," as the poet Carl Sandburg wrote, "of newmown hay swept over barn-dance floors," the London musical had been in a thirty-year state of shell-shocked retreat toward, at best, the Dickensian retreads of Lionel Bart (*Oliver*) or the two-piano nostalgic charms of Sandy Wilson (*The Boy Friend*). Mackintosh and Lloyd Webber realized that if Americans were once again to be drawn to British musicals, then Broadway had to be fought on its own prepackaged terms.

No real language or transatlantic travel problems here, no demands of different heritage or education, no cultural barriers to be stormed. Rice and Lloyd Webber drew *Joseph* and *Superstar* from familiar Bible stories, while *Evita* is the fictionalized biography of historical figure Eva Perón. *Miss Saigon* is at its very heart *Madame Butterfly; Les Misérables* and *Phantom* were both already filmed by the mid-1930s. Whereas many of the shows that once came to Britain from Broadway, from *Oklahoma!* onward to *A Chorus Line,* were definably about America, there is precious little about modern Europe in *Phantom of the Opera* or *Les Misérables* or *Cats;* in that sense, the British musical seems to have abandoned any role as a topical commentator. In order for something to succeed on both sides of the Atlantic, it has to be specifically about neither side of that ocean.

On honeymoon in New York in 1966, I saw on consecutive nights three musicals: *Hello, Dolly!, Funny Girl,* and *Mame,* and nobody was talking about that as being an especially good year. But the drought soon came, and what *Cats* proved was that for the first time Britain could assemble on home ground thirty singer-dancers as talented, versatile, and energetic as any of those who used to cross over from New York. Hits did not come any more smash than this one. *Les Misérables* marked a different leap forward. What mattered most was that, like Verdi's *Rigoletto* or, for that matter, Stephen Sondheim's *Sweeney Todd,* it set out to redefine the limits of musical theater. Like them, it tackled themes of universal social and domestic despair with energy and intensity.

But the impact of these shows and *Miss Saigon* was, if anything, still greater on Broadway than in the West End. In Manhattan, as one hotel manager once told me, a single smash hit can turn the whole city around; cab drivers and restaurant waiters look perceptibly happier if the reviews are good. That has never happened in London, where the connection between a healthy theater and a healthy tourist trade has never yet been even faintly recognized.

The name of the game now is familiarity and presell. Where once Richard Rodgers and Oscar Hammerstein gave us "take-home songs," the 11 o'clock numbers we sang in the shower the following morning, the demand now, at $65 a ticket, is for "take-in songs," ones we know we love before we take our seats. Today a musical can be comfortably staged in London at maybe half the cost of opening it in New York, made familiar on CDs and posters and T-shirts, and then brought to Broadway with little, if any, of the old risk of a sea change in its fortunes. Why else would Lloyd Webber's *Sunset Boulevard* have opened first in London?

"Now and forever." Maybe not with quite so many shows, but having established their place along the Great White Way, the Brits are not likely to be packing for home just yet. Not if Cameron Mackintosh and Andrew Lloyd Webber can help it.

SHERIDAN MORLEY

Divine Inspiration: Even before he transformed Broadway in the 1980s, Andrew Lloyd Webber (with Tim Rice) had scored big hits in the previous decade with both *Evita* and *Jesus Christ, Superstar, opposite.*

1 9 8 2

The *Thriller* Phenomenon

The deadline was fast approaching for Michael Jackson to turn in his next album to CBS Records.

Dog-tired from working on Steven Spielberg's *E.T. Storybook* album, for which he provided songs, narration, and arrangements, Jackson was left with two months to deliver the follow-up to his multi-platinum album *Off the Wall*. The pressure was greater than before, given that *Off the Wall* had been his big breakthrough solo album, selling over seven million copies worldwide and spawning such hits as the title track, "Don't Stop till You Get Enough," "Rock with You," and "She's Out of My Life." It had made Jackson the first artist to have four Top 10 singles from the same album on *Billboard*'s charts.

Ever the professional, Jackson realized that CBS was counting on the new album to be one of its bright spots of the Christmas 1982 season. And ever the businessman, he perhaps realized that the seasonal slot offered him his best chance at topping his previous album's sales. Working quickly with producer Quincy Jones, Jackson wrote the material, then recorded and mixed the disc, getting the package together just before the deadline.

The result of the hard work?

"It sounded like shit," admitted Jones. "It was in terrible shape."

The album in question was *Thriller,* destined to become the largest-selling record of all time, more than doubling its closest competitors and still going over the counter in impressive numbers to this day.

"We knew what we wanted," Jones said of the *Thriller* recording process, "but there was not time to think, no paralysis from analysis, as I say."

The problem with the initial recording was an unusual one: it contained too much music for the sonic-reproduction capabilities of a vinyl album, which was the main configuration of the audio industry back in the "dark ages" of the early 1980s. "Vinyl doesn't pick up that much information," Jones said. "On CD and cassette you can put everything on it, but if you go over nineteen minutes on one side of vinyl, the grooves aren't big enough. We knew we were in trouble, but when you're tired, you think you can defy technology."

Listening to the playback of the acetate version of the album, Jones and Jackson both realized that the sound was way too compressed. While several studio executives stood around popping champagne corks, those with an ear for the music real-

FACING PAGE

Record Success: Michael Jackson's *Thriller* album, released simultaneously with the artist's cutting-edge video for "Billie Jean," has sold an incredible 48 million copies to date, becoming the largest-selling record of all time.

ized that *Thriller* was in no way ready for the public's ears. Jones took Jackson back to his house and declined to head back to the studio until they were refreshed. "We took two days off, and then we decided to mix one song a day for eight days."

During the remixing process, *Thriller* became a far different album. It was time to slice and dice, and the Jackson/Jones team set to work, removing a long introduction to "Billie Jean" in one particularly memorable move. In addition, they reviewed album tracks and replaced four with new cuts. The new selections included "Pretty Young Thing," "Beat It," "Human Nature," and "The Lady in My Life," three of which would go on to become massive hits.

Finally, the album was ready. "We knew it was the best we could make it," Jones said.

The first single from *Thriller* was already on the streets, a typical record industry move to hype sales for a forthcoming album. "The Girl Is Mine," a duet with Paul McCartney, was a Top 10 hit, creating a buzz for the December 1, 1982, album release.

Even though Epic (a CBS division) and Jackson were holding a strong hand, they were not cautious. They decided to release the second and third singles within six weeks of each other, a risky move that could have cannibalized the commercial prospects of both. But "Billie Jean" and "Beat It" both clicked, and *Thriller* started its climb.

"The album had sold its first million in the first month, so we knew we had something," said Glen Brunman, Epic's West Coast director of publicity. Brunman was the man in charge of charting the album's progress for CBS and, as such, perhaps its closest liaison to Michael Jackson. "But the thing that made the difference was the video for 'Billie Jean.' That really transformed the way music videos were made."

Indeed, "Billie Jean," with its elaborate choreography and inventive set, which featured Jackson as a kind of magical figure whose feet left shiny footprints across the landscape, was unlike most videos up until that point. It was more like a movie, with Jackson in the Fred Astaire/Gene Kelly role. But there was only one hitch: MTV refused to include it in its regular rotation, allegedly because the channel did not feel that Jackson fit with the station's mix of video offerings, which, at the time, skewed heavily toward heavy metal and English alternative music.

Many are the stories of what CBS did to get MTV's attention. Some say former CEO Walter Yetnikoff threatened to pull every other CBS artist off the channel. Other tales suggest CBS threatened to cry racism at the channel's virtual exclusion of black videos. Brunman declines to be specific but admits, "The full strength of the company was brought to bear in trying to influence the exhibition of a video we thought was totally unlike anything that had been seen before."

Indeed, Jackson's entire album and video output from *Thriller* went on to surpass anything that had happened before. The milestones were many, with Jackson

Michael Jackson and producer Quincy Jones replaced four cuts on the *Thriller* album at the last minute, three of which went on to top the charts.

becoming the first artist to top the pop and rhythm and blues charts simultaneously. Then, when the album sat somewhere around sixteen million worldwide units sold, the *Thriller* short film was released, skyrocketing the album to another thirteen to fourteen million in sales.

Besides its raw sales, *Thriller* succeeded on yet another level: it brought around the hard-core audience of skeptics known as critics. "One interesting thing is that in the *Village Voice* poll, which came out in late January of 1983, *Thriller* finished number 19 for the year," Brunman said. "A year later, it finished number 1. So even the critics were somehow persuaded."

The album's legacy stands beyond sales and critics' praise. "It completely altered pop music for a number of years, changed the way people made records and videos," Brunman says. Edna Gundersen, chief pop critic for *USA Today,* agrees. "Not since the Beatles or Woodstock was there that kind of global consensus."

Which continues to this day. *Thriller* has now sold an incredible forty-eight million copies worldwide and still sells strongly, as old-timers gradually replace their vinyl records with compact discs.

BRUCE HARING

Ted Turner: King of Cable

Long before he was known in Hollywood circles as Jane Fonda's husband, Ted Turner was infamous for his purchase of the MGM film library. Paradoxically, that acquisition was the end product of an even bigger but failed deal. The America's Cup sailor, who had turned his dream of a twenty-four-hour news network into a powerful reality known as CNN, had some definite ideas about the future of television and believed he could best implement them through ownership of one of the Big Three broadcast networks.

Turner focused first on ABC, but Capital Cities beat him to the punch. He then turned his attention to CBS and spent the first six months of 1985 pursuing a Don Quixote-like takeover of the Tiffany network. However, the $5.4 billion bid prompted the press to paint him as a right-wing hick (Turner supported ultraconservative Senator Jesse Helm's concurrent effort to take over CBS) who was hell-bent on destroying a venerable news-gathering institution. In addition to bruising Turner's ego, the attempt cost his company, Turner Broadcasting System (TBS), more than $18 million. But instead of slinking back to his hometown, Atlanta, and laying low, the indomitable Turner set his sights on Hollywood.

MGM owner Kirk Kerkorian informed Turner in late July that he was putting the once-regal studio on the block for twenty-nine dollars a share. While Turner's CEO at the time, William Bevins, had valued MGM at roughly twenty-four or twenty-five dollars a share, and while investment bankers valued it at twenty-two (a number that financier Charles W. Knapp had offered Kerkorian for the company), Turner—much to general dismay—immediately accepted Kerkorian's price as long as he threw in 1,450 additional old movies from the RKO and Warner libraries. Because Kerkorian insisted that Turner commit irrevocably within two weeks of agreeing on terms of the deal, Turner was effectively forced into retaining Kerkorian's banker, Drexel Burnham, who already knew MGM's balance sheet inside out. Drexel's dominance of the junk-bond market would allow him to finance what many considered an unwise move.

Conventional wisdom said that Turner was simply trying to soothe his ego in

FACING PAGE

Cable Operator: When his attempts to take over ABC and CBS soured, Ted Turner turned his sights to Hollywood. Although his 1985 purchase of MGM soon collapsed as well, "The Mouth from the South" retained control of the studio's priceless library of film classics, laying the cornerstone for his fabulously successful Turner Network Television (TNT).

TED TURNER CLOSES

Management, Craft Unions Reach Terms For New 3-Year Contract

By DAVID ROBB

Hollywood, Aug. 6.

Terms of a new three-year contract for Hollywood's below-the-line craft unions were reached Thursday (1) morning after a 24-hour marathon bargaining session.

The agreement — reached between management's Alliance of Motion Picture & Television Producers and labor's Intl. Alliance of Theatrical Stage Employees and Basic Crafts — must now be approved by the unions' members. Ratification of the pact is expected within three weeks.

Included in the new pact is a $3-an-hour across-the-board wage increase, spread out over the life of the contract (90¢ per hour for the first year, $1 an hour for the second year and $1.10 an hour for the third year).

Pension benefits were also increased by 25% for active union members, and by 10% for retirees.

A settlement similar to those reached recently by the Directors

MCA Net Slips

MCA Inc. reported second-quarter earnings Tuesday (6) of $12,-298,000 or 25¢ a share on revenues of $416,382,000, vs. $19,953,000 (42¢) on revenues of $349,189,000 for the comparable period of fiscal 1984.

For the six months, company recorded net income of $30,675,000 (63¢) on revenues of $847,951,000, vs. $40,985,000 (85¢) on revenues of $741,630,000 last year.

MCA attributed the decreased second-quarter net to a "higher estimated effective income tax rate."

See MGM/UA's Gotham Pub Dept. In Place By Fall

Reversing two years of top-level management policy that ruled no

KERKORIA ALL ST

By RA

Ho

In what app deal marking th a major motior broadcaster sir Rubber acquir some 30 years a the Turner Broa close to annour ment.

For $29 a sha ly $1.5-billion, come a wholly TBS (see separa

Meanwhile, t New York mar up 4¾, Monda propelled share cious 2,055,200

"It appears agreement ha MGM/UA c Rockwell said. two or three sti parties at the

N ON LEO THE LION

GETS
K IN UA

DYND

od, Aug. 6.
o be a virtual
acquisition of
re studio by a
eneral Tire &
RKO Pictures
MGM/UA and
ing System are
merger agree-

approximate-
M/UA will be-
d subsidiary of
ry on page 41).

n roared on the
losing at 22⅝,
The velocity
ded to a fero-

a definitive
en reached,''
ate v.p. Art
er Monday (5),
points kept the
following a
itially reached

'Future,' 'Vacation' Top Natl. B.O.; 'Night,' 'Weird' Make Okay Bows

U.S. Boxoffice Report

Last Week	$102,400,000
1984	97,500,000
1983	104,900,000
Year To Date	$2,211,400,000
1984	2,460,900,000
1983	2,295,600,000

Source: *Variety.*

Thorn EMI Signs Up Slew Of Brit Indies To Production Pacts

London, Aug. 6.
In a move to gain a flow of British films, Thorn EMI Screen Entertainment is to play mother hen to a half-dozen leading independent producers via a deal one of them describes as ''too good to be true.''
The British major has created a $1,500,000 revolving development fund for various producers who

By JAMES GREENBERG

Hollywood, Aug. 6.
Late summer business at the national boxoffice continued to run ahead of action for the same period last summer. Main contributors this round were U's leggy ''Back To The Future,'' WB's ''National Lampoon's European Vacation'' and okay openings for Col's ''Fright Night,'' and U's ''Weird Science.''

With the opening of three new titles from the majors as compares to two last year, business for the top 10 pictures was 22% ahead of comparable figures for this time a year ago. Total of $42,669,629 represents a healthy jump over the $34,964,150 for Aug. 3-5, 1984. While business continued upbeat, early summer trough will still leave the overall seasonal figures well behind the $1.58-billion of a year ago.

Other new arrival this weekend was WB's ''Sesame Street Presents: Follow That Bird,'' not making much of a dent in the family market. New arrivals at this time last

Ted Turner's marriage to Jane Fonda is the entrepreneur's latest Hollywood acquisition.

PREVIOUS PAGES

Variety, **August 7, 1985:** Turner forked over $1.5 billion for MGM—a deal that later fell through.

the wake of the CBS fiasco. Others believe he acted so quickly because he was afraid the films might go to another suitor, even though another bona fide bidder was nowhere in sight. The fact that Turner focused so intently on the library—which included such classics as *Gone with the Wind, Casablanca,* and *Mutiny on the Bounty*—was an indication that his plans went far beyond the studio, with its film lab, real estate, and videocassette operation.

The deal began unraveling even before the ink was dry, as MGM movies bombed at the box office and studio cash flow plummeted. Drexel said the deal would have to be restructured to include only twenty-five dollars per share in cash and the rest in Turner stock. Under the new plan, Kerkorian and other MGM holders would receive fifty-three million shares of TBS preferred stock, and unless Turner repaid $900 million of his $2 billion debt within a year, the dividends for those shares would not be paid in cash but with new common shares.

When the $1.5 billion deal was finally completed in March of 1986, Kerkorian stood a fair chance of eventually gaining control over TBS, giving him the opportunity to sell MGM all over again. Awash in debt, Turner had no choice but to sell back to Kerkorian the studio, the videocassette business, and the MGM logo rights for $300 million, a substantial discount on his purchase price. In addition, he sold the real estate and the film lab to Lorimar Tele-Pictures for another $190 million. But those proceeds still were not enough to cover his crushing debt load. A consortium of cable operators including Tele-Communications and Time (now Time Warner) came to the rescue, buying $565 million worth of Turner's stock. While the bailout reduced Turner's ownership from 81 percent to 51 percent, it kept the company out of hostile hands.

The assessment at the time of the deal was that Kerkorian had taken Turner to the cleaners. "The Mouth from the South" had effectively paid about $1.2 billion for MGM's library of 3,301 movies plus the RKO and Warner Bros. titles. The consensus was that Turner had overpaid by approximately $300 million—based on the assumption that with annual cash flow of about $80 million, the library should have been valued at most at about $800 to $900 million. But Turner had always sought to portray the purchase as a strategic move needed to ensure the future of his company; studios and syndicators had become increasingly reluctant to sell TBS anything but their least desirable product, and he desperately needed to lock up his own program supply. For this reason he stuck to his original contention that the library was worth more to him than to anyone else.

Turner quickly set out to make the library even more valuable through colorization. Despite cries of "foul" from critics and directors, Turner forged ahead, colorizing about twenty-five films a year. While the process cost him about $250,000 per film, it increased the value of some as much as tenfold in syndication. That colorized library formed the cornerstone of the now fabulously successful Turner Network Television (TNT), which Turner launched three and a half years after purchasing the library. Debuting in seventeen million homes on October 3, 1988, the cable channel has grown into a profitable station airing everything from made-for-cable premieres to NFL football. But the foundation of the network—which today reaches approximately 58.6 million homes, or 63 percent of the viewing public—remains the movie classics Turner acquired from MGM. Those films have also bolstered Turner's Superstation, TBS, and allowed the company to build successful programming, home video, and sydication arms.

While at the time it seemed a disaster that Turner had given up autonomous reign over his company, the management control exerted by the cable consortium has also proven positive. Turner has been able to reduce debt via the effective use of capital markets, and the company was named among the ten winners of the 1991 Turnaround of the Year Award by the Turnaround Management Association.

Turner's buying habits also seem to have grown more conscientious. His most recent purchase (with joint venture partner Apollo Investment Fund) of animator Hanna Barbera Productions for $320 million raised no cries of overpayment from Wall Street. Using the MGM/TNT model, Turner utilized the cartoon library—which includes such characters as the Flintstones, Yogi Bear, and the Jetsons—to launch The Cartoon Network on October 1, 1992. By February 1993, the service reached 4.5 million subscribers.

While rumors still pop up from time to time about Turner wanting to own one of the Big Three networks, these days he seems temporarily content to work with them on special-event programming like the Olympics and his own Goodwill Games. Even so, his vision of someday owning both a working studio and one of the three has not died. The Federal Communications Commission's repeal of most of the financial interest and syndication rules has seemingly opened the door to network/studio pairings, and Turner has been in discussions with a cadre of industry heavyweights including CBS, Capital Cities/ABC, Paramount, and MGM about potential pairings. Eight years after his first attempts, Turner seems determined to reclaim those assets he so grudgingly left on the table—even if the Big Three are not so big anymore.

PAUL NOGLOWS

Ted Turner effectively paid $1.2 billion for the MGM library of 3,301 movies, colorizing classics such as *Casablanca* despite cries of sacrilege from critics and movie buffs.

CNN, Turner's twenty-four-hour news network, had already transformed the cable-television industry by 1985.

1 9 8 8

TV Tabloids—What Next?

Since the genre made its splash in 1988 with the launch of "A Current Affair," television has been awash in tabloid TV.

Surf the video waves on any day and, *click,* there is actual footage of a cop being blown away. *Click,* and a young girl, her eyes filled with tears, talks about the night she shot the lover who spurned her. *Click* again, and the final hours of Marilyn Monroe are replayed by a Marilyn look-alike, shot in hazy, pseudo-documentary style. *Click* once more, and secret cameras have captured scenes of chronic abuse in a veterans hospital.

"Cops," "America's Most Wanted," "American Detective," "Top Cops," "I Witness Video," "48 Hours," "Rescue 911": Each week on the four major networks there are at least thirteen hours of this kind of programming in prime time between 8 and 11 P.M. On top of that, there are over three hours of syndicated reality-based daily magazine shows such as "A Current Affair," "Hard Copy," and "Inside Edition," plus even more hours of talk shows dealing with similarly inflammatory subject matter, hosted by the likes of Phil Donahue, Sally Jesse Raphael, Geraldo Rivera, and Montel Williams. There is so much of this around that there are even a couple of cable stations that feature nothing but reality-based programming. And there will be more.

The genre has been vilified as tawdry titillation and, at its most extreme, a demented, demagogic call to violence. Somehow, though, all this noise about reality TV obscures what is really going on. Certainly, the provocative nature of these programs links them together. Their producers have realized that the limits of acceptable content have expanded and that the TV environment is like a crowded newsstand where, to get noticed, being provocative is one tried and true method. But these programs share something vital to television itself. Like MTV, this is programming created largely by and for a generation nurtured on the tube, exploiting properties unique to the medium. Generally, these shows are relatively cheap to produce and feed off young staffs that operate with a front-page can-do mentality.

The reasons for this flood of video reality represent a confluence of technology and economics, coupled with a societal hunger to make some sense of a world that often seems to have gone mad. New technologies—in particular, the spread of cable television—have changed everything. The public today has almost infinite viewing options, and the three premiere networks, ABC, NBC, and CBS, their profits

FACING PAGE

Mass Appeal: Ever since the Fox network launched tabloid TV with "A Current Affair" in 1988, prime-time programs like "Cops" have shocked and titillated television audiences with real-life tragedies and near-death adventures.

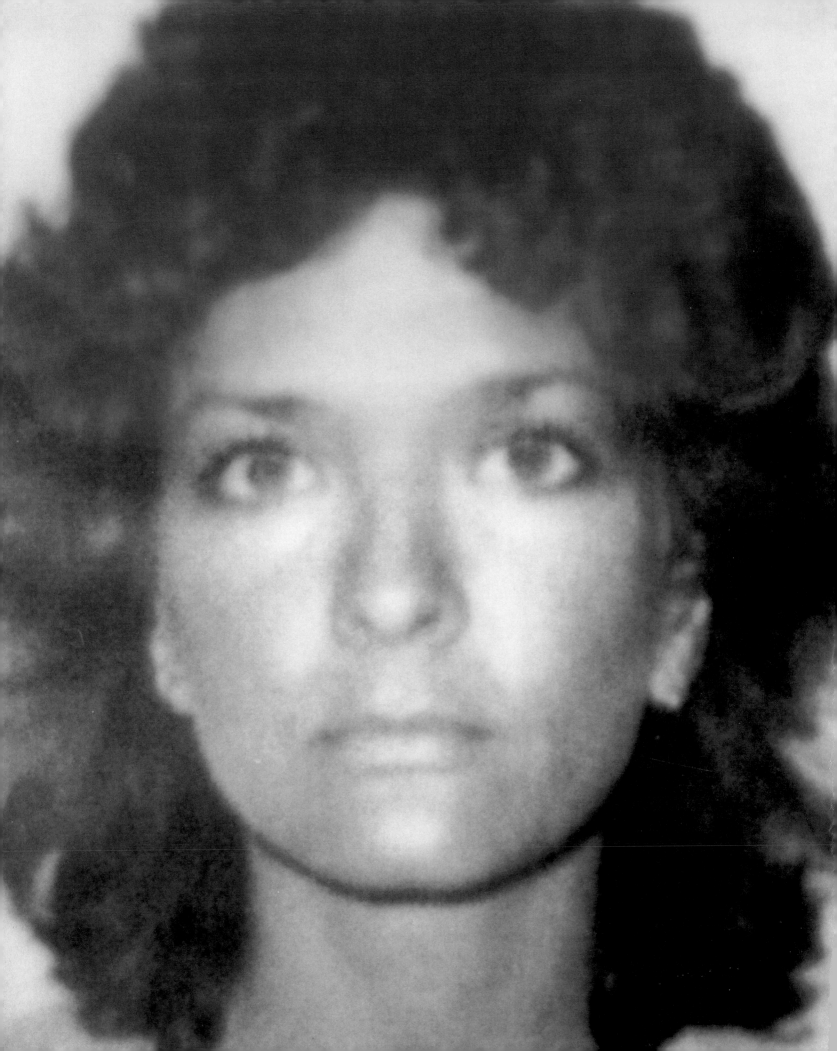

diminishing, have to look for a cheaper kind of programming. Now there is room in the TV game for new players who are not constricted by the old ways of doing things.

The reality TV genre really began to heat up in 1988. That year News Corporation chairman Rupert Murdoch, who had made his fortune in tabloid daily newspapers on three continents, launched his fledgling Fox network in the United States. Almost immediately, "A Current Affair," "America's Most Wanted," and "Cops" debuted on the upstart station. Murdoch's troops, many of them veterans of tabloids in Australia and the United Kingdom, brought a hell-bent, punk sensibility to the small screen. Their recipe for storytelling was borrowed straight from the print tabloid cookbook, spiced all the more by the audio and visual opportunities provided by the tube: garish tales about amazing, terrible things happening to ordinary people, as well as exposés of the rich, famous, and powerful—the whole enterprise heavily laden with sexual innuendo, slick camera work, and a pulsating soundtrack.

The big three networks watched the success of tiny Fox and quickly followed suit. It became clear that the reality genre represented a win-win proposition to television executives with bottom-line top of mind. Producing such programming generally costs only half as much as producing a situation comedy or drama. This is TV that can often be done in-house by a network news division, thus helping to amortize the cost of other news programming that either loses money or generates minimal profits. That reality gave birth to shows like "48 Hours," "Street Stories," "Primetime Live," and "Dateline NBC." The president of NBC News, Michael Gartner, recently remarked that, in order for a network news division to be success-ful today, it must have a successful prime-time news magazine show on the air. It *has* to be in the reality TV business.

Viewers eat most of this stuff up. Peter Brennan, creator of "A Current Affair," said: "What we do is show extraordinary things happening to ordinary people. People watch because they're thinking, 'There but for the grace of God go I.'" And savvy advertising executives know that a lot of these shows represent some of the best value on TV. Because of their controversial nature, they tend to offer advertis-ing rates that are lower than those for more timid fare. Admen also know that, for a lot of upscale viewers, such fare is a guilty pleasure. Unlike a newspaper tabloid, which somebody might see you buying at the checkout counter of the supermarket, nobody has to know that you enjoy a bit of sleaze in the privacy of your own home.

People also watch because this is television they feel empowers them. Shows like "America's Most Wanted" and the hit "Unsolved Mysteries" encourage viewers to call in if they have leads on the criminals whose horrible deeds they have just seen re-created with all the style of a slick MTV video. The shows tout each capture loudly. Bad guys are caught. Video vigilantism works. This is television that gives viewers a sense of security too. It is not surprising that shows like "Top Cops,"

Hosts of tabloid series, like John Walsh of "America's Most Wanted," are the "latest breed of news anchormen."

"America's Most Wanted," and "Rescue 911" are popular with elementary school children. These programs deliver an underlying all-American message that the institutions of government work.

At its best, the tabloid TV revolution has brought a more immediate, vital kind of storytelling to the medium. In part, its growth is a reaction to old-style TV news, which is all too often out of touch with the society it seeks to keep informed. The best shows of the genre, like "48 Hours" and "Primetime Live," often provide dynamic investigative reporting communicated with verve and style. And a show like "Cops" brings a gritty realism of America's mean streets into living rooms nationwide, providing a striking and often passionate picture of what is really going on in our society.

Of course, the genre can also push things too far. Too often, getting dramatic footage on the air to make a buck supersedes all other considerations. Voyeurvision sells and dignity suffers. And sometimes the cynicism of the producers, their drive to tell a compelling story, leads them to leave out essential information. The police on "Cops" and "Top Cops" are always heroes. This is not the Los Angeles Police beating Rodney King. Rather, these shows are cooperative efforts with the powers that be. Unfortunately, the lines between journalist and subject too often blur.

But, like it or not, tabloid TV is not going away any time soon. There is too much money at stake, and the people at home want more.

J. MAX ROBINS

Disney and the Animation Renaissance

On the Friday before Thanksgiving in 1989, Richard Cook, the Buena Vista Pictures Distribution executive in charge of releasing Disney and Touchstone Films, knew something different was happening with *The Little Mermaid*.

"Fridays rarely amounted to much [financially], because kids were still in school and parents were getting home from work," Cook says of the conventional wisdom going into the twenty-eighth animated Disney feature's first day of national release. "You never had a particularly large day. But as we started to get in results from the early matinees, you could tell that there was something different. The numbers, while they weren't gigantic, were sure a lot bigger than anything we had ever seen before for an animated picture."

That was just the beginning. *The Little Mermaid,* liberally adapted from the Hans Christian Andersen fairy tale by writer-directors Ron Clements and John Musker with a score of showstopping tunes by Howard Ashman and Alan Menken, earned more than $6 million in its first weekend at North American theaters. In less than two months, it grossed more than any other animated feature ever had in initial release, eventually topping out domestically at $84 million.

But Ariel, the rebellious, red-haired underwater princess with a yen for legs and surface lads, had many more laps to swim. *Mermaid* broke attendance records overseas, sold a platinum soundtrack album, and was shipped as some ten million videocassettes. It was the first full-length cartoon to win Academy Awards (for Menken's score and for his and lyricist Ashman's calypso crowd-pleaser "Under the Sea") in forty-eight years. Ariel and her friends—bellicose but loving ocean King Triton, Sebastian the singing crab, Ursula the octopusic sea witch—became favored denizens of Disney theme parks, and Ariel herself remains, according to a company source, the biggest merchandising property for girls in the world.

That still was just the tip of the iceberg *Mermaid* floated. Although it stumbled commercially with the follow-up 1990 holiday release *The Rescuers Down Under,* Disney's animation department came roaring back with 1991's *Beauty and the Beast.* A feminist rethink of the classic fable, it practically doubled *Mermaid*'s domestic gross

FACING PAGE

Welcome Back: Since Walt Disney's death in 1966, feature animation had been on life support for over two decades, before its rebirth with *The Little Mermaid* in 1989.

at $145 million and—just to top becoming the first cartoon feature to pass $100 million at the box office—was the first animated film in history nominated for a best picture Oscar. A year later, Musker and Clements's manically comical *Aladdin* blew *Beast* out of the box office record books. The Arabian Nights perennial—outrageously updated with Robin Williams's nonstop vocal improvisations as a rapid-fire, reality-shifting genie—was last seen taking a magic carpet ride to the $200 million gross mark, well out in front of any Buena Vista release, including 1989's *Pretty Woman,* the company's live-action champ.

Of course, Disney has squeezed as many drops of ancillary and licensing profits out of the later films as it did out of *Mermaid.* "What is so satisfying is that the length and the breadth of their power is stunning," enthuses Peter Schneider, the company's feature animation president. "These characters are not just around today. They'll last as long as Snow White or Cinderella."

Although Disney is the most obvious beneficiary of the cartoon tidal wave *Mermaid* triggered, the film's popular and critical success also opened the floodgates for other animators, both on television and in theaters. Where the mid-1980s averaged two or three new animation feature releases (with the inevitable Disney reissues once or twice) per year, 1992 alone saw *FernGully: The Last Rainforest;* Ralph Bakshi's *Cool World;* the first African-American cartoon comedy, *Bebe's Kids;* Disney defector Don Bluth's *Rock-A-Doodle; Little Nemo; Freddie as F.R.O.7.;* and Bill Plympton's nearly one-man show, *The Tune.* Meanwhile, cartoon programming, which like feature animation had been verging on extinction in the early eighties, spread all over the tube, from "The Simpsons," to Steven Spielberg's young Warner Bros. wabbits, "Tiny Toons," to cable's surreally slimy "Ren and Stimpy."

Of course, many of these developments were underway or being planned before *Mermaid* made its big splash. Spielberg had started reviving the feature animation form in 1986 with *An American Tail.* The profitable saga of nineteenth century immigrant mice was directed by Bluth, who had led an exodus of younger animators from the hidebound, Walt- and inspiration-less mouse factory in 1979, just as Disney was pouring money and talent into its greatest cartoon debacle, the morbid, $40 million bomb *The Black Cauldron* (1985). That disaster was perceived by many as the death knell for feature animation, which had been on life support for nearly two decades anyway. Since Walt's death in 1966, the studio that codified the genre with such timeless classics as *Snow White and the Seven Dwarfs, Fantasia, Bambi,* and *Sleeping Beauty* had grown increasingly listless. Ralph Bakshi, who had briefly breathed new life into the form with his X-rated *Fritz the Cat* (1972), had run out of creative and commercial steam by the 1980s as well.

Even in its darkest hour, though, Disney animation was being reborn. Although it took many years to produce, *Cauldron* was released shortly after Walt's nephew, Roy E. Disney, helped convince the stockholders of the raid-vulnerable corporation to hire the savvy team of Michael Eisner and Jeffrey Katzenberg away from

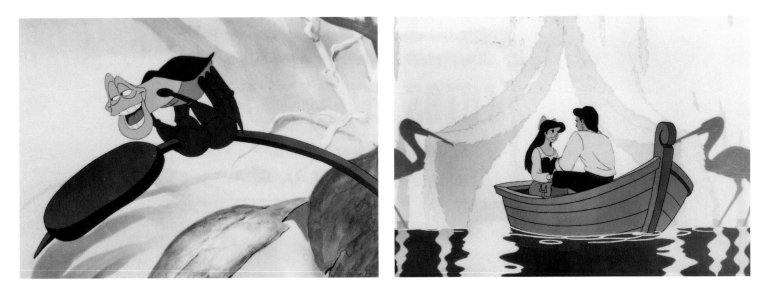

Paramount Pictures. The energetic Hollywood operators set about turning the film division into a competitive major player and exploiting the company's every asset as never before. Within a few years, the results included consistent top theatrical market shares, unprecedented profits from all corporate divisions, and, from film chief Katzenberg, a promise to give Roy Disney the money and freedom he needed to revitalize the animation department. The first cartoon to benefit from this new approach was Musker and Clements's maiden directing effort, a modest but adequately attended Sherlock Holmes knockoff called *The Great Mouse Detective* (1986).

It was a Disney alliance with Spielberg's Amblin Entertainment, however, that really indicated animation could break out of the kiddie film ghetto and into the big profits—and serious artistic consideration—that mainstream films enjoyed. 1988's *Who Framed Roger Rabbit?* was, in fact, a higher grossing film than either *Mermaid* or *Beauty and the Beast* would prove to be. A virtuosic intermingling of live action and cartoon craziness, the Robert Zemeckis-directed feature employed both Disney animators and a crew of London-based artists working for animation director Richard Williams. Like the Disney features that followed, *Roger* also unleashed an avalanche of merchandising and theme park ancillary activity, but it did not start a trend as *Mermaid* did.

While the Disney/Spielberg collaboration was the summer of 1988's biggest hit, the two companies were competing with each other by fall, when Amblin's Bluth-directed dinosaur epic, *The Land before Time,* opened on the same day as Buena Vista's twenty-seventh animated feature, an updated, Americanized, cat-and-dogged Dickensian musical called *Oliver and Company.* Both features did excellent business, *Oliver* setting a company record, first-release gross of $53 million, *Time* earning enough to push the two films' cumulative ticket sales past the $100 million mark.

If all of that was not enough to prove that feature animation was back with a vengeance, what was? Despite all the positive signals from the 1988 releases, Disney remained painfully unconvinced.

ABOVE AND FOLLOWING PAGES Not only did Disney's *The Little Mermaid* gross more than any other animated feature in the history of Hollywood ($84 million domestically), it was the first full-length cartoon to win Academy Awards in forty-eight years.

"The real decision was, how good do you have to make them?" Peter Schneider remembers. "We wrestled for days—and years—arguing about what to put in or things to take out. To make it better? To make it cheaper? To make it more expensive? To spend money or not spend money? The movies are wildly expensive to make [although Disney does not reveal their price tags, industry observers have estimated the last three fairy tales each cost somewhere in the high $20 million to mid-$30 million range], and before *Mermaid* came out, it was not clear that this was a good business to be in."

As *Mermaid*'s release date approached, indications of the film's potential began growing. The first screening for exhibitors had the tough-judging, all-adult audience laughing in all the right places and applauding each production number. When the film ended, distribution head Richard Cook recalls, "There was a pause—then, all of a sudden, the place just came unglued."

Released eight days before Thanksgiving in a few major markets, *Mermaid* earned generally positive reviews. Calling it "the best animated Disney film in at least thirty years," the *New York Times*'s Janet Maslin recognized that "it is designed to delight filmgoers of every conceivable stripe." The *Los Angeles Times*'s less enthusiastic Michael Wilmington nonetheless dubbed *Mermaid* a triumph, noting, "It's a different kind of film from the old classics. Coming after four decades of limited animation and MTV, it looks more hyperactive than *Snow White* or *Pinocchio*. There's a heightened element of sexual sophistication in the story—partial nudity and double entendres, despite a "G" rating—and it shows off new wrinkles like computer animation."

Indeed, the factors Wilmington mentioned distinguish *Mermaid* and her offspring from the juvenile-skewed animation that preceded it. *Mermaid, Beast,* and *Aladdin* all employ more sophisticated color schemes than earlier Disney features, songs that any Broadway show would envy ("What Disney's doing here are musicals," says Menken, who scored all three. "It really has become the best place for musical theater artists to work"), and attitudes cannily updated from Walt's fustier,

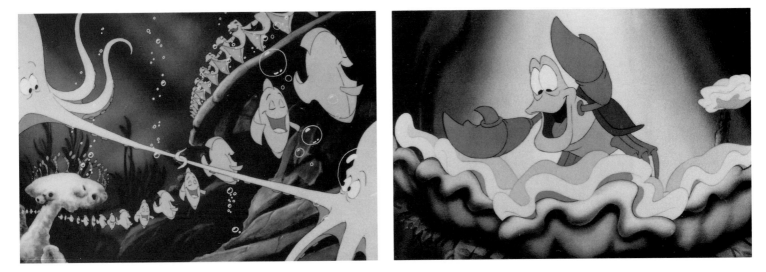

more naïve sensibility. In other works, the Disney artists have successfully strived to impress adults. "It's really a pleasure to see the audience broaden," Musker says. "We're making them for ourselves and hoping that they'll speak to kids as well as adults, and people won't feel condescended to. *Mermaid* helped break that down, and the other films went even further with that."

Adults sure did get involved with *The Little Mermaid*. The film's gender politics were debated widely, right-wing moralists blasted what they viewed as the film's endorsement of teenage rebellion, and a few alarmed parents even convinced themselves that a castle spire drawn on the videocassette's package was a phallic symbol— all relatively silly reactions, but indicative of the larger fact that adults finally were taking animation seriously. "Our goal when we started was to bring animation out of the ghetto of cartooning and make it a legitimate art form, to be taken seriously by our colleagues in the filmmaking business," Schneider says. "We have seen the general public and the professional public say, 'Gosh, this is an important moviemaking art form again.'"

That is easy to say—if you happen to work for the Walt Disney company. Non-Disney animated features have, to say the least, experienced rough sailing in *Mermaid*'s wake. She torpedoed her same-day release competition, Bluth's *All Dogs Go to Heaven,* and his Ireland-based cartooning company has been drowning in a sea of red ink practically ever since. When Spielberg's new (sans Bluth) Amblimation unit tried to open an *American Tail* sequel, *Fievel Goes West,* against *Beauty and the Beast,* the mouse western was flattened by Disney's box office stampede.

Indeed, almost all of the animated features released in 1992 performed dismally in theaters, although some will profit nicely from video sales to kids, by far the strongest revenue-generator for non-Disney products. Other films' inability to capture the Disney magic is due to a number of factors. There is a limited pool of talented artists in this work-intensive field, and the ever-expanding Disney operation can afford to hire most of them. Plus, Disney has strict storytelling guidelines and quality-control standards which, as the aimless likes of *Nemo*'s and *Freddie*'s quick disappearance demonstrated, are vital to an animated feature's success. Then there is Cook's marketing machine, perhaps the finest tuned sales force on earth.

Still, the possibility of slicing off some of Disney's success, coupled with costs and risks that are relatively low compared to live-action production, continues encouraging others to test *Mermaid*-charted waters. "It's not so much that *Aladdin*'s going to make $200 million and they're all doing better than ever," says 20th Century-Fox worldwide production president Tom Jacobson, whose studio's *FernGully* was the only non-Disney animated feature to turn a profit in 1992. "It's more the phenomenon of the whole family film business. People want to go see films with their kids again." Unsurprisingly, Fox has the most ambitious feature animation plans of the majors outside Disney, with *Once upon a Forest* and the semi-animated *Pagemaster,* with young superstar Macaulay Culkin (*Home Alone*), in the works. But Fox is far from alone in the animation sweepstakes. Amblimation has another dinosaur show, *We're Back;* Bluth's back in business with *Thumbelina, A Troll in Central Park,* and others on the drawing board; *Roger Rabbit*'s Richard Williams has long been at work on *The Thief and the Cobbler;* and Ted Turner's bankrolling *Tom and Jerry: The Movie.*

Jacobson cautions that "like any movie, quality is the key" to a feature cartoon's success. He also says that Fox is "not trying to reinvent the form," insisting that animation, like any genre, has certain conventions through which audience expectations must be satisfied. Others, like Tom Wilhite of Hyperiod Pictures, the company that made *Bebe's Kids,* believe that non-Disney success necessitates different approaches. "Certainly, there is an opportunity for an animation renaissance," he says. "There's a receptivity among studios and others to finance it, because there's clearly a large audience for animated films. But everything shouldn't be measured against the *Beauty and the Beast* yardstick. Animated films must have the same opportunity for variety that live-action films have."

Disney itself seems to agree that diversity is the stuff of animation's future. The studio has a stop-motion model feature for the 1993 holiday season, Tim Burton's *The Nightmare Before Christmas,* and is in production on cartoon features about African animals, Native Americans, and even an all-computer-animated comedy.

"There are no rules about Disney animation," insists film boss Katzenberg. "We want every single movie to be as distinctive as it possibly can be. It is not an accident that *Aladdin* is so incredibly different from *Beauty and the Beast*. That was not a business decision, it was a creative decision. The artists have got to be challenged, they have to do different work. We are not just going to sit here and do classic, romantic fairy tales. We'd get bored with 'em before you'd get bored with 'em, and you'd get bored with 'em pretty quick."

BOB STRAUSS

FACING PAGE

The Beauty of the *Beast*: Released in 1991, *Beauty and the Beast* doubled *The Little Mermaid*'s domestic gross and became the first animated film in history nominated for a best-picture Oscar. A year later, *Aladdin* blew *Beast* out of the box-office record books.

The Rising Sun Over Sunset Boulevard

Sony's purchase of Columbia Pictures Entertainment on September 27, 1989, was treated more like an invasion than an acquisition. From *Newsweek*'s memorable "Japan Invades Hollywood" cover headline on down, the media treated the Japanese electronics giant's deal as though enemy foreigners had landed on the beach.

At $4.7 billion, it was the largest U.S. buy to date by a Japanese concern. There was already general resentment about Japan's acquisition of American real estate, notably Rockefeller Center in New York. Although Americans seemed not to be bothered with the Sony name emblazoned right below their television screens, it was another thing to see it *on* the screen—a pointed reminder that foreigners controlled an important piece of American popular culture. Sony tried to soothe the flag-wavers by promising it had not come to Hollywood to churn out movies featuring Japan's biggest homegrown movie star, Godzilla, and that it would not impose its own cultural sensibilities on Columbia films.

Three years later Sony Corporation of America president and CEO Michael Schulhof, seated in his office in Sony's music headquarters in New York, is thinking back on that turbulent period. Much has changed since then. Foreign money in American movie studios is now commonplace: following Sony's buy, a Japanese rival, Matsushita, bought MCA/Universal; Australia-born Rupert Murdoch owns Twentieth Century-Fox; and MGM/UA gets its marching orders from the French lender Credit Lyonnais, and was nearly acquired by Italian entrepreneur Giancarlo Parretti.

"I was surprised only by the extent of the media coverage, not by the direction of the coverage," says Schulhof, the nuclear physicist who engineered the Sony deal with Coca-Cola, which previously owned 49 percent of the studio. "We had anticipated that the acquisition of any Hollywood studio by a foreign electronics company would cause a media reaction. During the year preceding the actual announcement of our intention to do an acquisition, there had been all kinds of speculation in the press about many kinds of transactions. The surprise was to see the *Newsweek* headline and the front-page attention it received in the *New York Times* and other media. Frankly, I was proud of the deal; I was proud that Sony, as

FACING PAGE

Variety, September 27–October 3, 1989: A foreign invasion of Hollywood began when Japanese electronics giant Sony plunked down $4.7 billion for Columbia Pictures.

RIETY

NEWSPAPE

® Second Class P.O.

NEW YORK, SEPT. 27-OCT. 3, 1989   **THE INTERNATIONAL ENTERTAINMENT WEEKLY**   **$2.75 Canada**

TURE IS SONY-SIDE-U

Hardware-software giant looms as Sony bids $4.7-billion for studio

By CHARLES KIPPS

New York The other shoe dropped, finally, over the weekend as Sony Corp. firmed up a long-gestating offer for Columbia Pictures Entertainment.

Sony has bid $27 per share for all outstanding shares in CPE, placing the cash value of the purchase at about $3.3-billion. Since Sony also must assume $1.3-billion in debt and purchase $100-million in preferred stock from the Coca-Cola Co., the total value of the proposed transaction weighs in at $4.7-billion.

The offer, which was tendered Sept. 24, was reviewed at a meeting of the CPE board of directors Sept. 26 and could be accepted as

Pictures. The significant financial ramification of the merger was the reduction of the Coca-Cola Co.'s stake in CPE to 49%.

"If you can afford to own 100% of a company," Paine Webber's Lee Isgur noted of Coca-Cola, "why would you own half?"

Stating that "Not only do you need a willing buyer, but also a willing seller," Isgur added that the merger signaled Coke's willingness to sell CPE.

When the CPE corporate structure was further consolidated in March 1989, the Sony rumor gained considerable momentum.

Whether or not the proposed transaction takes place is contingent on two blocks of stock: the 49% owned by Coke and a 4%

IRVING BER DIES AT 101

By JOSEPH McBRIDE

Hollywood Irving Be

l into a ith Max ed in a ling "Is-

Lorimar

an innovative company, was the first one to do a really major acquisition. And obviously not the last."

Sony, which was accused of overpaying for CBS Records (which it had acquired for a whopping $2 billion in 1987), was similarly criticized for the Columbia deal. It hired Hollywood insiders Jon Peters and Peter Guber to run its new studio, but it had to buy their production company for over $200 million (including $50 million in direct payments to the duo), as well as settle up with Warner Bros., which had the team under exclusive contract. Sony was also forced to trade its 35 percent interest in Burbank Studios to purchase the old Metro-Goldwyn-Mayer studio in Culver City from Warner Bros.

Sony clearly was investing for the long term, and just three years later, Schulhof likes the way the deals look on paper. "Using the typical multiple that Wall Street applies, our combined entertainment companies [movies, TV, music, electronic publishing, and theaters] probably have a capitalized value today of close to $13 billion to $15 billion," Schulhof says. "Our total acquisition cost for everything was $8 billion. I don't have any doubt of the value and the financial benefits of those acquisitions."

According to Schulhof, even the purchase of the old MGM studio—which Warner Bros. insisted upon to drop a lawsuit over the Guber-Peters exit—filled a Sony need. "The arrangements we made with Warner have given us a total of forty soundstages—a first-class facility that is probably the most hi-tech Hollywood studio running. This has propelled us to the forefront of all the motion picture companies. When I look now at our financial results, we are as strong as Warner, Disney, Paramount, any of the other studios. In fact, I think we are stronger than most of them."

Shortly after Sony bought CBS Records in an attempt to marry a software music production entity to its line of hardware, it began to look for a film studio for the same reason. The company fished around Hollywood, and in a year's time it had discussions with each studio, making serious overtures to MGM. Once the Australian concern Qintex made an agreement to buy that studio (a deal that later fell through), Sony set its sights on Columbia.

"I spent twelve months talking to the heads of every Hollywood studio," Schulhof recalls. "MGM was one, but at various times we spoke to principals of each company, not because we were prowling to find whatever was available, but because we were trying to understand the nature of Hollywood, the individuals and the weaknesses of each company. It was important to know which company would fit best with us."

Sony eventually plunked down twenty-seven dollars per share to buy Columbia, a studio that had a solid film library, and theater and television divisions, but whose movie division's results were lagging as the result of various regime changes. Several costly disasters, such as *Ishtar* and *Leonard Part VI,* persuaded Coke to stick to soda pop and leave pop culture to others. Despite this, the studio was alluring to suitors.

"Columbia had terrific assets," Schulhof says. "The library was first-class. The television group was first-class. The exhibition group was first-class. The main thing it was lacking was [film] production, and after deciding we would hire Guber and Peters, we were comfortable that we would be in a position to attract top-flight management talent, and the management talent would be able to take care of bringing current production up to the level of the other studios. In hindsight, we've been proved absolutely right. Sony Pictures—if you include Columbia, TriStar, Carolco, and Sony Picture Classics—has been the number one studio in terms of box office share for two years in a row [1991 and 1992]."

Not that there have not been bumps in the road. First, Walter Yetnikoff, the volatile CBS Records head who helped broker the studio deal and was poised to steer both divisions, left the company. Schulhof later assumed the music post himself. Then, Jon Peters, half of the management team for which Sony had paid hundreds of millions of dollars, stepped aside, leaving only Guber. Dawn Steel, who headed Columbia Pictures when Sony made the deal, had mixed results trying to pull the studio out of a slump caused by the eclectic slate of the previous studio head, David Puttnam. She was quickly removed and replaced by Frank Price, whose own tenure was short.

It had long been rumored that Guber wanted to bring in his own man, Mark Canton, who was the executive on big-budget Guber-Peters projects like *Batman* at Warner Bros. Canton felt frustration in not being able to green-light pictures himself at Warner Bros. and came aboard in late 1991. All of these changes were costly for the studio, with multimillion-dollar parachutes providing soft landings for outgoing execs.

Columbia has turned itself around nicely, however. Rather than throw out his predecessor's projects, as many incoming studio chiefs do, Canton nurtured many of them. Though 1992 started off badly with the disastrous *Radio Flyer,* the studio changed course by early summer. The Penny Marshall-directed *A League of Their Own* grossed $107 million, and the hits kept coming. *My Girl, Single White Female, Honeymoon in Vegas,* and *A River Runs Through It* all did well, and the studio ended the year strongly with *Bram Stoker's Dracula* and *A Few Good Men.* Columbia captured 12.5 percent of the market in 1992, up from a paltry 4.9 percent in 1990.

Its sister studio, TriStar, has not fared as well. It got only 6.6 percent of the 1992 market share, down from 9 percent in 1990. Carolco, which did *Terminator 2,* has been the studio's main supplier of blockbusters, but has run into financial troubles as well. Other films, such as *Bugsy, City of Joy,* and *Wind,* underperformed. Even *Husbands and Wives,* the Woody Allen film whose story line is eerily reminiscent of his affair with Mia Farrow's daughter, Soon-Yi Previn, did not draw, even though its release date was moved up to exploit the controversy.

Sony hired Barbra Streisand's former boyfriend, producer Jon Peters, to help run its film studio and allay fears of a Godzilla-like takeover of Hollywood.

While there has been speculation that TriStar will either be sold or absorbed by Columbia, the studio has started to show signs of life. Though his 1992 holiday film *Chaplin* was silenced quickly at about a $10 million gross, TriStar topper Mike Medavoy signed a deal with prolific producers Scott Rudin, Dan Melnick, and Eric Pleskow and Barry Spikings. The group could provide some big-ticket pictures if Carolco's fortunes do not improve. They intend to fund four "event" pictures per year, including the $35 million actioner *The Chinese Bandit*.

Schulhof says the turnaround is right on schedule. "I told everybody that it takes three years to restructure a company and three years to build a slate of films," he says. "I think we did it in less than that. I was never surprised by the amount of time it took."

He stresses that the success is all due to the management team, which, Schulhof says, has been left alone. "We're a global company, and global companies can only succeed when they learn to respect the business environment in each of the countries where they operate," he says. "We have established the United States operation, which has more assets now than the Japanese operation. We have $13 billion in assets in the U.S.; only $8 billion in Japan. We have 23,000 employees in the United States, and the company is run and managed by Americans. So our style here hasn't been a question of treating the U.S. as a branch sales office of Japan. We've grown because we have developed capable management and have expanded locally in the United States. I don't believe that any entertainment company can succeed into the next decade, much less the next century, unless it treats its overseas operations as fully integrated business operations, and not merely branch sales offices designed to market the export homegrown product."

And what about TriStar's plan to make a Godzilla movie?

"That was management's choice," Schulhof insists. "Peter Guber came to me and said, 'We want to make *Godzilla*. Can you give us some help getting hold of the people who own the rights in Japan?' I said, 'Sure, if that's what you want to do. I'll arrange an introduction to Toho, the Japanese film company that owns the *Godzilla* rights.' The decision we made was that we wouldn't interfere with the creative decisions, and that's absolutely true, straight down the line.

"But if they think they can make money on a Godzilla movie…well, that's a decision made by Medavoy and Guber and Mark Canton."

MICHAEL FLEMING

FACING PAGE

Variety, **December 3, 1990**: One year after the Columbia purchase, Sony rival Matsushita paid a whopping $6.6 billion for MCA/Universal.

VARIETY

THE INTERNATIONAL ENTERTAINMENT WEEKLY ▪ DEC. 3, 1990

収者よ、ご用心を

ollywood isn't MCA's new owners

financial seers Tanii of Mat- de a great deal at $66 a share, things they're ndeed, both in

STEEP WOES

BINS

There were no real winners in the November sweeps.

The first-place network, NBC, was real- y the biggest oser, taking a e from last year. k that gained ed last among

Hollywood and on Wall Street some serious questions are being uttered about the deal and what it portends — questions the sho-gun of Matsushita would do well to ponder.

▪ The most basic question: Does Akio Tanii really understand what he's got himself into? His meandering responses to press queries about creative controls and the Israeli boycott would suggest that the Japanese leader thinks of MCA as just another product line, like Panasonic. If so, he may be sorely mistaken.

MCA is, on one level, a cultur-al asset — the sort of enterprise which the governments of France or, indeed, Japan, would not allow to be sold to a foreign corporation. In acquiring MCA, *Turn to page 8*

Japanese giant bucks overspendin

By PAUL NOGLOWS and CHARLES FLEMING

NEW YORK Matsushita's purchase of MCA for $6.6 billion is the priciest foreign acquisition ever of a U.S. media and entertainment company. But unlike most other foreign buys of U.S. media, Wall Street experts seem to think this

time the purchase price is more in line with the company's actual value.

When Sony Corp. last year bought Columbia Pictures for $5 billion, and then had to spend an additional $800 million to secure the talents of Peter Guber and Jon Peters, observers concluded that the Japanese company had substantially overpaid to acquire

the studio.

"The genera Sony paid a v Columbia," sa analyst Harolo Lynch. "Espec in that Colum tioning at full be revved up acquire Guber-ment, which ra nificantly."

The same wa $2 billion purc ords in 1987. neering buyin, can marketpla Neuman, senic entertainment te & Touche. " in high and ha done."

Analysts va in the $69 to $7 (any ultimate s will push the higher end). industry's lon that MCA wou

BIG BROTHER IS (STILL) WATCHING EURO TV

LONDON Television in Europe may be getting more competi-tive and commercially oriented, but politicians of all persuasions are still pulling strings.

As private tv proliferates across the Continent and direct

government control of the air-waves diminishes, political influ-ence on broadcasting nonethe-less remains pervasive.

In some countries, privatiza-tion may mean more politics, not less. And for those building media and broadcasting empires, it clear-ly helps to have friends in high places.

A VARIETY survey found:

▪ Political power over broad-

Great Scott! Hot vid vanishes

By MAX ALEXANDER

NEW YORK Just when the video industry thought they had it all figured out, along came "The Rocky Horror Picture Show."

IN

The Mighty Carson Retires

Johnny Carson's last night as host of "The Tonight Show" turned out to be a surprisingly subdued final curtain for an entertainer who had presided over a TV series (and the American bedroom) longer—twenty-nine years, seven months, to be precise—than any other performer in showbiz history.

"We deliberately planned it that way," says Fred de Cordova, who served as executive producer of "The Tonight Show, Starring Johnny Carson" on NBC for twenty-three of those years, referring to the final episode of the late-night talk show on May 22, 1992. "We decided not to invite any guests, because we wanted to be careful not to offend the people who didn't get invited."

The night before, Carson had booked only two guests, Robin Williams and Bette Midler, both of whom were in top form. Williams launched into his usual hilarious free-form mimicry, which got Carson laughing so hard he ended up in tears. Midler drenched her segment in savvy, ingratiating schmaltz, and when, looking into Carson's eyes, she crooned "One More for the Road," the sentimentality of the occasion soon plunged him into an extended crying jag.

The exhilarating success of the May 21 edition carried over into the next day, but as the time edged closer to 5:30 P.M., when Carson was to tape the final hour, "we began to feel a kind of shock," says de Cordova. "In essence, we weren't just coming to the end of an episode of the show, we were saying good-bye."

The final hour went smoothly, highlighted by brief, tantalizing clips culled from three decades' worth of shows, featuring dozens of the guests who had made their pilgrimage to the most successful late-night TV series ever. After the taping, cast and crew journeyed out to Carson's beach house in Malibu for what de Cordova calls "a lavish wrap party," but the atmosphere was less than jovial. "We couldn't help but feel a sense of personal sadness," he says. "Something we'd enjoyed doing for so long was now over."

While it lasted, Carson's reign at the helm of "The Tonight Show" was unprecedented. No one else even comes close to him in man (or woman) hours logged in front of a camera on network television. And no performer has pocketed anywhere near as much money as Carson over the years. To cite one example, Jay Leno's yearly paycheck as Carson's replacement resides at somewhere around $3

FACING PAGE

Jump Start: In 1953, Johnny Carson was already honing the middle-American shtick on his ill-fated "Carson's Cellar" that would land him "The Tonight Show" nine years later.

million. Carson was taking home $4 million a year back in 1977, a figure that esca-lated over the next fifteen years to approximately $20 million at his retirement.

But when NBC initially came after him to host "The Tonight Show" after Jack Paar retired in March 1962, Carson turned the offer down. He was then hosting one of the highest rated daytime game shows, ABC's "Who [sic] Do You Trust?" "The gulf between chatting with unknown contestants for half an hour every after-noon," wrote Kenneth Tynan in a *New Yorker* magazine profile of Carson, "and matching wits with celebrities for what was then an hour and forty-five minutes every night seemed unnervingly wide, and he doubted his ability to bridge it." But NBC became desperate when other potential candidates for host (such as Bob Newhart, Jackie Gleason, Joey Bishop, and Groucho Marx) said no. The network set its sights on Carson again, and this time it broke down his resistance.

Carson brought with him Ed McMahon, his announcer on "Who Do You Trust?", who was to stick with the show for the full span of Carson's tenure. Like his predecessors Steve Allen (1954 to 1957) and Paar (1957 to 1962), Carson did "The Tonight Show" out of New York for the first ten years of his dominion before relocating to California. (Sadly, as Carson pointed out in the final episode, NBC did not preserve any of the tapes of those first ten years. The retrospective segment on the last show had to make do with still photographs of the host convers-ing with everybody from Bobby Kennedy and Nelson Rockefeller to Joan Crawford and Judy Garland.)

Over the first few years, Carson gradually honed the format that would become as ritualized as Kabuki theater and that set the standard for every subsequent talk show. Each episode opened with a monologue stuffed with jokes tied to the day's headlines. Then, after the first burst of commercials, he did another piece of comedy material, often drawing on his inventory of characters. The most enduring of these was Carnac the Magnificent, a send-up of the show-biz mountebanks who once toured the vaudeville circuit wowing audiences with their supposed psychic powers. Carnac, decked out in a huge rhinestone-studded turban and diaphanous black cloak clasped at the neck, would take an envelope from McMahon, hold it up to his temple, and, eyes closed, pretend to conjure up a word or phrase that was the answer to a question written on a card sealed within. For example, he would come up with the word "saucepan" from his otherworldly divination, then tear open the envelope and read the question: "Who was Peter Pan's alcoholic brother?"

Others in the pantheon of Carson alter egos included Aunt Blabby, a wisecrack-ing granny whose zingers dealt mostly with the indignities of old age; Art Fern, a fast-talking pitchman who evoked the early days of TV when con artist-type sales-men used to host movie showcases on local stations and deliver commercials for everything from used-car dealerships to the regional grocery chain; and Floyd R. Turbo, the know-nothing, camera-transfixed rube who represented the average right-wing Joe getting his moment in the spotlight to answer a bleeding-heart station editorial that has rubbed him the wrong way.

Following this comedy bit—and another ubiquitous burst of commercials (the heavy commercial load made "Tonight" the consistently most profitable show on NBC)—Carson started bringing out the guests. The typical lineup consisted of a big-name celebrity (usually an actor or comedian) first, then a singer or musical group, then a stand-up comic (often a young man or woman who had not yet achieved enough status to join Johnny at his desk), and finally, if there was still time, an offbeat guest like the author of a book that would appeal to a late-night audience, or a man who had won a birdcalling contest.

The highest rated Carson show of all time was the night Tiny Tim, the ukelele-strumming camp crooner of golden oldies, got married, on camera, to a woman named Victoria Budinger, on December 17, 1969. Probably the most famous single piece of shtick on the show took place in 1964 when Ed Ames, who was playing an Indian on the "Daniel Boone" TV series, agreed to instruct Carson in the art of tomahawk throwing. With the silhouette of a man as the target, Ames flung the tomahawk, scoring a direct hit to the target's crotch. This "frontier briss," as Carson called it, ended up on just about all of the year-end primetime "Best of the Tonight Show" wrap-ups.

While other talk show hosts tried to outdo each other in sucking up to their guests, Tynan calls Carson's interviewing style "glacial." Carson "operates on a level of high, freewheeling, centrifugal banter that is well above the snow line," he says. "Which is not to say that he is hostile. Carson treats you with deference and genuine curiosity. But the air is chill; you are definitely on probation."

Trying to explain Carson's longevity, Jane and Michael Stern, in their *Encyclopedia of Pop Culture,* say, "Polite, clean-cut, energetic, a good sport, and slick as polished chrome, with a midwestern face you knew you could trust and a mischievous—but never actually mean—sense of humor, Johnny Carson is the most purely American character in popular culture since Mark Twain invented Tom Sawyer."

The all-purpose talk show model that Carson perfected—opening monologue, some variation of the host seated behind a desk with guests perched on a couch to his right, a band attached to the show—became standard issue for all competing networks trying to put a dent in Carson's ratings. ABC, with "The Joey Bishop Show," mounted the first serious challenge in the spring of 1967. Bishop, a stand-up comedian, had harvested good reviews as a frequent guest host of "The Tonight Show." Despite being able to draw on a wider pool of big-name celebrity talent because it originated in Los Angeles, the Bishop show never made enough headway in the ratings to pose a threat to Carson's late-night hegemony.

Bishop's run lasted for two and a half years, giving way in December 1969 to "The Dick Cavett Show," which tried a more highbrow approach to luring viewers away from Johnny. That strategy almost guaranteed that it would not reach mass

The king of late-night TV, pictured here in 1971 with Muhammad Ali and sidekick Ed McMahon, perfected the all-purpose talk-show format. For thirty years, CBS and ABC tried in vain to put a dent in Carson's unassailable ratings.

audience levels, but it hung in nightly until January 1973, when it was downgraded to one week a month as part of an umbrella series called "ABC's Wide World of Entertainment." In that format, Cavett rotated with a week of "Jack Paar Tonite," Friday night Dick Clark–produced "In Concert" music specials, plus a mix of various TV movies and variety programs.

While ABC was having no luck in the late-night sweepstakes, CBS put forward its first talk show competitor, "The Merv Griffin Show," in August 1969. Griffin had no more success against Carson than Bishop or Cavett on ABC. In February 1972, Griffin bowed out of the network wars, shifting his show to daytime syndication. CBS went down in flames seventeen years later when it launched its second major foray at Carson, "The Pat Sajak Show." Sajak is the host of the most successful game show in TV history, "Wheel of Fortune" (created and produced, ironically enough, by Merv Griffin), but as a talk show host, the super-slick Sajak came off as bland and facetious. He also found himself competing with a new syndicated talk-variety hour, "The Arsenio Hall Show," which, since its debut on January 3, 1989, has carved out a solid late-night niche by focusing on guests who appeal particularly to young adults.

Carson's retirement triggered a battle royal among the networks to divvy up lucrative chunks of the late-night audience. NBC designated Jay Leno, who had become the sole guest host during Carson's vacations and frequent days off, as the new star of "The Tonight Show" (comedienne Joan Rivers had once been slated for that honor, but split from NBC in the mid-80s to star in her own short-lived talk show on the new Fox network). The choice of Leno angered David Letterman,

whose post-Carson hour-long talk show had chalked up surprisingly high Nielsens for NBC since it kicked off on February 1, 1982. Letterman's unhappiness caused him to ankle NBC and shift his base of operations to CBS in the late summer of 1993, going head-to-head with Leno. The Fox network also weighed in with "The Chevy Chase Show" in the fall of 1993, with most affiliates running it at 11 P.M., E.S.T., to give it a half-hour jump on Leno and Letterman.

But the general industry consensus is that no one will ever come close to matching Carson's late-night dominance, because most cable systems throughout the country are planning to double or triple their channel capacity over the next few years. This explosion of choices will so fragment viewers' attention that it will be almost impossible for any one show to command the audience share that the mighty Carson swallowed up in his heyday.

JOHN DEMPSEY

CONTRIBUTORS

SCOTT BALDINGER is a writer and the Features Editor of *Harper's Bazaar.*

CARI BEAUCHAMP, who is currently writing a biography of Frances Marion and women screenwriters of the 1920s and 1930s, is co-author of *Hollywood on the Riviera: The Inside Story of the Cannes Film Festival* with HENRI BÉHAR, who covers the North American cultural scene for the French daily *Le Monde.*

PORTER BIBB, a writer and investment banker, was producer of *Gimme Shelter* for Maysles Films and the first publisher of *Rolling Stone* magazine. He is the author of the new biography of Ted Turner, *It Ain't As Easy As It Looks.*

JOHN BRODIE, a television reporter for *Daily Variety* and formerly the staff writer for *Spy* magazine, has written for the *New York Times, The New Republic, Gentleman's Quarterly,* and the *Village Voice.*

MICHELLE CONLIN, a freelance writer, studied acting under Morris Carnovsky at the Eugene O'Neill Theatre Center in New York City.

PETER COWIE, *Variety's* European Publishing Director and the founding editor of the *International Film Guide,* has written numerous books on film, most recently a biography of director Francis Ford Coppola.

JOHN DEMPSEY, a television reporter for *Variety,* was previously a reporter for the *Baltimore Sun,* a movie critic for the *Boston Herald Traveler,* a reporter for the Associated Press, and the Associate Editor of *Broadcasting* magazine.

MICHAEL FLEMING, a *Variety* reporter, writes the magazine's weekly "Buzz" column, as well as the "Dish" column for *Daily Variety.* He was formerly a reporter for *New York Newsday.*

BARBARA GELB is the co-author with her husband Arthur Gelb of *O'Neill,* a biography of Eugene O'Neill.

JEREMY GERARD, *Variety's* Theater Editor and Chief Theater Critic, was previously a reporter for the *New York Times* covering Broadway and television, the Chief Theater Critic of the *Dallas Morning News,* and a staff critic at *Soho Weekly News.* He has written for *Vanity Fair, New York, Esquire,* the *New York Times Magazine, American Theater,* and *TV Guide,* among others.

BRUCE HARING, a music editor for *Daily Variety,* was formerly an assistant news editor at *Billboard* magazine and a pop critic for the *Newark Star-Ledger.*

DAVID HORII researched Mary Wilson's best-selling autobiography, *Dreamgirl—My Life As a Supreme.*

JOSEPH HURLEY is a New York-based theater and film critic.

LEE ISRAEL, the author of *Kilgallen, Miss Tallulah Bankhead,* and *Estée Lauder: Beyond the Magic,* is currently working on a biography of Vanessa Redgrave and on a collection of celebrity letters.

HARLAN JACOBSON, a writer, film critic, and former reporter for *Variety,* is the contributing editor for culture of *New Democrat* magazine.

TODD MCCARTHY, *Variety*'s Chief Film Critic, codirected and wrote the acclaimed documentary *Visions of Light: The Art of Cinematography,* won an Emmy for writing *Preston Sturges: The Rise and Fall of an American Dreamer,* and cowrote the documentary *Hollywood Mavericks.* He also coedited *Kings of the Bs.: Working Within the Hollywood System,* and has written for numerous film magazines and newspapers.

STUART MILLER is a freelance writer working on a book about New York City. A former *Variety* reporter, he has written for *Gentleman's Quarterly, New York,* the *Daily News, TheaterWeek,* and *Playboy.*

SHERIDAN MORLEY writes "Strands," *Variety*'s fortnightly London theater column, and serves as Drama Critic of the *International Herald Tribune* and *The Spectator.* He has written or edited thirty film and theater books, including a new biography of his father, actor Robert Morley, to be published this fall.

KHOI NGUYEN, a New York-based writer, has written for *Town & Country, Vanity Fair,* and *People.*

PAUL NOGLOWS, a *Variety* reporter who covers Wall Street and the financial markets, was an adjunct associate professor of journalism at New York University. He has written for *TV Guide* and a number of European trades, including *Television Business International.*

CHARLES PAIKERT, an associate editor at *Variety,* has written about entertainment, business, and culture for publications including the *New York Times* and *Premiere.*

BROOKS PETERS is a writer on theater, design, and the arts whose work has appeared in *Vanity Fair, Architectural Digest,* and *Mirabella.* He is currently at work on a novel.

DANIEL PINCHBECK is a New York-based writer and a contributing editor of *Art & Antiques* magazine.

J. MAX ROBINS, *Variety*'s Television Editor, writes the magazine's weekly "Wired" column. Formerly a senior editor at *Channels* magazine, he has written for publications such as the *New York Times* and the *Village Voice* and has commented on the media business for "CBS Evening News," "NBC Nightly News," CNBC, and CNN.

TONY SCOTT, a founder of the Los Angeles Drama Critics Circle and the Vice-President of the Los Angeles Author's Club, is a TV reviewer for *Daily Variety.*

RICHARD SETLOWE, whose most recent novel is *The Black Sea,* is a former staff writer for *Daily Variety.*

BOB STRAUSS, the Film Critic for the *Los Angeles Daily News,* writes regularly on film for the *Chicago Sun Times* and the *Boston Globe.*

ANNE THOMPSON, the West Coast Editor of *Film Comment* and a contributing editor of *Entertainment Weekly,* writes the "Risky Business" column for *L.A. Weekly.*

KEVIN ZIMMERMAN, a music columnist and reporter for *Variety,* has written about the music business for *Spin* and *Spy* magazines. He is currently working on a novel.

INDEX

PHOTO CREDITS

THE BETTMANN ARCHIVE
Pages 1, 4, 18, 40, 42, 43, 64, 83.

UPI/BETTMANN
Pages 76 (top), 81, 104, 107, 124, 165, 177.

SPRINGER/BETTMANN FILM ARCHIVE
Page 8.

Pages 7 (Nelson Evans), 15, 16, 21, 23, 59 (© 1932 MGM), 75,
76 (© 1939 MGM), 77 (© 1939 UA), 98, 99 (© Gabi Rona), 110, 148,
167 (© 1979 Omni/Zoetrope), 169 (© 1979 UA), 205 (© 1991 Disney),
213 (© Sid Avery), 224 (© 1932 MGM).

ARCHIVE PHOTOS
Pages 10, 13, 31, 37, 41, 48, 51, 61, 65 (American Stock), 66, 69, 72, 79, 97,
102, 103, 109, 119 (Alpha Blair), 129, 145, 147, 156, 181 (LDE),
183 (Fotos Int'l), 185 (Fotos Int'l), 191 (top), 201–203 (Fotos Int'l),
209 (Fotos Int'l), 216 (Alpha Blair).

THE KOBAL COLLECTION
Pages 45, 74, 77 (top), 199.

CULVER PICTURES, INC.
Pages 49, 57, 71, 115.

EVERETT COLLECTION
Pages 53, 54, 55, 56, 58, 125, 127, 135, 136, 141, 142, 154,
155, 162, 171, 172, 173, 174, 193, 194, 195, 197, 217.

SYGMA
Pages 87 (© Leo Mirkine), 91 (© F. Darmigny), 150 (© J. P. Laffont),
151 (© J. P. Laffont), 159 (© Ira Wyman), 187 (© Randy Taylor),
190 (© Les Stone), 191 (bottom, © Randy Taylor).